THE STORY OF A SOUL

A New Translation

St. Thérèse of Lisieux

Complete and Unabridged

Translated and Edited by
ROBERT J. EDMONSON, CJ

PARACLETE PRESS
Brewster, Massachusetts

2008 Fourth Printing
2007 Third Printing
2006 First and Second Printing

Copyright © 2006 by Paraclete Press, Inc.
ISBN 978-1-55725-487-0

Library of Congress Cataloging-in-Publication Data
Thérèse, de Lisieux, Saint, 1873–1897.
   [Histoire d'une âme. English]
   The story of a soul : St. Thérèse of Lisieux, a new translation /
translated, with an introduction by Robert J. Edmonson, CJ.—Complete
& unabridged [ed.].
      p. cm.
   ISBN 1-55725-487-7
1. Thérèse, de Lisieux, Saint, 1873–1897.
2. Christian > saints—France—Lisieux—Biography.
3. Lisieux
(France)—Biography. I. Edmonson, Robert J. II. Title.
BX4700.T5A3 2006
282.092—dc22   2005035832

10 9 8 7 6 5 4

Published by Paraclete Press
Brewster, Massachusetts
www.paracletepress.com
Printed in the United States of America.

Contents

When in 1997 Pope John-Paul II declared Thérèse of Lisieux a Doctor of the Church, the number of saints with this title rose to thirty-three, of whom only three are women: Catherine of Siena, Teresa of Avila, and the humble saint whose story is told in these pages.

Thérèse would probably be surprised to find herself designated a Doctor, even though her life's aim was, as she told her father at an early age, to be "a great saint." Was she extra-ordinary? To be sure. But she taught us that ordinary people can have an extraordinary love for God *if* our hearts are turned to God as hers was.

No better explanation of Thérèse's contribution to all of Christendom can be given than that of Pope John Paul II, in his homily of October 19th, 1997:

"Thérèse of the Child Jesus and the Holy Face is the youngest of all the 'Doctors of the Church,' but her ardent spiritual journey shows such maturity, and the insights of faith expressed in her writings are so vast and profound that they deserve a place among the great spiritual masters. . . .

"Thérèse of Lisieux did not only grasp and describe the profound truth of Love as the centre and heart of the Church, but in her short life she lived it intensely. It is precisely this convergence of doctrine and concrete experience, of truth and life, of teaching and practice, which shines with particular brightness in this saint, and which makes her an attractive model especially for young people and for those who are seeking true meaning for their life.

"Before the emptiness of so many words, Thérèse offers another solution, the one Word of salvation which, understood and lived in silence, becomes a source of renewed life. She counters a rational culture, so often overcome by practical materialism, with the disarming simplicity of the 'little way' which, by returning to the essentials, leads to the secret of all life: the divine Love that surrounds and penetrates every human venture. In a time like ours, so frequently marked by an ephemeral and hedonistic culture, this new Doctor of the Church proves to be remarkably effective in enlightening the mind and heart of those who hunger and thirst for truth and love."

The Historical Setting

St. Thérèse of Lisieux was born on January 2nd, 1873, and baptized two days later as Marie-Françoise-Thérèse Martin. This was just two years after the Franco-Prussian War had ended with the collapse of the French armed forces, the ending of France's Second Empire, and the creation of the Third Republic. The nineteenth-century Church into which Thérèse was baptized had fallen greatly from its former glory. The leaders of the French Revolution ravaged the Church during the latter part of the eighteenth century, and even after the restoration of the French monarchy in 1814, other revolutions broke out in 1830 and 1848, creating conditions that would prevent the Church from ever regaining its pre-Revolutionary power. And yet, in 1815 the Carmelite order was reintroduced into France, and by 1880 there were 113 convents of Discalced nuns.

The Carmelites take their name from Mount Carmel, a group of mountains in the Holy Land. Inspired by the prophet Elijah, who had defeated the prophets of Baal on these same mountains, a thirteenth-century group of men comprised of former Crusaders and pilgrims settled on Mount Carmel and took the name of the Brothers of the Blessed Virgin Mary. In 1206, Saint Albert of Jerusalem gave these hermits a Rule of Life, and the Church officially recognized them as an Order. In 1452, Blessed John Soreth, then Prior General of the Order, added a Second Order of Carmelites, comprised of women religious, and a Third Order of Carmelites, also called the Carmelite Order Secular, or Tertiaries, consisting of lay persons who felt called to live in harmony with Carmelite spirituality outside of convents or monasteries.

In the sixteenth century, the great Spanish Carmelite mystic St. Teresa of Avila was inspired to renew the fervor of the order and return it to its spiritual beginnings. Aided by St. John of the Cross, she began a reform movement that spread to the friars as well. After her death, convents and monasteries of her reform were established in France and Belgium, and from these two countries daughter houses were founded in England, Scotland, and Wales. Today Carmelite convents and monasteries can be found in almost every country of the world.

Founded in 1838, the Carmel of Lisieux was based on the reformed rule of St. Teresa of Avila. Five nuns from the Carmel of Poitiers established the new Carmel, including two senior nuns, Mother Elizabeth of St. Louis, the Prioress; and Mother Geneviève of St. Teresa, the Sub-Prioress and Novice Mistress, who died in 1891, soon after Thérèse entered the convent.

In the mid-1890s, the Carmel of Lisieux was comprised of twenty-six nuns—twenty-two choir nuns and four lay Sisters. Its superior at the time of Thérèse's entrance, Mother Marie de Gonzague, was an educated woman, a refined member of the nobility. In 1893, Thérèse's elder sister Pauline, who had entered the community before Thérèse and had taken the name of Sister Agnes of Jesus, was elected prioress. Mother Marie and Mother Agnes were to alternate as prioress for a number of years.

At age fourteen and a half, Thérèse found the courage to speak to her father, Louis Martin, about becoming the fourth daughter in her family to enter a religious order.

Thérèse's Quest to Enter Carmel

Thérèse struggled, however, with how best to approach her father. "How was I to talk to him about letting go of his queen, he who had just sacrificed his three oldest ones? . . . Oh! What inner struggles I suffered before feeling the courage to talk about it! . . . However, I had to come to a decision. . . . In order to make my great revelation I chose the day of *Pentecost*. All day long I pleaded with the Holy Apostles to pray for me, to inspire in me the words that I was going to have to say. . . . Were they not the ones in fact who had to help the timid child that God was destining to become the apostle of apostles through prayer and sacrifice? . . .

"It was only in the afternoon when, coming back from Vespers [a late afternoon church service], I found the opportunity to talk to my dear father. . . . Through my tears I confided in him my desire to enter Carmel. Then his tears began mingling with my own, but he didn't say a word to turn me away from my vocation, being simply content to point out that I was still quite young to make such a serious determination. But I defended my cause so well, that with Papa's simple and upright nature, he was soon convinced that my desire was that of God Himself, and in his deep faith he cried out that God was giving him a great honor to ask him for his children in this way."

Having received her father's permission, Thérèse thought her path to Carmel would be smooth. But she did not anticipate her Uncle Isidore's firm refusal. However, seeing Thérèse's determination, and recognizing that she truly had a vocation, her uncle relented.

Thérèse later recalled the next hurdles: "A few days after I obtained my uncle's consent, I went to see you, beloved Mother [Pauline], and I told you about my joy that now my trials had passed. But how surprised and disappointed I was at hearing you tell me that the Superior would not consent to my entrance before the age of twenty-one. No one had thought about that opposition, the most invincible of all."

However, the Little Flower was a force to be reckoned with. Thérèse went immediately with her father and Céline to visit their priest, who coldly refused to

hear of such a young girl's entrance into an austere religious order. "Finally he ended by adding that he was
only the *bishop's delegate,* and that if the bishop wanted
to let me enter Carmel, he himself would have nothing
more to say. . . ."

No sooner said, then done! On October 31st, All
Saints' Eve, Thérèse and her father made their way to
Bayeux for an appointment with Bishop Hugonin and
his grand vicar, Fr. Révérony. "His Excellency asked me
if I had wanted for a long time to enter Carmel. 'Oh, yes!
Your Excellency. . . .' 'Let's see,' began Fr. Révérony,
laughing, 'you can't say that you've had this desire for
fifteen years.' 'That's true,' I replied, smiling as well, 'but
there aren't many years to subtract, because I've wanted
to become a nun beginning with my reaching the age of
reason, and I desired to enter Carmel as soon as I got to
know it well, because in that order I found that all the
aspirations of my soul would be fulfilled.' . . .

"His Excellency, thinking that he was being kind to
Papa, tried to make me stay a few more years with him.
So he was not a little *surprised* and *edified* to see him
stand up for me, interceding for me to obtain the permission to leave the nest at the age of fifteen. However,
it was all of no use. He said that before he made a decision a meeting with *the Superior of Carmel* was
absolutely necessary. I couldn't have heard anything
that would have given me greater suffering, because I
knew about the total opposition of our rector."

One last recourse remained open to Thérèse, and that
was to ask permission from the Holy Father, Pope Leo
XIII himself.

Appeal to the Pope

One week after the meeting with Bishop Hugonin, Thérèse, her sister Céline, and Louis Martin boarded a train for Rome in the company of a group of pilgrims who were journeying to the Eternal City to celebrate Pope Leo XIII's Golden Jubilee as a priest.

The long-awaited audience with Pope Leo XIII came on November 20th, 1887. "Leo XIII was seated on a great chair. . . . We passed before him in procession; each pilgrim knelt in turn, kissed Leo XIII's foot and hand, and received his blessing. . . . I was quite resolved *to speak,* but I felt my courage weaken when I saw, at the Holy Father's right hand, Fr. *Révérony!* . . . Almost at the same moment we were told on *his behalf* that he *forbade us to speak to* Leo XIII, since the audience was going on too long. . . .

"I turned toward . . . Céline, in order to learn her opinion. 'Speak,' she told me. A moment later I was at the Holy Father's feet and had kissed his slipper, and he was extending his hand out to me. But instead of kissing it, I joined my hands together and, lifting toward his face my eyes bathed in tears, I cried out, 'Most Holy Father, I have a great grace to ask of you! . . .' Then the Supreme Pontiff lowered his head toward me in such a way that my face almost touched his, and I saw his *dark* and *deep eyes* fix on me and seem to pierce me to the depths of my soul. 'Most Holy Father,' I said to him, 'in honor of your jubilee, allow me to enter Carmel at the age of fifteen! . . .'

"Emotion had without a doubt made my voice tremble, so, turning around toward Fr. Révérony, who was looking at me with surprise and discontent, the Holy Father said, 'I don't understand very well.' . . . 'Most Holy Father,' replied the Grand Vicar, 'this is *a child* who wants to enter Carmel *at the age* of fifteen, but the superiors are examining the question right now.' 'Well, my child,' the Holy Father continued as he looked at me kindly, 'do what the superiors tell you.' Then, placing my hands on his knees, I attempted one last effort, and I told him with a pleading voice, 'Oh! Most Holy Father, if you were to say yes, everyone would be willing! . . .' He looked at me fixedly and pronounced these words, emphasizing each syllable: 'All right. . . . All right. . . . *You will enter if it is God's will.*'

"The Holy Father's kindness was so encouraging that I wanted to speak to him some more, but the two gentlemen of the Papal Guard *touched me politely* to make me stand. Seeing that that wasn't sufficient, they took me by the arms, and Fr. Révérony helped them lift me up, because I was remaining there with my hands clasped together, leaning on Leo XIII's knees, and it was *by force* that they tore me away from his feet. . . . At the moment when I had been made to *stand up* in this way, the Holy Father put his hand over my lips, then raised it to bless me. . . . The two Papal Guards carried me so to speak as far as the door, and there, a third one gave me a Leo XIII medal."

Thérèse had pleaded her case before the highest authority in the Church, and now the audience was over. The remainder of the pilgrimage passed in a blur, and the three Martins returned home. Immediately Thérèse went to visit Pauline at Carmel and told her every detail of the trip. Pauline told her to write His Excellency the bishop to remind him about his promise. Thérèse did so, and then waited. But Christmas came, and there was no response.

On the day before her fifteenth birthday, Thérèse received the news that her desire had been granted—but she would have to wait: "The first day of the year 1888, Jesus made me another present of His cross, but this time I was alone in carrying it, because it was all the more sorrowful since it was not understood. . . . A *letter from Pauline* [now Sr. Agnes of Jesus] arrived, letting me know that His Excellency the bishop's reply had arrived on December 28th, the feast day of the *Holy Innocents,* but that she hadn't let me know about it, having decided that my entrance would not take place *until after Lent.*"

The ninth of April, 1888, was chosen for Thérèse's entrance. "The morning of the big day, after casting one last look about Les Buissonnets, that graceful nest of my childhood that I was not to see again, I left on the arm of my dear king to climb the mountain of Carmel. . . . After embracing all the members of my beloved family, I knelt before my incomparable father, asking for his blessing. In order to give it to me he *knelt as well* and blessed me while weeping. . . . A few moments later, the doors of the blessed ark [Carmel] closed on me, and there I received the welcoming embraces of the *dear Sisters. . . .* Finally my desires had been accomplished, and my soul felt such sweet and such deep PEACE that it would be impossible for me to express it.'"

Life at Carmel

Despite her youth, Thérèse understood the sacrifice that was now required of her: "With what deep joy did I repeat these words, 'It's forever, forever that I'm here!' This happiness wasn't fleeting. It wasn't to fly away with 'the illusions of the first days.' As for the *illusions,* God gave me the grace *not to have* ANY as I entered Carmel. I found the religious life to be as I had conceived it. No sacrifice surprised me, despite the fact that, as you know, my dear Mother, my first steps met with more thorns than roses! . . . Yes, suffering held out its arms to me, and I threw myself into those arms with love. . . ."

Thérèse's life at Carmel was much more demanding than the picture she paints in her writing. Daily life was rigorous, from rising at 4:45 AM until bedtime at 11 PM. Prayer, occupying about seven hours, was the nuns' most important duty. Work, occupying about five hours, was performed in solitude; it consisted of such tasks as doing laundry, washing dishes, baking, gardening, and caring for the sick. The nuns slept for six hours in the summer and seven in the winter.

Thérèse followed a time-honored path in becoming a nun: Her postulancy of nine months ended with her taking the Carmelite habit on January 10th, 1889. The next stage was her period as a Novice, lasting until her Profession—the taking of religious vows—on the

Blessed Virgin Mary's birthday, September 8th, 1890, and her taking of the veil on September 24th.

A year after Thérèse took her vows, she had the blessing of being present at the death of Mother Geneviève, the revered co-foundress of the convent. Soon afterward, Thérèse had a vivid dream: "One night after Mother Geneviève's death, I had a dream that was . . . comforting. I dreamed that she was making her testament, giving to each Sister one thing that had belonged to her. When my turn came, I thought I wouldn't receive anything, because she had nothing left. But standing up, she said three times with a penetrating accent, "To you, I leave my *heart.*"

Mother Geneviève's saintly heart was evident in Thérèse's behavior during the epidemic of influenza that attacked the convent in the winter of 1890-91. "The day of my nineteenth birthday was celebrated by a death, followed soon by two others. At that time I was the only one in the sacristy. The head Sister for this duty being gravely ill, I was the one who had to prepare the burials, open the grilles of the choir at the time of Mass, etc. God had given me many graces of strength at that time. . . . Death was the rule everywhere. The sickest ones were cared for by those who could hardly walk. As soon as one Sister had given up her last breath, we were obliged to leave her alone."

When the surviving members of the community recovered, Thérèse had gained acceptance. Most of the members of the Carmel community saw Thérèse as a simple little girl who became a good nun, but nothing more. In her nine years in the convent, Sr. Thérèse worked in the sacristy, cleaned the refectory [the dining room], painted pictures, wrote short pious plays for the Sisters—including two about Joan of Arc, and composed poems.

St. Thérèse's Little Way

In a letter to her sister Marie, Thérèse described one of her best-known legacies—her "little way":

"I want to seek the means of going to Heaven by a little way that is very straight, very short, a completely new little way.

"We're in an age of inventions. Now there's no more need to climb the steps of a staircase. In rich homes there are elevators that replace stairs to great advantage. I would also like to find an elevator to lift me up to Jesus, because I'm too little to climb the rough staircase of perfection. So I sought in the holy books the indication of the elevator that is the object of my desire, and I read these words that come from the mouth of Eternal Wisdom: 'Let all who are *simple* come to my house' [Isa. 9:4]. So I came, suspecting that I had found what I was looking for, and wanting to know, God, what You would do with the simple little one who would respond to Your call.

"I've continued my search, and here is what I've found: 'As a mother comforts her child, so I will comfort you. . . . [Y]ou will nurse and be carried on her arm and dandled on her knees' [Isa. 66:13, 12]. Oh! Never have words more tender, more melodious, come to rejoice my soul. The elevator that must lift me up to heaven is Your arms, Jesus! For that I do not need to become big. On the contrary, I have to stay little—may I become little, more and more."

Writing Down The Story

Were it not for the Holy Spirit's leading her sister Pauline, who in 1893 was elected prioress of Carmel, Sr. Thérèse of the Child Jesus of the Holy Face might have passed into obscurity. But in the winter of 1894, Pauline asked Thérèse to write the memoirs of her childhood. Over a period of time, Thérèse wrote the charming recollections that have come down to us as "Manuscript A," comprising chapters one through eight of the traditional editions of her writings, including this one.

In September, 1896, a few months after Thérèse showed the first symptoms of tuberculosis, her sister Marie asked her to write a memoir of a retreat she had taken. Thérèse wrote some of her loftiest words in this treatise that she called "My Vocation: Love," which has come down to us as "Manuscript B," comprising chapter nine of this edition.

As Thérèse's illness worsened, she was finally confined to the infirmary. There, at Mother Marie de Gonzague's direction, less than three months before her death, she penned her last writings, known as "Manuscript C," comprising chapters ten and eleven of this edition.

Sensing Thérèse's impending death, her sister Marie told her she would be very sorry when Thérèse died. "Oh! No, you will see," replied Thérèse. "It will be like a shower of roses. After my death, you will go to the mailbox, and you will find many consolations." The advancing tuberculosis ravaged Thérèse's frail body, and on September 30th, 1897, her exile came to an end. At the young age of twenty-four, she had found what she so longed for as a child: "the eternal rest of Heaven, the *Sunday* where the sun never sets in the *Homeland!*"

Yes, heaven would be a place of rest. But in another well-known passage, Thérèse presented a concept of eternity that shows the thinking of her mature years. Heaven is no longer seen as a time of rest, but a time of action: "I will spend my heaven doing good on earth." Millions bear testimony that Thérèse is continuing to do good, even today.

Publishing The Story of a Soul

Sensing the importance of the writings Thérèse had left behind, her sister Pauline, now Mother Agnes of Jesus, proposed to Mother Marie de Gonzague, who in 1896 had been reelected prioress, to publish them in place of the obituary that it was customary to send around to other Carmelite houses when a Sister died. Mother Marie agreed, and Mother Agnes set about organizing and editing the lengthy manuscripts. In March, 1898, Mother Marie sent the revised copy to Dom Godefroid Madelaine, a longtime friend of the community who had preached retreats there. Dom Madelaine suggested a few changes, including dividing the work into chapters and giving it the title *The Story of a Soul.*

The original printing of 2,000 copies of the book was completed in time for the anniversary of Thérèse's death on September 30th, 1898. It was an instant success, and reprint after reprint was made. In 1901 the book was translated into English, and by 1906 it had been published in six languages. By the time Thérèse was canonized in 1925, over twenty million copies had been sold in France alone.

Widespread interest in the original, unedited text brought about the publication of a facsimile edition of Thérèse's manuscripts in 1956. The Centenary Edition—a critical edition of Thérèse's complete works—was published in 1988. Further research brought the publication in 1992 of the New Centenary Edition, a copy of which was presented to Pope John Paul II on February 18th, 1993.

Much discussion has been conducted about Mother Agnes's contribution to the original text. Did she make excessive changes or edits to the original text? But when the edited book is compared to Thérèse's letters, which have been published verbatim, it becomes clear that it is Thérèse who speaks in *The Story of a Soul,* not Mother Agnes. As Thérèse's lifelong confidante, Mother Agnes understood her sister's heart better than any other person, and produced a work that has been described as accurate, simple, and clear. She understood that Thérèse wrote a personal memoir that was never aimed at publication. The facsimile and critical editions reveal that Mother Agnes was inspired to cut away certain childhood stories, references to third parties, and tedious passages, allowing her sister's true voice to come through clearly and succinctly. Still, the proof of the value of Mother Agnes's work lies in the millions of lives that have been touched by the book that resulted.

About this Edition

Many editions of the original French version of *The Story of a Soul* are in the public domain. For this edition, I obtained two of them. One was closer to Mother Agnes's edited version in that it did not contain Dom Madelaine's chapter divisions. The other contained the chapter divisions and subheadings that characterize most French editions. I compared the two editions word for word and found them nearly identical. In the few cases where there were variants, I chose the variant that most closely followed the spirit of the rest of the text.

Out of respect for the writings of this Doctor of the Church, I have given the complete and unabridged text. Every word that appeared in Mother Agnes's edited version appears in this edition, including obscure references that most abridged editions leave out. I retained the author's use of italics and her use of capitalization in places where current usage might call for lower case. I kept her frequent use of ellipsis points, an important aspect of her personal writing style that represents a transition in thought, not an omission from the text. I also retained the author's style of referring to herself in the first person and in the third person, often within the same paragraph. As much as is possible in a translation, I wanted this edition to retain the same feel as the original French version.

To make the text more understandable and pleasing to the eye, I retained Dom Madelaine's chapter divisions and the traditional subheadings. One area in which I did exercise editorial discretion was in dividing very long paragraphs into shorter ones.

Since in manuscripts A (chapters one through eight) and C (chapters ten and eleven), Thérèse wrote in conversational style, I used the English conversational convention of contracting words such as "I'm" and "can't" instead of using the more formal "I am" and "cannot." For manuscript B (chapter nine), which is written in a more formal style of French, I used a more formal style of English.

To avoid confusion between religious persons and Thérèse's natural relatives, I used initial lower case when referring to her sisters, her mother, and her father. The convention in this edition is therefore that nuns and priests are Sisters, Mothers, and Fathers, with initial capitals. When "Sister" and "Father" are followed by a name, their titles are abbreviated as "Sr." and "Fr."—for example, "Sr. Marie," "Fr. Pichon."

Following the practice of many editions, the French sources contained numerous Scripture references, most of which I incorporated into the text within brackets. In many cases I added additional references suggested by the text.

Thérèse knew the Bible intimately and made constant allusions to Scripture. The Bible she read was based on the Latin Vulgate text by St. Jerome. In most cases modern Bible versions, translated from the original languages, read much the same as the Vulgate. In keeping with the flowing style of Thérèse's writing, I have used *Today's New International Version* to render most Scriptures into English. In a few cases, the Vulgate read differently enough from modern versions that to accurately convey the point Thérèse was making, I used the Douay-Rheims version of the Bible that was translated into English using the Vulgate. Scriptures taken from the Douay-Rheims version are marked "D-R."

Thérèse's words were written to persons who would know the people she described, the events that occurred on dates she mentioned, and the religious terminology she used. To clarify passages that might not easily be understandable, I have added brief explanations in brackets within the text itself, rather than use footnotes or endnotes.

For well over a century, St. Thérèse of Lisieux's words have brought a spiritual shower of roses to all who have read them. It is to that aim that this new edition is offered.

Robert J. Edmonson, CJ
Orleans, Massachusetts

Chapter 1
Alençon
1873–1877

Springtime story of a little white Flower written by herself and dedicated to the Reverend Mother Agnes of Jesus [my sister Pauline, the current prioress of the Carmelite Convent at Lisieux]

It is to you, beloved Mother, to you who are twice my Mother, that I am coming to entrust the story of my soul. . . . The day you asked me to do this, it seemed to me that it would consume my heart needlessly by causing it to be engrossed with itself. But afterward Jesus made me feel that by simply obeying I would be pleasing to Him. Besides, I'm going to only do one thing: begin to sing of what I ought to repeat forever: *"The mercies of the Lord!!!"* [cf. Ps. 89:1] . . .

Before taking my pen in hand, I knelt before the statue of Mary (the one that gave us so many proofs of the Queen of Heaven's motherly partiality for our family), and I begged her to guide my hand so that I might not write a single line that would not be pleasing to her. Then, opening the Gospels, my eyes fell on these words: "Jesus went up on a mountainside and called to him those he wanted, and they came to him" [Mk. 3:13]. Now this is the mystery of my calling, of my whole life, and above all the mystery of Jesus' privileges over my soul. He doesn't call those who are worthy, but those He *wants*, or, as St. Paul puts it: "'I will have mercy on whom I have mercy, and I will have compassion on whom I have compassion.' It does not, therefore, depend on human desire or effort, but on God's mercy" [Rom. 9:15-16].

For a long time I wondered why God showed partiality, why all souls don't receive the same amount of graces. I was astounded to see Him lavish extraordinary favors on the Saints who had offended Him, such as St. Paul and St. Augustine, and whom He so to speak forced to receive His graces. Or when I read the life of Saints whom Our Lord was pleased to embrace from the cradle to the grave, without leaving in their path any obstacles that might hinder them from rising toward Him, and granting these souls such favors that they were unable to tarnish the immaculate brightness of their baptismal robes, I wondered why poor primitive people, for example, were dying in great numbers without even having heard the name of God pronounced. . . .

Jesus consented to teach me this mystery. He placed before my eyes the book of nature; I understood that all the flowers that He created are beautiful. The brilliance of the rose and the whiteness of the lily don't take away the perfume of the lowly violet or the delightful simplicity of the daisy. . . . I understood that if all the little flowers wanted to be roses, nature would lose its springtime adornment, and the fields would no longer be sprinkled with little flowers. . . .

So it is in the world of souls, which is Jesus' garden. He wanted to create great saints who could be compared to lilies and roses. But He also created little ones, and these ought to be content to be daisies or violets destined to gladden God's eyes when He glances down at His feet. Perfection consists in doing His will, in being what He wants us to be. . . .

I understood that Our Lord's love is revealed as well in the simplest soul who doesn't resist His grace in anything, as in the most sublime of souls. In fact, since the essence of love is to bring oneself low, if every soul were like the souls of the holy Doctors who have shed light on the Church through the clarity of their doctrine, it seems that God wouldn't come down low enough by coming only as far as their great hearts. But He created the child who doesn't know anything and only cries weakly, He created poor primitive persons who only have natural law as a guide—and it is to their hearts that He consents to come down: Here are wildflowers whose simplicity delights Him. . . .

By bringing Himself low in this way, God shows His infinite greatness. Just as the sun shines at the same time on the tall cedars and on each little flower as if it were the only one on earth, in the same way Our Lord is concerned particularly for every soul as if there were none other like it. And just as in nature all the seasons are arranged in such a way as to cause the humblest daisy to open on the appointed day, in the same way all things correspond to the good of each soul.

Doubtless, dear Mother, you're wondering with surprise where I'm going with all this, because until now I haven't said anything that looks like the story of my life. Yet you've asked me to write without holding back anything that might come to my thoughts. But it isn't about my life, properly speaking, that I'm going to write, it's about my thoughts concerning the graces that God has consented to grant me. I find myself at a point in my life when I can take a look back at the past. My soul has matured in the crucible of outward and inward trials. Now, like a flower strengthened by the storm, I lift my head, and I see that the words of the twenty-third psalm are coming true in me. ("The LORD is my shepherd, I lack nothing. He makes me lie down in green pastures, he leads me beside quiet waters, he refreshes my soul. . . . Even though I walk through the darkest valley, I will fear no evil, for you are with me; your rod and your staff, they comfort me.") Always the Lord has been for me "compassionate and gracious, slow to anger, abounding in love" [Ps. 103:8].

So, Mother, it is with happiness that I come to sing near you of the mercies of the Lord. . . . It is for you alone that I'm going to write the story of the *little flower* picked by Jesus. So I'm going to talk without restraint, without worrying about the style or the many digressions that I'm going to make. A mother's heart always understands her child, even when the child doesn't know how to do anything but stammer, so I'm sure that I'll be understood and read by you who formed my heart and offered it to Jesus! . . .

It seems to me that if a little flower could talk, it would tell simply what God has done for it, without trying to hide its blessings. Under the pretext of a false humility it wouldn't say that it is unsightly and lacking in perfume, that the sun has taken away its beauty and its stem has been broken, while it recognizes just the opposite in itself.

The flower that is going to tell its story rejoices in having to publish abroad the completely undeserved kindness of Jesus. It recognizes that nothing in itself was capable of attracting His divine glance, and that His mercy alone has made everything that there is of good in it. . . . It is He who caused it to be born on holy ground and, as it were, completely imbued with a *virginal perfume*. It is He who caused it to be preceded by eight dazzlingly white Lilies [my older sisters and brothers]. In His love, He wanted to preserve His little flower from the poisoned breath of the world. Hardly had its petals begun to open when the divine Savior transplanted it onto the mountain of Carmel, where already the two Lilies who had surrounded it and gently rocked it in the springtime of its life [my sisters Pauline and Marie] were spreading forth their sweet perfume. . . .

Seven years have passed since the little flower took root in the garden of the Bridegroom of virgins, and now *three* Lilies wave their scented petals around her [now that my sister Céline has also entered Carmel]. A little farther away one more lily [my sister Léonie] is blossoming under Jesus' gaze, and now the two blessed stalks who produced these flowers [Papa and Mama] are reunited for eternity in the heavenly homeland. . . . There they have found once again the four lilies [my two brothers and two sisters who died at an early age] whom the earth did not see in bloom. . . . Oh! May Jesus consent not to leave long on the far shore the flowers who remain in exile; may the branch of lilies be soon complete in heaven!

Mother, I have just summarized in a few words what the Good Lord has done for me. Now I'm going to enter into the details of my life as a child. I know that where another would only see a boring tale, your *motherly heart* will find charms. . . .

And then the memories that I'm going to bring up are also yours, since it is by your side that my childhood flowed, and I have the happiness of belonging to the incomparable parents who surrounded us with the same care and the same tenderness. Oh! May they consent to bless the littlest of their children and help her sing of the mercies of the Lord! . . .

In the story of my soul up to my entrance into Carmel I distinguish three very different periods. The first, in spite of its shortness, is not the least fruitful in memories: It extends from the awakening of my reason, up to the departure of our dear mother for the homeland of heaven.

God gave me the grace to open my intelligence quite early and to engrave so deeply in my memory the remembrances of my childhood that it seems to me that the things that I'm going to tell about happened yesterday. Without a doubt, Jesus wanted, in His love, to make me know the incomparable mother that He gave me, but whom His Divine hand was hastening to crown in Heaven! . . .

All my life it pleased the Good Lord to surround me with *love*. My earliest memories are imprinted with smiles and the most tender of embraces! . . . But if He had placed much *love* near me, He had also placed love into my little heart, creating it to be loving and sensitive. So I loved Papa and Mama very much, and showed them my tenderness in a thousand ways, because I was very expansive. Only the means that I used were sometimes strange, as a passage from a letter from Mama shows: "The baby is an unparalleled imp; she comes and gives me a hug and tells me she wants me to die: 'Oh! How I wish that you would die, my poor little mother! . . .' She's scolded, and she says, 'But it's so that you will go to heaven, since you say that you have to die to go there.' In the same way she wishes death for her father when she's in the midst of her excesses of love."

On the twenty-fifth of June, 1874, when I was barely eighteen months old, here is what Mama said about me: "Your father has just installed a swing. Céline [three and a half years older than Thérèse] is an unparalleled joy, but you ought to see the little one swing—it makes me laugh. She holds herself like a big girl; there's no danger that she'll let go of the rope, but when it doesn't go high enough, she cries out. We attach another rope onto her in front, but in spite of that I'm uneasy when I see her perched up there.

"A funny adventure happened to me recently with the little one. I'm in the habit of going to Mass at 5:30 AM. In the early days I didn't dare to leave her alone, but when I saw that she never woke up, I wound up deciding to leave her. I put her to bed in my own bed, and I pulled the cradle so close that it was impossible for her to fall out. One day I forgot to push the cradle into place. When I got home the little one wasn't in my bed. At the same time I heard a cry, so I looked around, and I saw her sitting on a chair across from the head of my bed. Her little head was lying on the cross bar, and she was asleep there—sleeping badly, because she was uncomfortable. I couldn't understand how she had fallen into that chair in a sitting position, because she'd been lying in bed. I thanked God that nothing had happened to her. This was really providential—she ought to have rolled off onto the floor. Her guardian Angel watched over her, and the souls in purgatory to whom I pray every day for the little one protected her. That's how I figure this . . . go figure it out for yourself! . . ."

At the end of the letter, Mama added, "The little baby has just passed her little hand over my face and kissed me. This poor little one doesn't want to leave me, she's with me continually. She loves to go to out in the garden, but if I'm not there she doesn't want to stay and cries until she's brought back to me. . . ." (Here's a passage from another letter:) "Little Thérèse was asking me the other day if she would go to heaven. I told her yes, if she was very good; she replied, 'Yes, but if I weren't cute, I'd go to hell. . . . But I know what I'd do, I'd fly up to be with you who would be in heaven. How would God do to take me? . . . You would be holding me tight in your arms?" I saw in her eyes that she positively believed that God couldn't do anything to her if she were in her mother's arms. . . .

"Marie [twelve years older than Thérèse] loves her little sister a lot—she finds her very cute. It would be very difficult for her not to, since the poor little one is very afraid of hurting her. Yesterday I wanted to give her a rose, knowing that that would make her happy, but she started begging me not to cut it, because Marie had told her not to. She was red in the face with emotion, but in spite of that, I gave her two of them. She didn't dare to appear in the house. It didn't matter that I told her the roses belonged to me. 'No, no,' she said, 'they're Marie's.'

"She's a child who easily gets emotional. As soon as some little bad thing happens to her, the whole world has to know about it. Yesterday after she unwittingly dropped a little corner of the tapestry, she was in a pitiful state, and then her father had to be told right away. He came home four hours later. Nobody was thinking about it any more, but very quickly she went to Marie and told her, 'Tell Papa that I tore the paper.' She was like a criminal awaiting the judge's sentence, but she has in her little head that she's going to be forgiven more easily if she accuses herself."

I loved my dear *godmother* [my oldest sister, Marie] very much. Without looking like it, I paid a lot of attention to everything that was being done and said around me. It seems to me that I had as much judgment about things as I do now. I used to listen attentively to what Marie was teaching Céline so I could do as she did. After she left the Visitation school, in order to be granted the favor of being allowed in her room during the lessons that she was teaching Céline, I was very good and I did everything she asked. So she showered me with presents, which, in spite of their being of little value, gave me a great deal of pleasure.

I was quite proud of my two big sisters [Marie and Pauline], but the one who was my *ideal* as a child was Pauline. . . . When I started to talk and Mama asked me, "What are you thinking about?" the answer was an invariable, "Pauline! . . ." Another time, I was tracing my little finger over the floor tiles, and I said, "I'm writing 'Pauline'! . . ." Often I used to hear that of course Pauline was going to be a *nun.* So, without knowing too much about what that was, I thought, *I'm going to be a nun, too.* That's one of my earliest memories, and ever since, I've never changed my resolve! . . .

You were the one, dear Mother [Pauline], whom Jesus chose to engage me in marriage to Himself. You weren't at my side then, but a link had already been formed between our souls. . . . You were my *ideal,* I wanted to be like you; and it was your example that, from the age of two, drew me to the Bridegroom of virgins. . . . Oh! What sweet thoughts I would like to confide in you! But I need to pursue the story of the little flower, its complete and general story, because if I wanted to talk in detail about my relationship with "Pauline," I'd have to leave everything else out! . . .

Dear little Léonie [my middle sister, nine years older than I] also held a big place in my heart. She loved me a lot. In the evening she was the one who watched me when the whole family used to go for a walk. . . . It seems as if I can still hear the gentle songs that she used to sing in order to help me go to sleep. . . . In everything she looked for a way to please me, so I would have been very upset if I gave her trouble. I remember her first Communion very well, especially the moment when she carried me in her arm to take me with her into the rectory. It seemed so beautiful to be carried by a big sister dressed all in white like me! . . . That night I was put to bed early because I was too little to stay at the big dinner, but I can still see Papa coming in, bringing his little darling some pieces of the dessert. . . .

The next day, or a few days later, we went with Mama to Léonie's little girlfriend's house. I think that that was the day our dear Mother took us behind a wall to give us some wine to drink after the dinner (that poor Mrs. Dagorau had served), because she didn't want to hurt the good woman, but she also didn't want us to miss out on anything. . . . Ah! How delicate is the heart of a mother! How it translates its tenderness into a thousand watchful caring acts that no one would think about!

Now it remains to me to talk about my dear Céline, my little childhood friend, but I have such an abundance of memories that I don't know which ones to choose. I'm

going to excerpt a few passages from letters that Mama
wrote you at the Visitation school, but I'm not going to
copy everything—that would take too long. . . . On July
10th, 1873 (the year I was born), here is what she told
you: "The wet nurse brought back little Thérèse on
Thursday. All she does is laugh. She especially liked little
Céline, and she burst into laughter with her. You might
say that she already wants to play; that will come soon.
She holds herself up on her little legs, stiff as a little post.
I think she's going to walk early and that she will have a
good character. She seems very intelligent and gives the
appearance of having a good future. . . ."

But it was especially after I came home from the wet
nurse's that I showed my affection for dear little Céline.
We got along very well, only I was livelier and more naïve
than she was. Although I was three and a half years
younger, it seemed to me that we were the same age.

Here's a passage from one of Mama's letters that will
show you how sweet Céline was and how naughty I was:
"My little Céline is completely given over to virtue—it's
the innermost feeling of her being; she has a truthful soul
and hates evil. As for the little imp, it's hard to know
how she'll turn out, she's so little, so scatterbrained! She
has more intelligence than Céline, but she's not as sweet,
and her hardheadedness is practically unshakable. When
she says 'no' nothing can make her give it up. You could
put her in the cellar for a whole day and she'd go to sleep
there rather than to say 'yes.'

"Yet she has a heart of gold. She's full of hugs and
says exactly what she thinks. It's curious to see her run
after me and confess, 'Mama, I pushed Céline just

once, I hit her once, but I won't do it again.' (It's like that for everything she does.)

"Thursday evening we were taking a walk near the train station when she absolutely wanted to enter the waiting room to look for Pauline. She ran ahead with a joy that pleased me, but when she saw that we had to go back home without getting on board the train to go get Pauline, she cried all the way home."

This last part of the letter reminds me of the happiness that I felt when I saw you come back from the Visitation school. You, Mother, took me in your arms, and Marie took Céline. Then I gave you lots of hugs and I bent over backward in order to admire your big pigtail. . . . Then you gave me a chocolate bar that you had been keeping for three months. You can imagine what a treasure this was for me! . . .

I also remember the trip that I took to Le Mans; this was the first time that I went on a train. What a joy it was to be traveling alone with Mama! . . . However, I don't know why anymore, but I began to cry, and all our dear Mother could present to my aunt in Le Mans was a little *ugly duckling*, all red with the tears that she had shed on the way. . . .

I don't remember anything about that visit, but only the moment when my aunt passed me a little white mouse and a little cardboard basket full of candies on which were *enthroned* two little sugar rings, just about the thickness of my finger. Immediately I cried out, "Such happiness! There will be a ring for Céline!"

But, such sadness! I took my basket by the handle, gave my other hand to Mama, and we left. After a few steps I looked at my basket and saw that my candies were almost all strewn on the street, like Tom Thumb's stones. . . . I looked closer and saw that one of the precious rings had suffered the deadly fate of the candies . . . I didn't have one to give to Céline! . . . Then my sorrow burst out, and I asked to go back; Mama didn't seem to be paying attention to me. It was all too much—my *tears* were followed by my *cries*. . . . I couldn't understand why she didn't share my pain, and that very much increased my suffering. . . .

Now I'll come back to the letters in which Mama talked to you about Céline and me. They're the best means I can use to let you know my character. Here's a passage in which my faults stick out like a sore thumb: "There's Céline, who plays a dice game with the little one. They argue from time to time, and Céline gives in, in order to have a pearl in her crown. I'm obliged to correct the little baby, who flies into terrible rages. When things don't go the way she wants them to, she rolls on the ground like a madwoman who thinks all is lost. There are times when it gets so strong that she loses her breath. She's quite a nervous child, but she's cute and very intelligent—she remembers everything." You see, Mother, how far I was from being a little girl with no faults!

Nobody could even say about me that "I was good when I was asleep," because at night I was even more wiggly than during the day. I would send the covers flying, and then (asleep all the while) I would crash against the wood of my little bed. The pain would wake me up, and I would say, "Mama, I've been *bumped*." My poor dear mother had to get up and establish that I did in fact have knots on my forehead, and that I had been *bumped*. She would cover me up securely and go back to bed. But after a short time I started *being bumped* again, so that they had to *tie me in* my bed. Every night, little Céline would come and tie the several cords that were intended to keep the little imp from getting *bumped* and waking up her mama. This method finally worked, so from then on I was *good* while I was *asleep.* . . .

Another fault I had (when I was awake) and which Mama didn't talk about in her letters, is that I was very conceited. I'm only going to give you two examples so as not to make my story too long. One day Mama told me, "Dear little Thérèse, if you want to kiss the ground, I'm going to give you a penny." A penny was quite a lot of money for me. In order to get it I didn't have to lower my *great* height, because my *little* height didn't put a big distance between me and the ground. However, my pride revolted at the thought of *kissing the ground,* so, standing up very straight, I told Mama, "Oh! No, Mother, I'd rather not have a penny! . . ."

Another time we were supposed to go to Grogny to Mrs. Monnier's. Mama told Marie to dress me in my pretty, sky-blue, lace-trimmed dress, but not to leave my arms bare so the sun wouldn't burn them. I let myself be dressed with the indifference that children my age should have, but inside I was thinking that I would have been much nicer if my little arms were bare.

With a nature like mine, if I had been brought up by parents who lacked virtue, or even if like Céline I had

been spoiled by Louise [our maid], I would have
become bad and perhaps would have become lost. . . .
But Jesus was watching over His little bride-to-be. He
wanted everything to turn out for her good, even her
faults, which, curbed early on, have been used for her
growth in perfection. . . . Since I was full of *self-love*
and also *love* of *good*, as soon as I began to think seriously (which I did when I was quite little) it was
enough for someone to tell me that something wasn't
good, for me not to want to repeat it twice. . . .

I'm pleased to see in Mama's letters that as I grew up
I gave her more consolation. Since all I had around me
were good examples, I naturally wanted to follow
them. Here's what Mama wrote in 1876: "Even
Thérèse sometimes wants to get involved in religious
practices. . . . She's a charming child, fine as a shadow,
very quick, but her heart is sensitive. Céline and she
love each other a lot. They're all each other needs to
keep from getting bored. Every day right after dinner
Céline goes and gets her little rooster doll. She suddenly
catches Thérèse's hen doll—I can't get over it!—but
she's so quick that she grabs it on the first jump. Then
they both take their animals and sit beside the fire and
play nicely together for a long time. (It was little Rose
who had given me the hen and the rooster as a present,
and I had given the rooster to Céline.)

"The other day Céline was sleeping with me, and
Thérèse was sleeping on the second floor in Céline's
bed. She had begged Louise [our maid] to take her
downstairs so they could dress her. Louise went up to
look for her and found the bed empty. Thérèse had

heard Céline and had gone down to be with her. Louise said to her, 'So you don't want to go down and get dressed?' 'Oh no, poor Louise, we're like the two little chickens, we can't be separated!' And when she said that, the two girls kissed and hugged each other. . . . Then that evening, Louise, Céline, and Léonie left for the Catholic circle and left poor Thérèse, who understood very well that she was too little to go. So she said, 'If only they wanted to put me to bed in Céline's bed! . . .' But no, they didn't want to. . . . She didn't say anything and stayed alone with her little lamp, and fifteen minutes later she was fast asleep. . . ."

Another day Mama wrote again: "Céline and Thérèse are inseparable; you can't imagine two children loving each other more. When Marie comes to get Céline to teach her her lesson, poor Thérèse dissolves into tears. Alas, what is going to become of her? Her little friend is going to go away! . . . Marie feels sorry for her, she takes her along, too, and the poor little one sits on a chair for two or three hours. They give her pearls to string or a rag to sew. She doesn't dare budge and often heaves great sighs. When her needle loses its thread she tries to rethread it. It's curious to see her, not managing to get it threaded and not daring to disturb Marie; soon you can see two big tears running down her cheeks. . . . Marie quickly comforts her, rethreads the needle, and the little angel smiles through her tears. . . ."

In fact I can remember that I couldn't be separated from Céline. I would rather leave the table before finishing my dessert than not follow her as soon as she got up to leave. I would turn in my high chair and ask to be put down, and then we would go play together. Sometimes we went with a little friend, which pleased me to no end because of the park and all the beautiful toys that she used to show us, but it was really to please Céline that I would go.

What I really preferred was to stay in our little yard *to scratch the walls,* because we would pull off all the little shiny flakes of stone that we would find there, and then we would go *sell them* to Papa, who would buy them, looking very serious.

On Sundays, since I was too little to go to services, Mama stayed to watch me. I was very good, and I would only walk on tiptoe during the Mass. But as soon as I saw the door open, there was an unparalleled explosion of joy. I would rush in front of my *pretty* little sister, who was then *decked out like a chapel . . .* and I would say, "Oh, dear Céline, quick, give me some blessed bread!" Sometimes she didn't have any, since she had arrived there too late. . . . What could I do now? It was impossible for me to go without it; it was *my Mass.* The answer was quick in coming: "You don't have any blessed bread? Well, make some!" No sooner said, then done. Céline would take a chair, open the cupboard, take out some bread, cut a mouthful, and very *seriously* recite a *Hail Mary* over it, then present it to me. And I, after making the sign of the Cross with it, would eat it with *great devotion,* claiming that it *tasted* exactly like *blessed bread.*

Often we would do *spiritual teachings.* Here's one example that I'm borrowing from Mama's letters:

"Our two dear little ones, Céline and Thérèse, are angels of blessing, two little angelic natures. Thérèse is Marie's joy, happiness, and glory; it's unbelievable how proud she is of her. It's true that she comes up with answers that are quite unusual at her age; she shows up Céline, who's twice as old as she is. The other day Céline was saying, 'How is that God can be in such a little Communion host?' Little Thérèse said, 'That's not so surprising since God is all-powerful.' 'What does that mean, "all-powerful"?' 'Well, it means He can do what He wants! . . .'"

One day Léonie, thinking she was now too big to play with dolls, came and found us both with a basket full of dresses and pretty little pieces of cloth intended to make others; on top was sitting her doll. "Here, little sisters," she said, "you *choose,* I'm giving you all this." Céline stuck out her hand and took a little ball of yarn that she liked. After thinking about it for a moment, I in turn stuck out my hand and said, "*I choose all!*" And I took the basket without further ceremony. Those who were watching the scene thought it was quite fair—Céline herself didn't think to complain. (Besides, she had no lack of toys; her godfather showered her with presents, and Louise found a way to get her anything she wanted.)

This childhood trait sums up my whole life. Later, when perfection made its appearance to me, I understood that in order to become *a saint* you have to suffer a lot, always be in search of what is the most perfect, and forget yourself. I understood that there are many degrees of perfection, and that each soul is free to respond to

Our Lord's advances, to do little or much for Him—in a word, to *choose* among the sacrifices that He requires. Then, just as in the days of my childhood, I cried out, "Dear God, *I choose all*. I don't want to be a *halfway saint*. It doesn't scare me to suffer for You; I'm afraid of only one thing, and that is to hold onto my *will*. Take it, because '*I choose all*,' all that You want! . . ."

I have to stop here. I shouldn't talk yet about the time of my youth, but about the little four-year-old imp. I remember a dream that I must have had around that age and that is deeply engraved in my imagination. One night I dreamed that I was going out to take a walk alone in the garden. Arriving at the foot of the steps that I had to go up to get there, I stopped, paralyzed with fear. In front of me, near the arbor, stood a barrel of lime, and on that barrel two *horrible* little *devils* were dancing with surprising agility in spite of the clothing irons they had on their feet. Suddenly they cast their flaming eyes on me, but just at the same time, looking more scared than I was, they jumped off the barrel and went and hid in the laundry that was just across the way. When I saw how un-brave they were, I wanted to know what they were going to do, and I went up to the window. The poor little devils were there, running on the tables, not knowing what to do to escape my looks. Sometimes they would go up to the window, looking out with a troubled expression to see if I were still there. When they saw me still there, they started running around again like madmen.

No doubt this dream is nothing out of the ordinary, but nonetheless I think that God allowed me to remember it in order to prove to me that a soul in the state of grace has nothing to fear from demons, who are cowards, capable of running away from a child's glance. . . .

Here's another passage that I found in Mama's letters: Poor Mother was already sensing that the end of her earthly exile was coming: "The two little ones don't worry me, they both get along so well. They are chosen natures; certainly they will be good. Marie and you will be perfectly able to raise them. Céline never commits the slightest voluntary fault. The little one will be good, too. She would never lie for all the gold in the world. She has a mind and a spirit like I've never seen in the rest of you.

"The other day she was at the grocer's with Céline and Louise, and she was talking about her religious practices and was discussing this strongly with Céline. The lady said to Louise, 'What does she mean, when she plays in the garden and all she hears about is religious practices? Mrs. Gaucherin sticks her head out her window to try to understand what this debate about religious practices is all about.' . . .

"This poor little one is our happiness, she will be good, you can already see it coming. All she talks about is God; she wouldn't miss saying her prayers for anything. I wish you could see her reciting little fables; I've never seen anything so nice. All by herself she finds the expression that she needs to give, and the tone, but it's especially when she says, 'Little blond-haired child, where do you think God is?' When she comes to 'He's up there in the blue sky,' she turns her face upward with an angelic expression. We never get tired of having her do it, it's so beautiful. There's something so heavenly in her look that we're quite taken by it! . . ."

Oh, Mother! How happy I was at that age. Already I was beginning to enjoy life. Virtue had its charms for me, and I was, it seems to me, already disposed in the same way I am now, already having great control over my actions. Ah! How quickly they passed by, those sunny years of my early childhood, but what a sweet imprint they left on my soul!

I remember with happiness the days when Papa took us to the *cottage;* the slightest details are engraved on my heart. . . . I especially remember the Sunday walks when Mama always went with us. . . . I can still feel the deep and *poetic* impressions that were born in my soul at the sight of the wheat fields spangled with *cornflowers* and wildflowers. Already I loved *faraway places.* . . . The spaces and the giant pine trees with branches touching the ground left in my heart an impression like the one I still feel today at the sight of nature. . . .

Often during these long walks we used to meet poor people, and it was always little Thérèse whose duty it was to give them alms, and she was happy to do so. But also, Papa often would find that the route was too long for his little queen, so he would take her home earlier than the others (much to her great displeasure). So, to comfort her, Céline would fill her pretty little basket with daisies and give them to her when she got back home. But alas! The poor "granny" would find that her "granddaughter" had too many of them, so she would take a good part of them to [place in front of the statue of] the Blessed Virgin. . . . Little Thérèse didn't like that, but she was careful not to say anything about it, having adopted the good habit of never complaining, even when something that belonged to her was taken away, or when she was unjustly accused. She preferred to hold her tongue and not excuse herself. This wasn't merit on her part, but natural virtue. . . .

What a shame that this good disposition vanished! . . . Oh! truly, everything on earth was smiling at me: I found flowers under every one of my steps, and my happy character also contributed to making my life pleasant. But a new period was going to begin for my soul. I was going to have to pass through the crucible of trials and to suffer, beginning in my childhood, in order to be able to be offered sooner to Jesus. In the same way as the springtime flowers begin to germinate under the snow and begin to open at the first rays of the Sun, even so the little flower whose memories I'm writing about had to pass through the winter of trial. . . .

CHAPTER 2

At "Les Buissonnets"
1877–1881

Mama's death
Lisieux
Papa's tenderness
First confession
Family holidays and Sundays
Prophetic vision
Trouville

All the details of our dear mother's sickness are still present in my heart. I especially remember the last weeks that she spent on earth. Céline and I were like little exiles. Every morning Mrs. Leriche would come and get us, and we would spend the day at her place. One day we hadn't had the time to say our prayers before leaving, and as we went, Céline whispered to me, "Should we tell her that we haven't said our prayers? . . ." "Oh, yes," I answered. So, timidly, she told Mrs. Leriche, who replied, "Well, little girls, you're going to say them." And then, putting us both in a big room, she left. . . . Then Céline looked at me, and we said, "Oh, that's not like Mama. . . . She always had us say our prayers with her! . . ."

When we played with other children, the thought of our dear mother always stayed with us. Once Céline

was given a beautiful apricot. She leaned over and
whispered to me, "We aren't going to eat it; I'm going
to give it to Mama." Alas, our dear little mother was
already too sick to eat the fruits of the earth. She was
no longer able to have her hunger *satisfied* except in
Heaven, filled with the *glory* of God, and her thirst
assuaged except by *drinking* with Jesus *the mysterious
wine* that He talked about in His Last Supper, when He
said that He would share it with us in His Father's
kingdom [Mt. 26:29].

The touching ceremony of Last Rites is also imprinted
on my soul. I can still see the place where I stood beside
Céline. All five of us stood, from oldest to youngest,
and our dear father was also there, sobbing. . . .
   The day after Mama left us, or perhaps the next, he
took me in his arms and said, "Let's go kiss your poor little mother one last time." And without saying anything,
I reached my lips to my dear mother's forehead. . . . I
don't remember crying a lot; I didn't talk to anyone
about the deep feelings I was experiencing. . . . I watched
and listened in silence. . . . Nobody had the time to be
concerned with me, so I saw lots of things that they
might have wanted to keep hidden from me. Once, I
found myself standing in front of the coffin lid. . . . I
stopped and considered it for a long time. I had never
seen anything like it, but nevertheless I understood. . . . I
was so little that despite Mama's short stature, I was
obliged to *raise* my head to see the top, and it seemed
very *big . . . very vast* to me. . . .

Fifteen years later I found myself in front of another coffin, that of Mother Geneviève [the co-foundress of the Carmel at Lisieux]; it was the same size as Mama's, and I thought I was back in the days of my childhood. . . . All my memories crowded in. It really was the same little Thérèse who was watching, but she had *grown up* and the coffin looked little to her. She didn't have to *raise* her head to see it; she no longer *raised* it except to contemplate *heaven,* which seemed *quite joyful* to her, because all her trials had come to an end and the winter of her soul had passed away forever [Song 2:10-11]. . . .

The day when the Church blessed the mortal remains of our dear mother, who was now in heaven, it was God's will to give me another mother on earth, and He wanted me to choose her freely. All five of us were together, looking at each other sadly. Louise [our maid] was there, too, and upon seeing Céline and me, she said, "Poor little girls, you don't have a mother any more! . . ." Then Céline jumped into Marie's arms and said, "Well! You will be Mama now." Now, I was accustomed to doing just as she did, but this time I turned toward you, Mother, and, as if the veil over the future had already been torn open, I threw myself into your arms and cried out, "Well, for me, Pauline will be Mama!"

As I said before, beginning with this time in my life I had to enter the second period of my existence, the most painful of the three, especially after the entrance into the Carmelite convent of the one whom I had chosen to be

my second "Mama." This period stretches from the age
of four and a half until my fourteenth year, the period
when I found my character as a *child* again, while yet
entering into the seriousness of life.

I have to tell you, Mother, that starting with Mama's
death, my happy character changed completely. I, who
had been so lively, so expansive, became timid and
mild, sensitive to excess. One look was enough to make
me burst into tears. I was happy only when nobody
was bothering with me. I couldn't stand the company
of strangers, and I resumed my customary high spirits
only when I was with the intimate family. . . .

Nonetheless, I continued to be surrounded by the
most delicate *tenderness*. Papa's heart, which was so
tender, had joined a truly motherly love to the love that
he already had! . . . Weren't you, Mother, and Marie
the *most tender,* the most impartial of mothers to me?
. . . Oh! If God hadn't lavished His kindly *rays* on His
little flower, she would never have been able to become
acclimated to the earth. She was still too weak to
endure rain and storms; she needed warmth, gentle
dew, and springtime breezes. She never went without
these blessings; Jesus caused her to find them, even
underneath the snows of trials!

I wasn't upset at leaving Alençon. Children like change,
and I was pleased to go to Lisieux. I remember the trip
and arriving in the evening at my aunt's. I can still see
Jeanne and Marie [my cousins] who were waiting for
us at the door. . . . I was so happy to have such nice
little cousins. I loved them a lot, as well as my aunt

[Céline Guérin] and especially my uncle [Isidore Guérin, Mama's brother]—only I was afraid of him, and I didn't feel at ease in his home as I did at "Les Buissonnets" ["The Hedges," our family's rented house]—it was there that my life was truly happy. . . .

In the morning you would come see me and ask me if I had given my heart to God. Then you would dress me while talking about Him, and then, at your side, I would say my prayers. After that came my reading lesson. The first word I could read by myself was this: "Heaven." My dear godmother [my sister Marie] was in charge of the writing lessons, and you, Mother, were in charge of all the others. I didn't find it very easy to learn, but I had a good memory. Catechism and sacred history were my favorites. I used to study them with joy, but grammar often brought me to tears. . . . "Remember which French nouns are masculine and which are feminine!"

As soon as my class was over, I would climb up on the belvedere [a small, roofed pavilion] carrying my little red chalk and my note for Papa. How happy I was when I could tell him, "I got a five without any *exceptions. Pauline* was the one who said it *first!* . . ." That's because when I asked you if I got a five without any exceptions and you said yes, in my eyes it was one point less. You also used to give me points for being good. When I had accumulated a certain number of them, I got a reward and a day off. I remember that those days seemed much longer to me than the others, and that pleased you, since that showed that I didn't like to sit around doing nothing.

Every afternoon I would go on a little walk with Papa. We would go visit the Blessed Sacrament, visiting a different church each day, and that's how I entered the chapel of the Carmelite convent for the first time. Papa showed me the grille in the choir and told me that there were nuns behind it. I certainly didn't suspect that nine years later I would be one of them! . . .

After our walk, during which Papa always used to buy me a little gift for a small coin or two, I would go back home. Then I would do my homework, and then all the rest of the time I would stay to go skipping in the garden around Papa, because I didn't *know how* to play with dolls.

It was a great joy to me to prepare "herb teas" using little grains from tree bark that I would find on the ground. I would then take them to Papa in a pretty little cup. Poor Papa would leave his work and then, smiling, pretend to drink it. Before giving me back the cup he would ask me (sort of on the sly) if he should toss the contents. Sometimes I would say yes, but more often I would take away my precious herb tea, wanting to serve it several times. . . .

I used to love to cultivate my little flowers in the garden that Papa had given me. I would have a good time making little altars in the hollow that was in the middle of the wall. When I had finished, I would run to Papa, and, leading him along, I would tell him to shut his eyes tight and open them only when I told him to. He did everything I wanted, and let himself be led to my little garden. Then I would cry out, "Papa, open your eyes!"

He would open them and gush in order to give me pleasure, admiring what I thought was a masterpiece! . . .

I'd never stop if I told you the thousand little stories like that one that come crowding into my memory. . . . Oh! How could I tell you all the tenderness that Papa showered on his little queen? There are things that the heart feels, but that words and even thoughts can't manage to express. . . .

Those were beautiful days for me, days when my "dear king" used to take me fishing with him. I used to love the country, the flowers, and the birds so much! Sometimes I would try to fish with my little fishing pole, but I preferred to go sit *alone* on the flower-covered ground. Then my thoughts were very deep, and without knowing what it meant to meditate, my soul would plunge into real prayer. . . . I would hear distant noises. . . . The murmur of the wind and even the distant, indistinct music of soldiers whose sounds came to my ears would bring a sweet melancholy to my heart. . . . The earth seemed to me a place of exile, and I would dream of heaven. . . .

The afternoon would pass by quickly, and soon we would have to go back to "Les Buissonnets." But before leaving I would take out the snack that I had brought in my little basket. The *beautiful* bread and jam that you had prepared for me had changed in appearance: Instead of its bright color I saw only a light rose tint, old and worn out. . . . Then the world seemed still sadder, and I understood that only in heaven would joy be without clouds. . . .

Speaking of clouds, I remember that one day the beautiful blue sky of the countryside covered over and soon a storm began to rumble. Lightning streaked across the dark clouds, and I saw thunderbolts strike. Not at all frightened, I was thrilled. It seemed that God was so close to me! . . . Papa was not at all as happy as his little queen; it was not that the storm made him afraid, but the grass and the big daisies (which were as tall as I was) shimmered with raindrops like precious stones. We had to cross several meadows before finding our way, and my dear father, fearing that the diamonds would get his little girl wet, picked her up, despite his baggage of fishing poles, and carried her on his back.

During the walks that I used to take with Papa, he liked to have me give alms to the poor people we met. One day we saw a man who was hobbling along painfully on crutches. I approached him and offered him a small coin, but, not finding himself poor enough to receive charity, he looked at me, smiling sadly, and refused to take what I was offering him. I can't say what happened in my heart; I would have like to give him some comfort, some relief. Instead of that I thought I had hurt him. No doubt the poor invalid guessed what I was thinking, because I saw him turn around and smile at me.

Papa had just bought me a cake. I really wanted to give it to the man, but I didn't dare. But I wanted to give him something that he couldn't refuse, because I felt great sympathy for him. So I remembered hearing that on the day of your first Communion you get whatever you ask for. This thought comforted me, and even though I was only six years old, I told myself, "I'll pray for *my poor person* on the day of my first

Communion." I kept my promise five years later, and I hope that God heard and granted the prayer that He had inspired me to direct toward Him for one of His suffering children. . . .

I loved God very much, and I often gave Him my heart using the little formula that my mama had taught me. One day, however, or rather one evening in the beautiful month of May, I committed a fault that's well worth the trouble of being reported. It gave me quite an opportunity to be humbled, and I believe that I've made perfect contrition for it.

Since I was too little to go to the special devotions for Mary's month [the month of May], I stayed with our maid, Victoire, and with her I made my devotions in front of *my little Mary's month*, which I arranged in my own way. Everything was so little: candleholders and pots of flowers, which two wax "Vesta" matches illumined perfectly. Sometimes Victoire would surprise me with two little wax tapers, but that was rare.

One night everything was ready for us to begin our prayers, when I said, "Victoire, would you please start the 'Memorare' ['Remember'—a prayer asking for the Virgin Mary's protection]? I'm going to light the matches." She pretended to begin, but she didn't say anything and looked at me, laughing. As I watched my *precious matches* burning quickly down, I begged her to start the prayer, but she continued to keep quiet. Then, getting up, I started telling her that she was very naughty, and, departing from my usual mildness, I stamped my feet as hard as I could. . . . Poor Victoire didn't feel like laughing any more; she looked at me with surprise and showed me the wax tapers that she had brought me. . . . After having shed tears of anger, I now cried tears of sincere repentance and made a firm resolve not to do that ever again!

Another time I had an adventure with Victoire, but I didn't have any cause for repentance that time, because I stayed perfectly calm. I wanted to have an inkwell that was kept on the mantel in the kitchen. Since I was too little to get it, I asked Victoire very *nicely* to give it to me, but she refused, telling me to get up on a chair. I pulled out a chair without saying anything, but I was thinking that she wasn't very kind. Wanting to make her feel that, I searched in my little head for what was the most offensive thing to me, which was that when she was annoyed with me she often called me a "little brat," and that humiliated me a lot. So, before *jumping off* my *chair*, I turned with *dignity* and told her, "Victoire, you're a *brat!*" Then I ran off, leaving her to meditate on the profound word that I had just spoken to her. . . .

The result was unexpected: Soon I heard her crying out, "Miss Marie . . . Thérèse just told me that I'm a *brat!*" Marie came and made me apologize, but I did it without being sorry, finding that since Victoire hadn't wanted to extend *her big arm* to do me a *little favor,* she deserved the title of *brat.* . . .

Nonetheless, she liked me a lot, and I liked her a lot too. One day she pulled me out of a *grave danger* that I had fallen into through my own fault. Victoire was ironing, having next to her a bucket with water in it. I was watching her while swinging (as was my custom) on a chair. Suddenly the chair gave way and I fell, not

on the floor, but into the *bottom* of the *bucket!* . . . My
feet touched my head and I filled the *bucket* like a little
chick fills an egg! . . . Poor Victoire looked at me with
extreme surprise, never having seen such a thing. I really
wanted to get out of my *bucket* immediately, but it was
impossible. My prison was so tight that I couldn't move
an inch. With a little bit of trouble she saved me from
my *great danger.* Not so with my dress and all the rest
of my clothing, which she was obliged to change,
because I was soaked.

Another time I fell into the fireplace, but fortunately
the fire wasn't lit. Victoire's only misfortune was to
pick me up and shake off the ashes that I was covered
with. It was on Wednesdays, when you were off at
chant with Marie, that all these adventures used to
happen to me.

It was also on a Wednesday that Fr. Ducellier came to
pay a visit. When Victoire told him that nobody was
home except little Thérèse, he came into the kitchen to see
me and look at my homework. I was very proud to wel-
come *my confessor,* because a short time before that I had
gone to confession for the first time. What a delightful
memory that was for me! . . . Oh, dear Mother! With
such care you prepared me! telling me that it wasn't to a
man, but to God, that I was going to tell my sins. I was
really quite convinced of that, so I made my confession
with a great spirit of faith, and I even asked you if I
should tell Fr. Ducellier that I loved him with all my heart
because I was going to talk to God through him. . . .

Well instructed in what I should say and do, I went
into the confessional and knelt down, but when he

opened the grille Fr. Ducellier didn't see anyone. I was so little that my head was below the little shelf on which people fold their hands. So he told me to stand up. Obeying immediately, I stood up and, turning directly toward him so I could see him well, I made my confession like a *big girl*, and I received his blessing with *great devotion*, because you had told me that at that moment the *tears* of the *Baby Jesus* were going to purify my soul. I remember that the first exhortation that was addressed to me invited me especially to devotion to the Blessed Virgin, and I promised to redouble my tenderness toward her.

When I left the confessional I was so happy and so light that I've never felt so much joy in my soul. Afterward I returned to confess at every important holiday, and it was a true celebration for me each time I went.

Holidays! . . . Oh! how this word brings back memories! . . . *Holidays!* How I loved them so much! . . . You knew how to explain to me, dear Mother, all the mysteries hidden underneath each one of them so that they were truly, for me, days from Heaven. I especially loved the processions of the Blessed Sacrament. What a joy it was to cast flowers under God's feet! . . . But before letting them fall there I would throw them as high as I could, and I was never so happy as when I saw my leafless roses *touch* the sacred monstrance [a receptacle in which the consecrated host was placed in an opening through which it could be viewed]. . . .

Holidays! Oh! If the big ones are rare, each week brings one that's quite dear to my heart: "Sunday!"

What a day it is, this day called *Sunday!* . . . It was
God's holiday, the day of *rest*. First of all I stayed *in bed*
longer than on other days. And then Mama Pauline
would spoil her little daughter, bringing her hot chocolate
as she lay in bed. And then she would dress her up like
a little queen. . . . The godmother [Marie] curled the
hair of her *goddaughter,* who wasn't always nice when
her hair was pulled. But then she was quite happy to go
take the hand of her king who, on that day, kissed her
even more tenderly than usual. And then the whole
family would leave to go to Mass.

All along the way and even in church, little "Papa's
queen" would give him her hand. Her place was at his
side, and when we were obliged to go down for the
sermon he had to find another two chairs side by side.
This wasn't hard to do; everybody looked as if they
found it so nice to see such a *handsome* elderly man
with *such a little girl* that people moved aside to give up
their places. My Uncle, who used to sit in the church-
wardens' pew, was delighted to see us arrive. He used
to say that I was his little ray of sunshine. . . .

I hardly worried about being looked at, and I listened
quite attentively to the sermons, even though I could
hardly understand anything about them. The first one
that I *understood* and that *touched me deeply* was a
sermon on the Passion preached by Fr. Ducellier, and
after that I understood all the other sermons.

When the preacher would talk about St. Teresa, Papa
used to bend over and whisper to me, "Listen, my little
queen, they're talking about your Patron Saint." In fact
I was listening, but I used to look at Papa more often

than at the preacher; his beautiful face told me so many things! . . . Sometimes his eyes used to fill with *tears* that he would try in vain to hold back. He seemed already not to hold on to earth, so much did his soul love to plunge into eternal truths. . . . However, his course was far from being finished; long years were to pass before beautiful heaven was to open to his delighted eyes and the Lord was to wipe away the *tears* of his good and faithful servant! . . . [cf. Rev. 21:4, Mt. 25:21]

But I'll come back to my day on Sundays. This *joyful* day, which passed so quickly, had its own tinge of *melancholy.* I remember that my happiness was unmixed until Compline [the evening service]. During that service I used to think how the day of *rest* was going to end . . . and the next day I'd have to go back to life, work, and learning lessons, and my heart would feel the *exile* of the world. . . . I would long for the eternal rest of heaven, the *Sunday* where the sun never sets in the *Homeland!* . . .

It wasn't until the walks that we used to take before going back to "Les Buissonnets" that a feeling of sadness would enter my soul, since the family wasn't complete anymore. That's because to please my uncle, every Sunday evening Papa would leave Marie *or Pauline* with him. Only I was quite happy when I stayed, too. I liked that better than being invited all alone, because they paid less attention to me. My greatest pleasure was to listen to everything my uncle used to say, but I didn't like it when he would ask me questions, and I was quite scared when he would put me on *only one* of his knees and sing "Bluebeard" with gusto.

It was with pleasure that I would see Papa come back to get us. On my way home I would look at the *stars* that were twinkling gently, and that sight would fill me with delight. . . . There was especially one group of *golden pearls* that I noticed joyfully, finding that it had the shape of a T (well, that's about what its shape was . . .). I would show it to Papa and tell him that my name was written in the heavens [Lk. 10:20], and then, not wanting to see anything on the horrid old earth, I would ask him to guide me while, without watching where I was stepping, I would thrust my little head into the air, never growing tired of contemplating the starry sky! . . .

What can I say about winter evenings, especially Sunday evenings? Oh! How sweet it was after the *checkers game* to sit with Céline on Papa's lap. . . . With his beautiful voice, he would sing songs that filled the soul with deep thoughts. . . . Or sometimes, rocking us gently, he would recite poems full of eternal truths. . . . Then we would go up to say our prayers together, and the little queen would be alone with her king, having only to watch him to know how the Saints pray. . . .

At the end we would all come in order of age to say good night to Papa and get a kiss. Naturally, the *queen* was last, and to give her a hug the *king* would take her by the *elbows* and she would cry out, "Good night, Papa, have a good night, sleep well." That's the way it was every night. . . .

Then my dear mama would take me into her arms and carry me to Céline's bed, and I would say, "Pauline, have I been cute today? . . . Are the *little angels going to fly around me?*" The answer was always yes—otherwise I would have spent the whole night crying. . . . After giving me a hug, as well as my dear godmother, *Pauline* would go back downstairs, and poor little Thérèse would be all alone in the dark. It was in vain that she would try to imagine the *little angels flying around her.* Soon dread would overtake her; the shadows would make her afraid, since from her bed she couldn't see the stars that were gently twinkling. . . .

I see it as a true grace to have become accustomed by you, dear Mother, to overcoming my fears. Sometimes you would send me alone at night to get an object from a distant room. If I hadn't been so well trained, I would have become quite fearful, but instead now it's really hard to scare me. . . . I sometimes wonder how you could have raised me with so much *love* and sensitivity without spoiling me, because it's true that you never let me get away with a single imperfection. You never reproached me without a cause, but you never took back anything that you had decided on. I knew this so well that I would have neither been able to nor wanted to take a single step if you had told me not to.

Papa himself was obliged to conform to your will. Without *Pauline's* consent I wouldn't go out for walks, and when Papa would tell me to come, I would answer, "Pauline doesn't want me to." Then he would come and ask for me to go, and sometimes to please him *Pauline* would say yes. But little Thérèse could see by the look on her face that it wasn't willingly that she said yes, so little Thérèse would start crying inconsolably until *Pauline would say yes and give her a big hug!*

When little Thérèse was sick, something that happened every winter, it's impossible to say with what motherly tenderness she was taken care of. Pauline would put her in her own bed (an incomparable favor), and then she would give her everything she wanted.

One day Pauline pulled out from underneath the bolster a *pretty little knife of hers,* and, giving it to her little girl, left her plunged into indescribable delight. "Oh! Pauline," she cried out, "so you love me so much that for me you're depriving yourself of your pretty little knife that has a *mother of pearl star?* . . . But since you love me so much, would you sacrifice your *watch* in order to keep me from *dying?* . . ." "Not only to keep you from dying would I give you my watch, but just to see you get well soon, I'd make that sacrifice in an instant." When I heard those words of *Pauline's,* my great surprise and my thankfulness were so great that I can't begin to express them. . . .

In the summer I sometimes used to have a stomach ache. Again, Pauline would take care of me tenderly. In order to cheer me up, which was the best of remedies, she would *wheel me in a wheelbarrow* all around the garden, and then, helping me down, she would put in my place a pretty little head of daisies that she would *wheel* very *carefully* up to my garden, where it was placed with great ceremony. . . .

Pauline was the one who heard my most intimate confidences, who enlightened all my doubts. . . . One time I was expressing surprise that God should not give equal glory in heaven to all His elect, and I was afraid that everyone would not be happy. Then Pauline told me to go get Papa's big glass and to put it next to my little dice cup, and to fill them with water. Then she asked me which one was the most full. I told her that one was as full as the other and that it was impossible to put in more water than they could hold. Then my dear mother helped me understand that in Heaven, God would give to His elect as much glory as they could hold, and so the last would have nothing to envy about the first. This is how, by placing within my grasp the most sublime of secrets, you knew, Mother how to give my soul the nourishment that it needed. . . .

With what joy I came every year to the end-of-school-year distribution of prizes! There, as always, *justice* was respected; I would receive only the rewards that I had earned. Standing *all alone* in the midst of the *noble assembly,* I would hear my sentence, read by the king of France and Navarre [as I called Papa]. My heart would beat fast as I received the prize and the crown. . . . For me this was like an image of the Last Judgment! . . . Right after the distribution of prizes, the little queen would take off her white dress, and then they would hurry to disguise her so she could take part in *the big play!* . . .

Oh! How joyful were these family celebrations. . . . How far I was then, when I saw my dear king so radiant, from foreseeing the trials that were to visit him! . . . One day, however, God showed me in a really extraordinary *vision*, the *living* image of the trial that it was His will to prepare us for in advance, since his cup of suffering was already filling up.

Papa had been away on a trip for several days, and he wasn't supposed to come home for two more days. It could have been two or three o'clock in the afternoon. The sun was shining brightly, and all of nature seemed to be celebrating. I was alone in the window of a dormer overlooking the big garden. I was looking ahead of me, my mind filled with cheerful thoughts, when I saw, in front of the wash-house just across the way, a man dressed absolutely like Papa, with the same height and the same walk, only he was *much more hunched over*. . . . His *head* was covered with a sort of apron of an indistinct color in such a way that I couldn't see his face. He wore a hat that looked like the ones Papa wore. I saw him approach with measured steps, walking through my little garden.

Suddenly a feeling of supernatural dread invaded my soul, but in an instant I decided that no doubt Papa had come back home and that he was hiding in order to surprise me. So I called out loudly, my voice trembling with emotion, "Papa, Papa! . . ." But the mysterious person didn't seem to hear me, and continued his measured steps without even turning around. Following him with my eyes, I saw him heading toward the woods that cut the big driveway in two. I expected to see him reappear on the other side of the big trees, but the prophetic vision had vanished! . . . All of this lasted only an instant, but it was engraved so deeply on my heart that today, after fifteen years . . . the memory is still as present as if the vision were still before my eyes. . . .

Marie was with you, Mother, in a room adjoining the one where I was. When she heard me calling Papa, she felt an impression of dread, feeling, she told me later, that something extraordinary must have happened. Without letting me see her emotion she ran to me and asked what had come over me to make me call Papa, who was in Alençon. So I told her what I had just seen. To reassure me, Marie told me that no doubt it was Victoire who, to scare me, had hidden her head under her apron. But when she was asked, Victoire assured us that she hadn't left her kitchen. Besides, I was quite sure that I saw a man, and that this man had Papa's appearance. Then all three of us went behind the stand of trees, but when we didn't find any sign indicating that someone had passed by, you told me not to think about this anymore. . . .

Not to think about it wasn't in my power. Quite often my imagination would bring back the mysterious scene that I had seen. . . . Quite often I would try to lift the veil that hid its meaning, because deep in my heart I had the inner conviction that this vision had a *meaning* that was going to be revealed someday. . . .

That day was a long time in coming, but after four-teen years God Himself tore open the mysterious veil. I was on leave with Sr. Marie of the Sacred Heart [my sister Marie], and we were talking as always about things of the other life and our childhood memories, when I recounted the vision that I had had at the age of six or seven. Suddenly as we recalled the details of that strange scene, we both understood at the same time what it meant. . . . It really was *Papa* that I had seen, trudging forward, hunched over by age. . . . It really was Papa, bearing on his venerable face, on his head white with age, the sign of his *glorious* trial. . . . Like Jesus' adorable face, which was veiled during His Passion [Lk. 22:64], the face of His faithful servant was to be veiled during the days of his suffering, in order to shine in the heavenly Country with his Lord, the Eternal Word! . . .

It was in the midst of that indescribable glory, when he was reigning in heaven, that our dear Papa obtained for us the grace to understand the vision that his little queen had had at an age when there's no need to be afraid of illusion! It's from the midst of that glory that he obtained for us that sweet comfort of understanding that ten years before our great trial, God was already showing it to us, as a Father who sets before His children the glorious future that He's preparing for them and is pleased to consider in advance the priceless riches that are to be their lot. . . .

Oh! Why was I the one to whom God showed this light? Why did He show such a little child something that she was unable to understand, something that, if she had understood it, would have caused her to die with suffering—why? . . . Herein lies one of the mysteries that no doubt we will understand in heaven and that will be the source of our unending admiration. . . .

How good God is! . . . How He apportions out trials according to the strength that He gives us. Never, as I have just said, would I have been able to stand even the thought of the bitter pains that the future held in store for me. . . . I couldn't even think without shuddering that Papa *was going to die.* . . . Once he had climbed up on a ladder, and as I was standing just under him he called out, "Step away, little dearie—if I fall I'm going to land on top of you." When I heard that I felt an inner revolt; instead of stepping away, I clung to the ladder, thinking, "At least if Papa falls, I'm not going to have the suffering of watching him die, since I'm going to die with him!"

I can't say how much I loved Papa. Everything about him caused me admiration. When he would explain his thoughts to me (as if I had been a big girl), I would tell him naïvely that of course if he said all that to the great men of the government, they would take him and make him king, and then France would be happy as it had never been. . . . But in my heart I was happy (and I reproached myself for thinking this out of selfishness) that I was the only one who *knew Papa well,* because if he had become the king *of France* and *Navarre* I knew that he would have been unhappy, since that's the fate of all monarchs, and especially because he would no longer have been my king and mine alone!

I was six or seven years old when Papa took us to Trouville. I'll never forget the impression that the sea made on me. I couldn't keep myself from looking at it without stopping. Its majesty, the roaring of its waves, everything spoke to my soul about the Greatness and the Power of God. I remember that during the walk that we were taking on the beach, a gentleman and a lady watched me playing joyfully around Papa. Approaching, they asked him if *I were his,* and they said that I was a very nice little girl. Papa told them yes, but I became aware that he was making signs to them not to pay me compliments. . . .

This was the first time that I heard that I was nice, and that gave me a lot of pleasure, because I didn't believe it. You gave a lot of attention, dear Mother, not to let me near anything that might tarnish my innocence, especially not to let me hear a single word that might be capable of letting vanity slip into my heart. Since I paid attention only to your words and Marie's, and you had never addressed a single compliment toward me, I didn't attach much importance to the lady's words and admiring glances.

That evening, at the time when the sun seems to swim in the immensity of the waves, leaving before it a *luminous wake,* I went to sit on a rock all alone with *Pauline.* Then I remembered the touching story of "The Golden Wake." I contemplated that shiny wake for a long time, the image of grace lighting the path that the little vessel with the gracious white sail was to take. . . . Near Pauline, I made a resolution never to distance my soul from Jesus' gaze, so that my soul might sail in peace to its heavenly homeland!

My life flowed along, tranquil and happy. The affection with which I was surrounded at "Les Buissonnets" made me, so to speak, grow up. But I was no doubt big enough to begin to struggle, to begin to become familiar with the world and the distresses that fill it. . . .

CHAPTER 3

Sorrowful Years
1881–1883

Pupil at the abbey
Free days
Céline's First Communion
Pauline at Carmel
Strange illness
The Virgin's smile

I was eight and a half years old when Léonie [my middle sister] left school and I took her place at the Abbey. I've often heard that time spent at school is the best and the sweetest time of life. That's not how it was for me; the five years I spent there were the saddest of my life. If I hadn't had my dear Céline [the youngest of my sisters, three and a half years older than I] with me, I wouldn't have been able to stay a single month without falling sick. . . . The poor little flower had been accustomed to plunging her fragile roots into *chosen ground,* made especially for her, so it seemed to her that it was very hard to see herself among flowers with all kinds of roots that were often not very delicate, and to be obliged to find in *common ground* the sap that was necessary to her subsistence! . . .

You had taught me so well, dear Mother, that upon arriving at the school I was the most advanced of the children my age. I was placed in a class of pupils who were all bigger than I was. One of them, aged thirteen or fourteen, was not so intelligent, but she knew how to impress the students and even the teachers. Seeing that I was so young, almost always the first in my class, and beloved by all the nuns, she no doubt felt a jealousy that was quite forgivable for a schoolgirl, and she made me pay for my little successes in a thousand ways. . . .

With my timid and delicate nature, I didn't know how to defend myself, and I was content to weep without saying anything, not complaining *even to you* about what I was suffering. But I didn't have enough virtue to rise above these griefs that life brings, and my poor little heart suffered a great deal. . . .

Fortunately, each night I would go home to my father, and there my heart would expand. I would jump into my king's lap, telling him about the grades that had been given to me, and his kiss would make me forget all my troubles. . . . With what joy I announced the results of my *first composition* (a composition on sacred history). *A single point* was all I needed to get a perfect paper—I didn't know the name of Moses' father. So I was first in the class, and I had brought home a beautiful silver decoration.

As a reward Papa gave me a *pretty little coin* worth four pennies, and I placed it in a box that was destined to receive, nearly every Thursday, a new coin always of the same *size*. . . . (I used to go into that box on certain important feast days when I wanted to give an offering from my purse, either for the propagation of the Faith or for other similar works.) *Pauline,* delighted with the

success of her little pupil, made her a gift of a pretty hoop
to encourage her to continue to study hard. The poor
little one had a real need for these joys in the family.
Without them, life in school would have been too hard.

Thursday afternoons were time off from school, but
these were not like *Pauline's times off;* I wasn't in the
belvedere with Papa. . . . I had to play, not with my
Céline, which I liked when I was *all alone with her,* but
with my little cousins and the little girls from the
Maudelonde family.

For me this was truly painful, not knowing now to
play like the other children. I wasn't pleasant company,
but nonetheless I did my best to be like the others, but
without success, and I was bored a lot, especially when
I had to spend a whole afternoon *dancing the quadrille.*
The only thing I liked was to go to the *star garden.*
Then I was the first one everywhere, picking flowers in
profusion. Since I knew how to find the prettiest ones,
I excited the envy of my little classmates. . . .

What pleased me still more was when by chance I
was alone with little Marie [Marie Guérin, my cousin].
Not having Céline Maudelonde with her any more to
drag her into her *ordinary games,* she would leave me
free to choose, and I would choose a completely new
game. Marie and Thérèse became two *hermits,* having
only a little hut, a little wheat field, and a few vegetables
to cultivate. Their life was spent in continual contem-
plation, that is, one of the *hermits* replaced the other in
prayer when it became necessary to be concerned with
the active life. Everything was done with understanding,
silence, and such religious etiquette that it was perfect.

When my aunt would come and get us for our walk, our game would continue even on the road. The two hermits would recite the Rosary together, using their fingers so as not to show their devotion to an indiscreet public. One day, however, the youngest hermit forgot herself, and having received a piece of cake at snack time, before eating it she made a great sign of the Cross over it, which made all the irreverent folks of this age laugh. . . .

[My cousin] Marie and I were always of the same opinion. We even had the same tastes, and one day our *union of wills* passed all limits. On the way back from the Abbey one evening, I told Marie, "Guide me, I'm going to close my eyes." "I want to close mine, too," she replied. No sooner said, then done; *without discussing it,* each one did *her will.* . . . We were on a sidewalk, so there was no need to be afraid of carriages, so after a pleasant walk lasting several minutes, having savored the delights of walking without seeing where they were going, the two little scatterbrains fell *together* on some boxes outside the door of a store. Or rather, they made the *boxes fall.* The merchant came out quite angrily to pick up his merchandise. The two voluntarily blind girls had gotten back up and started walking, taking *big steps,* eyes *wide* open, while listening to the just reproaches of Jeanne [my other cousin], who was as angry as the merchant! . . . So, to punish us she resolved to separate us, and from that day on Marie and Céline would go together while I would go with Jeanne. This put an end to our great *union of wills,* and this wasn't a bad thing for the older girls, who on the contrary were never of the same opinion and used to argue all along the way. So the peace was complete.

I haven't said anything yet about my close relationship with Céline. Oh! If had to tell it all, I wouldn't be able to finish. . . .

At Lisieux, the roles had changed. It was Céline who had become a clever little imp, and Thérèse was no longer anything more than a sweet little girl who was a *big cry-baby.* . . . That didn't prevent Céline and Thérèse from loving each other more and more. Sometimes there were little spats, but it was nothing serious, and in their hearts they were always of the same mind. I can say that my dear little sister *never* gave me any *trouble,* but that she was for me like a ray of sunshine, giving me joy and always comforting me. . . . Who can say with what fearlessness she defended me at the Abbey when I was accused of something? . . . She took such good care of my health that it bothered me sometimes.

What didn't bother me was to *watch her playing.* She would put the whole group of our dolls in rows and would teach them a class like a gifted schoolmistress, only she would take care that her girls were always well behaved, while mine were often sent out the door because of their bad behavior. . . . She would tell me all the new things that she had just learned in her class, which amused me a lot, and I looked at her as a fountain of knowledge.

I had received the title of "Céline's little girl," so when she was angry with me, her biggest sign of discontent was to say to me, "You aren't my little girl any more, it's over, I'll *always remember what you did!*"

Then all I had to do was cry like a baby, begging her to treat me like her little girl again. Soon she would hug me and promised *not to remember anything* again! . . . To comfort me she would take one of her dolls and would say to her, "My dear, hug your aunt." One time the doll was in such a hurry to hug me tenderly that she put her two little arms around *my nose*. . . . Céline, who hadn't done it on purpose, looked at me totally shocked, with the doll hanging off my nose. *The aunt* didn't take long to push away the too-tender embrace of her *niece* and start laughing with all her heart at such a remarkable adventure.

The funniest thing was to see us buy our New Year's gifts, together at the bazaar; we would carefully hide from each another. Having ten small coins to spend we needed five or six different objects, so it was up to us to buy the most *beautiful things*. Delighted with our purchases, we would wait impatiently for New Year's Day in order to offer our *magnificent presents* to each other. The one who woke up before the other would hurry to wish her a Happy New Year. Then we would give each other our *New Year's gifts*, and each would be in ecstasy over the *treasures* given for ten small coins! . . . These little gifts gave us almost as much pleasure as the *beautiful New Year's gifts* given by my *uncle*. However, this was only the beginning of the joyous times. That day we would get dressed quickly and each one would lie in wait to jump on Papa's neck, as soon as he came out of his room. There would be shouts of joy in the whole house, and poor dear father would seem happy to see us so content. . . .

The New Year's gifts that Marie and Pauline used to give to their little girls weren't worth a lot, but they gave them *great joy.* . . . Oh! It was just that at that age we weren't blasé. Our souls in all their freshness were opening like flowers that are happy to receive the morning dew. . . . The same breeze caused our petals to flutter, and what gave joy or sorrow to one did the same thing at the same time to the other. Yes, our joys were shared.

I was keenly aware of this on that beautiful day of my beloved Céline's first Communion. I wasn't attending school at the Abbey yet, since I was only seven, but I've preserved in my heart the sweet memory of the preparation that you, beloved Mother, had given Céline. Each night you used to take her on your lap and speak to her about the important act that she was going to do. I used to listen, keen to prepare myself as well. But often you would tell me to go away because I was too little. Then my heart would be quite heavy, and I used to think that four years were not too long to prepare oneself to receive God. . . .

One night I heard you say that beginning with first Communion, we must begin a new life. Immediately I resolved not to wait for that day but to begin a new life at the same time as Céline. . . . I had never felt so much that I loved her as I did during her three-day retreat. For the first time in my life, I was far from her, I wasn't going to sleep in her bed. . . .

The first day, forgetting that she wasn't going to come back, I kept a little sprig of cherries that Papa had bought for me, intending to eat them with her. When I didn't see her arrive I was quite upset. Papa comforted me by saying that he would take me to the Abbey the next day to see my Céline, and that I would give her another sprig of cherries! . . .

The day of Céline's first Communion left an impression on me like the day of my own. Waking in the morning all alone in the big bed, I felt myself *overcome with joy.* "It's today! . . . The big day has arrived. . . ." I never got tired of repeating those words. It seemed to me that I was the one who was going to take my first Communion. I think that I received great graces that day, and I consider it to be one of the most *beautiful* of my life. . . .

I've gone back in time a bit in order to recall that delicious, sweet memory. Now I have to speak about the painful trial that came and broke little Thérèse's heart, when Jesus took away from her, her dear *Mama:* her so tenderly beloved *Pauline!* . . .

One day, I had told Pauline that I would like to be a hermit and go away with her to a faraway deserted place. She answered that my desire was hers as well, and that she *would wait* until I was big enough to leave. No doubt this wasn't said seriously, but little Thérèse took it seriously, so what suffering it was one day to hear her dear Pauline talking with Marie about her upcoming entry into Carmel. . . . I didn't know what "Carmel" was, but I understood that Pauline was going to leave me to enter into a convent. I understood that she *wouldn't wait for me,* and that I was going to lose my second *mother.* . . . Oh! How can I tell you of the anguish in my heart? . . .

In an instant I understood what life was. Until then I hadn't seen it as so sad, but it appeared to me in all its reality, and I saw that it was only suffering and continual separation. I shed the most bitter tears, because I didn't understand yet the *joy* of sacrifice. I was *weak, so weak* that I see it as a great grace to have been able to endure a trial that seemed well beyond my strength! . . . If I had learned in a gentle way about my beloved Pauline's departure, perhaps I wouldn't have suffered so much, but since I learned it by surprise, I felt as if a sword had been thrust into my heart [Lk. 2:35].

I will always remember, beloved Mother, with what tenderness you comforted me. . . . Then you explained to me about the life at Carmel that seemed so beautiful to me. As I was going over in my mind everything that you had told me, I felt that Carmel was *the desert* where God wanted me as well to go and hide. . . . I felt it with so much strength that there wasn't the slightest doubt in my heart. This was not the dream of a child who lets herself be carried away, but the *certainty* of a Divine call. I wanted to go to Carmel, not for *Pauline,* but for *Jesus alone.* . . . I thought *many* things that words can't express, but which left a great peace in my soul.

The next day I confided my secret to Pauline, who, viewing my desires as the will of heaven, told me that soon I would go with her to see the Prioress of the Carmelite convent, and that I would need to tell her what God was making me feel. . . . One Sunday was chosen for this solemn visit. My perplexity was great when I learned that Marie Guérin [my cousin] was to stay with me, since I was still little enough to see the Carmelite Sisters.

Nonetheless, I had to find a way to be alone, so here is what came to my mind: I told Marie that since we had the privilege of seeing the Prioress, we had to be very nice and very polite. For that we had to confide *secrets* to her, so each one of us had to go out for a moment and leave the other one all alone. Marie took me at my word, and in spite of her dislike of having to confide *secrets that she didn't have,* we stayed alone, one after the other, with Mother Marie de Gonzague.

Having heard my *great confidences,* this good Mother believed in my vocation, but she told me that they didn't receive *nine-year-old* postulants, and that I would have to wait until I was sixteen. . . . I resigned myself to this, in spite of my strong desire to enter as soon as possible and to make my first Communion on the day that Pauline was to take the nun's habit. . . .

That was the day that I received compliments for the second time. Sr. Thérèse of St. Augustine came to see me and never got tired of saying that I was nice. But I wasn't counting on coming to the convent to receive praise. So after that time in the parlor, I never stopped repeating to God that it was for *Him alone* that I wanted to be a Carmelite.

I tried to take full advantage of my beloved Pauline during the few weeks that still remained to her in the world. Each day Céline and I would buy her a cake and some candies, thinking that soon she would no longer be eating any such thing. We were always at her side, not leaving her a minute's rest. Finally the *second of October* came, a day of tears and blessings, when Jesus gathered the first of His flowers, who was to be the *mother* of the ones who would be coming to join her a few short years later.

I can still see the place where I received *Pauline's* last kiss. Then my aunt took us all to Mass while Papa was going up on the mountain of Carmel to offer his *first sacrifice* [like Abraham as he was preparing to offer his son Isaac on Mount Moriah, Gen. 22:1–19]. . . . The whole family was in tears, so that when people saw us entering the church they looked at us with great surprise. But I paid no attention, and I couldn't keep myself from crying. I think that if everything had crumbled around me I wouldn't have paid any attention. I was watching the beautiful blue sky, and I was astounded that the sun could shine with so much brilliance, while my soul was flooded with sadness! . . .

Perhaps, beloved Mother, you might find that I'm exaggerating the pain that I felt. . . . I'm quite aware that it shouldn't have been so great since I held the hope of finding you at Carmel later, but my soul was FAR from being *matured;* I had to pass through many crucibles before attaining the end that I desired so much. . . .

October 2nd was the day appointed for going back to school at the Abbey. So I had to go in spite of my sorrow. . . . In the afternoon my aunt came and got us so we could go to the Carmelite convent, and I saw my *beloved Pauline* behind the *grille.* . . . Oh! How I suffered at that *meeting* at the Carmelite convent! Since I'm writing the story of my soul, I ought to tell everything to my dear Mother, and I admit that the sufferings that had preceded her entrance into the convent were nothing compared to the ones that followed it. . . .

Every Thursday we would go as a *family* to the convent, and I, who was used to speaking at length, heart to heart, with *Pauline,* obtained with great difficulty two or three minutes at the end of the meeting. Of course I spent them crying, and I went away with my heart broken. . . . I didn't understand that it was out of tactfulness toward my aunt that you preferred to address the conversation toward Jeanne and Marie [my cousins] instead of speaking to your little girls [your sisters]. . . . I didn't understand, and I would say deep in my heart, "Pauline is lost to me!!!" It's surprising to see how much my mind developed in the midst of suffering. It developed to such a point that it didn't take me long to fall sick.

The illness that struck me came most certainly from the devil, who was furious at your entry into Carmel. He wanted to take revenge on me for the wrong that our family was to do to him in the future. But he didn't know that the gentle Queen of Heaven was watching over her fragile little flower, and that she was *smiling* at her from her throne on high, and was getting ready to make the storm cease at the very moment when her flower was about to become crushed beyond return. . . .

Toward the end of the year I was taken with a headache that, though continual, almost didn't make me suffer. I was able to pursue my studies, and no one was worried about me. This lasted until Easter, 1883. Papa had gone to Paris with Marie and Léonie, so my aunt took me to her house, with Céline. One night my uncle, who had taken me with him, talked to me about Mama, about past memories, with a goodness that touched me deeply and made me cry. Then he told me that I was too tenderhearted, and that I needed to be distracted. So he resolved with my aunt to bring us some pleasure during the Easter vacation. That night we were to go to the Catholic circle, but finding that I was too tired, my aunt put me to bed. As I was getting undressed I was taken with a strange trembling. Thinking that I was cold, my aunt covered me with blankets and hot water bottles, but nothing could lessen my agitation, which lasted almost all night. When my uncle came back from the Catholic circle with my cousins and Céline, he was quite surprised to find me in a state that he deemed to be serious, but he didn't want to say so in order not to frighten my aunt.

The next day he went to find Dr. Notta, who concluded, like my uncle, that I had a very serious illness that had never struck such a young child. Everybody was quite dismayed. My aunt was obliged to keep me at her place and took care of me with truly *motherly* solicitude. When Papa came back from Paris with my big sisters, Aimée greeted them with such a sad face that Marie thought I was dead. . . .

But this illness was not so that I would die. It was rather like the one Lazarus had, so that God might be glorified [Jn. 11:4]. . . . And in fact He was, through the admirable resignation of my poor dear *father,* who thought "his little girl was going to go mad or that she was going to die." God was also glorified by *Marie's* resignation as well! . . . Oh! How she suffered because of me. . . . How grateful I am for the care that she poured out on me with so much unselfishness. . . . Her heart dictated to her what was necessary for me, and truly, a *mother's heart* is much more *knowledgeable* than a doctor's heart—it knows how to *guess* what is suited to its child's illness. . . .

Poor Marie was obliged to come live at my uncle's, because it was impossible to transport me to Les Buissonnets at that time. However, Pauline's taking of the habit was approaching. They avoided talking about it in front of me, knowing the pain that I felt at not being able to go. But I talked about it often, saying that I would be well enough to go see my beloved Pauline. And in fact God didn't want to refuse me that comfort, or rather, He wanted to comfort His beloved *Betrothed* [Pauline] who had suffered so much from the illness of her little girl [Thérèse]. . . .

I've noticed that Jesus doesn't want to send trials to His children on the day of their betrothal. That holiday should be cloudless, a foretaste of the joys of heaven. Hasn't He shown this five times already? So I was able to *kiss* my beloved mother [Pauline], *sit* on her *lap* and flood her with hugs. . . . I was able to contemplate her being so attractive, under the white garment of Bride [her Carmelite habit]. . . . Oh! That was a *beautiful day,* in the midst of my dark trial, but that day went by quickly. . . .

Soon I had to climb into the carriage that took me so far from Pauline . . . far from my beloved Carmel. Arriving at Les Buissonnets, they put me to bed. In spite of myself I assured them that I was perfectly well and no longer needed to be taken care of. Alas, I was still only at the beginning of my ordeal. . . . The next day I was stricken again like I had been before, and the illness became so serious that I wasn't supposed to survive it according to human calculation. . . . I don't know how to describe such a strange illness. I'm persuaded now that it was the work of the devil, but for a long time after I got well I thought that I had become sick on purpose, and that was a *true martyrdom* for my soul.

I told this to Marie, who reassured me as best she could, with her ordinary *goodness*. I told it at Confession, and there again my confessor tried to calm me down, saying that it wasn't possible to pretend to be sick to the point where I had been. God, who no doubt wanted to purify me and especially to *humble* me, left me with this *inner martyrdom* right up to my entrance into Carmel. There, the *Father* of our souls took away all my doubts as if it were with His own hand, and since then I have been perfectly peaceful.

It isn't surprising that I was afraid that I looked sick without in fact being sick, because I would say and do things that I wasn't thinking. I almost always seemed to be delirious, saying words that had no meaning, and nevertheless I'm *sure* that I wasn't *deprived for a single instant of the use of my reason.* . . . Often I appeared to have fainted, not making the slightest movement.

At that time I would have let be done to me anything anyone might have wanted, even kill me. Nonetheless I was hearing everything that was being said around me, and I still remember everything. It happened to me once that I stayed for a long time without being able to open my eyes, and yet I opened them for an instant while I was alone.

I think that the devil had received an *outward* power over me, but he couldn't approach my soul or my mind, unless it was to inspire in me *great fear* of certain things, for example, fears of the very simple remedies that people tried in vain to make me accept.

But if God was allowing the devil to come near me, He was also sending me visible angels. . . . Marie was always at my bedside, taking care of me and comforting me with the tenderness of a mother. She never showed the slightest irritation, despite the fact that I gave her a lot of trouble by not allowing her to leave me. Nonetheless she had to go to meals with Papa, but I wouldn't stop calling her the whole time she was away. Victoire, who was taking care of me, sometimes was obliged to go get my dear "Mama" since I was calling for her. . . . When Marie wanted to go out it had to be in order to go to Mass or to see *Pauline*, and then I didn't say anything. . . .

My uncle and aunt [Isidore and Céline Guérin] were also very good to me. My dear aunt came *every day* to see me and spoiled me a lot. Other people who were friends of the family also came to visit me, but I begged Marie to tell them that I didn't want any visits. I didn't like "seeing people sitting around my bed *all squashed together*, looking at me like some strange animal."

The only visitors I liked were my uncle and my aunt. Since that illness I couldn't tell you how much my affection for them increased. I understood better than ever that they were not ordinary relatives to us.

Oh! Poor dear father was quite right when he repeated so often the words that I have just written. Later he experienced the fact that he hadn't been wrong, and now [that he's in heaven] he must protect and bless those who poured out such devoted care on him. . . . But as for me, I am still in exile, and since I don't know how to show my gratefulness, I have only one means to relieve my heart: Pray for the relatives that I love, who were and still are so good to me!

Léonie was also quite good to me. She tried to entertain me as best she could. But sometimes I hurt her because she could see quite clearly that nobody could take Marie's place at my side.

And my dear Céline, what did she not do for her Thérèse? On Sunday, instead of taking a walk she would stay indoors for hours on end with a poor little girl who looked like an idiot. Truly, it would have taken love not to run away from me. . . . Oh! Dear sisters, how I made you suffer! No one had given you so much *trouble* as I, and no one had received so much *love* as you poured out on me. . . . Fortunately, I will have heaven to pay you back. My Bridegroom is very rich, and I will dig into His treasures of *love* in order to give you back a hundred times as much as all that you suffered because of me.

My greatest comfort while I was sick was to receive a letter from *Pauline*. . . . I read it and reread it until I knew it by heart. . . . One time, dear Mother, you sent me an hourglass and one of my dolls dressed up as a Carmelite nun. To say how much joy I felt would be impossible. . . . My uncle wasn't happy. He said that instead of making me think about Carmel I ought to put it out of my mind, but I felt on the contrary that it was the hope of being a Carmelite someday that kept me alive. . . .

My pleasure was to work for Pauline. I made her little objects of Bristol-board paper, and my greatest occupation was to made crowns of daisies and forget-me-nots for the Blessed Virgin. We were now in the beautiful month of May [Mary's month]. All of nature was adorning itself with flowers and breathing gaiety. Only the "little flower" was languishing and seemed to be forever wilted. . . .

However, she had one Sun near her, and that Sun was the *miraculous statue* of the Blessed Virgin that had spoken twice to Mama. And often, quite often, the little flower turned its petals toward that blessed Star. . . . One day I saw Papa go into Marie's room, where I was lying in bed. And giving her several gold coins with an expression of great sadness, he told her to write to Paris and have Masses said to Our Lady of Victories so that she would heal his poor little daughter. Oh! How touched I was at seeing the faith and love of my beloved king. I would have liked to be able to tell him that I was well, but I had already given him enough false joys. It was not my desires that could make a *miracle*, because it was going to take one to heal me. . . .

A *miracle* was needed, and it was Our Lady of Victories who did it. One Sunday (during the novena [nine days of Masses]), Marie went out into the garden, leaving me with Léonie, who was reading near the window. After a few minutes I started calling almost silently, "Mama . . . Mama." Léonie, who had become accustomed to hearing me call out like that, didn't pay attention to me. This went on for a long time, so I called out louder, and finally Marie came back in. I saw her clearly when she entered, but I couldn't say that I recognized her, and I continued to call out ever louder, "Mama."

I was suffering a lot from this strong and inexplicable struggle, and Marie was suffering from it perhaps even more than I. After vain efforts to show me that she was beside me, she got down on her knees beside my bed with Léonie and Céline, and then, turning toward the Blessed Virgin, and praying with the fervor of a mother who was asking for the life of her child, *Marie* obtained what she desired. . . .

Finding no help on earth, poor little Thérèse had turned toward her Heavenly Mother. She was praying to her with all her heart to finally have pity on her. . . . Suddenly the Blessed Virgin seemed *beautiful* to me, *so beautiful* that I had never seen anything so beautiful. Her face was breathing inexpressible goodness and tenderness, but what penetrated right to the depths of my soul was the "lovely smile of the Blessed Virgin." Then all my sufferings melted away, and two big tears burst from my eyelids and streaked silently down my cheeks—but these were tears of an unadulterated joy. . . . Oh! I thought, the Blessed Virgin smiled at me, how happy I am. . . . Yes, but I will never tell anyone about it, because then my *happiness would disappear.*

Without any effort I lowered my eyes and saw Marie, who was watching me with love. She seemed moved, and seemed to suspect the favor that the Blessed Virgin had granted to me. . . . Oh! It was to her, to her touching prayers, that I owed the grace of the *smile* of the Queen of Heaven. When she saw my gaze fixed on the Blessed Virgin, she had said to herself, "Thérèse has been healed!" Yes, the little flower was going to be born anew to life. The glowing *Ray* that had warmed her was not going to stop its blessings. It doesn't act suddenly, but sweetly, gently, it picked its flower back up and strengthened it in such a way that five years later it opened up on the fertile mount of Carmel.

As I said, Marie had guessed that the Blessed Virgin had granted me some hidden grace, so when I was alone with her and she asked me what I had seen, I couldn't resist her questions that were so tender and pressing. Surprised to see that my secret had been discovered without my having revealed it, I confided the whole story to my dear Marie. . . . Alas! Just as I had felt, my happiness was to disappear and change into bitterness. For four years the memory of the inexpressible grace that I had received was for me a true *suffering of the soul*. I was to find my happiness again only at the feet of Our Lady of Victories, but then it was given back to me in *all its fullness*. . . .

I will talk again later about this second grace of the Blessed Virgin. Now I have to tell you, dear Mother, how my joy changed into sadness. After hearing me tell my naïve and sincere story about "my grace," Marie asked me for permission to tell it to the Carmelite nuns—and I couldn't say no. On my first visit to this beloved convent, I was full of joy at seeing my *Pauline* with the habit of the Blessed Virgin [the nuns' habit was like the garments worn by the Blessed Virgin

Mary]. This was a very sweet moment for us both. . . .
There were so many things to say that I couldn't say
anything at all, my heart was too full. . . .

The good Mother Marie de Gonzague [the prioress]
was there as well, giving me many signs of affection. I
saw still other Sisters, and in front of them I was ques-
tioned about the grace that I had received. Marie asked
me if the Blessed Virgin was carrying the baby Jesus, or
if there was a lot of light, etc. All these questions troubled
me and gave me a lot of distress. I could say only one
thing: "The Blessed Virgin seemed to me to be *very
beautiful* . . . and I saw her *smile at me.*" It was her *face
alone* that had struck me, so when I saw that the nuns
were imagining something completely different (the
sufferings of my soul were already beginning concerning my illness), I figured that I *had lied.* . . .

No doubt, if I had kept my secret, I would have
kept my happiness. But the Blessed Virgin allowed
this torment for the good of my soul. Perhaps without it I would have had some thought of vanity.
Instead, *humiliation* became my lot. I couldn't look
at myself without a feeling of *deep horror.* . . . Oh!
What I suffered, I will be able to tell only in heaven!

CHAPTER 4

First Communion–
Boarding School
1883–1886

Pictures and reading
First Communion
Confirmation
Illness of scruples
Mrs. Papinau
Child of Mary
New separations

Speaking of visits to the Carmelites, I remember my
first one, which took place a short time after
Pauline's entrance. I forgot to mention it earlier, but it's
a detail that I shouldn't leave out. The morning of the
day when I was to go to the parlor, reflecting all alone
in my bed (because it was there that I prayed my deepest prayers and, contrary to the bride in the Song of
Songs, I always found my Beloved there [Song 3:1–4]),
I wondered what name I would have at Carmel. I knew
that there was a Sr. Thérèse of Jesus. However, my
beautiful name of Thérèse couldn't be taken away from
me. Suddenly I thought about the *Little* Jesus whom I
loved so much, and I told myself, "Oh! How happy I
would be to be called Thérèse of the Child Jesus!" I

didn't say anything in the parlor about the *dream* that I'd had while completely awake, but when dear Mother *Marie de Gonzague* asked the Sisters what name should be given to me, it came to her to call me by the name that I had dreamed about. . . . Great was my joy, and that happy meeting of thoughts seemed to me to be a gentle touch from my Beloved Little Jesus.

I have forgotten a few more details of my childhood before your entrance into Carmel. I haven't talked to you about my love of pictures and books. . . . And yet, beloved Mother, I owe to the beautiful pictures that you used to show me as a reward, one of the sweetest joys and the strongest impressions that have excited me in the practice of virtue. . . . I used to forget the time as I was looking at them; for example, *The Divine Prisoner's Little Flower* [a nineteenth-century poem made into a picture book] told me so many things that I was completely immersed in it. When I saw that the name of *Pauline* was written at the bottom of the little flower, I would have liked for Thérèse's to be there, too, and I used to offer myself to Jesus to be His *little flower.* . . .

If I didn't know how to play games, I loved reading a lot, and I would have spent my life doing it. Fortunately, I had as my guides earthly *angels* who chose books for me that, while entertaining me, nourished my heart and my mind. And then I was supposed to spend only a certain amount of time reading, and that was for me the subject of great sacrifices, since my reading was often interrupted in the middle of the most fascinating passage. . . .

This attraction to reading lasted until my entrance into Carmel. It would be impossible for me to say how many books passed through my hands, but God never allowed me to read a single one that was capable of harming me. It's true that as I read certain tales about knights, I didn't always feel at first glance the *truth* about *life;* but soon God let me feel that true glory is the one that will last forever, and that to obtain it, it isn't necessary to do outstanding works, but to remain hidden and to practice virtue in such a way that the right hand doesn't know what the left hand is doing [Mt. 6:3]. . . .

So, when I was reading the tales of the patriotic actions of French heroines, in particular those of the *Venerable* Joan of Arc, I had a great desire to imitate them. It seemed to me that I felt within me the same burning desire that stirred them, the same heavenly inspiration. Then I received a grace that I have always regarded as one of the greatest of my life, because at that age I wasn't receiving *enlightenment* like that with which I'm flooded now. I thought that I was born for *glory,* and in my search for the means of obtaining it, God inspired in me the feelings that I've just written about.

He also gave me to understand that my own glory wouldn't be apparent to mortal eyes, that it would consist in becoming a great *Saint!!!* . . . This desire might seem foolhardy if one were to consider how weak and imperfect I was, and how much I still am after seven years spent in the religious life, but nonetheless I still feel the same audacious confidence that I'll become a great Saint. That's because I'm not counting on my merits, since I have *none,* but I hope in the One who is Virtue, Holiness Itself. It is He alone who, being content with my feeble efforts, will raise me up to Himself and, covering me with His infinite merits, will make me a *Saint.* I wasn't thinking then that one has to suffer a great deal to arrive at sainthood, but God wasn't long in showing me this by sending me the trials that I told about earlier. . . .

Now I need to pick up my story at the point where I left off: Three months after I was healed, Papa took us on a trip to Alençon. This was the first time that I had gone back there, and great was my joy when I saw once again the places where I had spent my early childhood, especially to be able to pray over Mama's grave and to ask her to protect me always. . . .

God gave me the grace to know the *world* only enough to hold it in contempt and to remove myself from it. I could say that it was during my stay at Alençon that I had my *first entrance* into the *world.* Everything was joy and happiness around me. I was received with open arms, fussed over, admired—in a word, my life for two weeks was just strewn with flowers. . . . I admit that this life had charms for me. Wisdom was right to say, "the bewitching of the trifles of the world seduces even the spirit that is far from evil" [cf. Wis. 4:12]. At the age of ten the heart can easily let itself be dazzled, so I see it as a great grace not to have stayed in Alençon. The friends that we had there were too worldly. They knew too well how to mix the joys of the world with God's service. They didn't think about *death* enough, and yet *death* has come to visit a great number of persons whom I have known, young, rich, and happy! . . .

I love to return in my thoughts to the *enchanting* places where they lived, to wonder where they are, what use they now have of the castles and parks where I saw them enjoying the commodities of life. . . . And I see that all is a meaningless chasing after the wind under the Sun [Eccl. 2:11] . . . and that *the only good* is to love God with our whole heart and here below to be *poor* in spirit [Mt. 5:3]. . . .

Perhaps Jesus wanted to show me the world before the *first visit* that He was to pay me so that I might freely choose the path that I was to promise Him that I would follow. The period of my first Communion remains engraved on my heart, like a cloudless memory. It seems to me that I couldn't have been better disposed than I was, and then the troubles of my soul left me for nearly a year. Jesus wanted to cause me to taste as perfect a joy as is possible in this valley of tears. . . .

Do you remember, beloved Mother, the delightful little book that you gave me three months before my first Communion? . . . This is what helped me to prepare my heart in an unwavering and rapid manner, for if I had already been preparing it for a long time, I had to give it a new forward impulse, fill it with *new flowers* so that Jesus could find rest there with pleasure. . . . Each day I did a great number of practices that yielded as *many flowers*. I fulfilled a still greater number of objectives that you had written in my little book for each day, and these acts of love formed the flower *buds*. . . .

Each week you wrote me a lovely little letter that filled my soul with deep thoughts and helped me practice virtue. This was a comfort for your poor little daughter, who was making such a *great sacrifice* in accepting not being *prepared* by sitting on your lap every night as her dear Céline had been. . . .

It was Marie who took Pauline's place for me. I would sit on her lap, and there I would listen *avidly* to what she was telling me. It seemed to me that her whole heart, so *big, so generous,* was passing into me. Like those illustrious warriors who teach their children the craft of weaponry, that is how she spoke to me about the *combats* of life, about the palm that is given to those who are victorious. . . . Marie talked to me still more about the everlasting riches that it's easy to store up each day, about how unfortunate it is to pass by without wanting to take the trouble to reach out our hand to take them. Then she indicated to me the way to be *holy* through faithfulness in the smallest of things. She gave me the little booklet "On Renouncing Oneself," and I meditated on it with delight. . . .

Oh! How *eloquent* was my dear godmother! I would have wanted not to be the only one to hear her profound teachings. I felt myself so *touched* that in my naïveté I believed that the greatest sinners would have been touched as I was, and that leaving right there their perishable riches, they would no longer have wanted to gain anything but the riches of heaven. . . .

At that time no one had taught me yet how to pray at length. I certainly wanted to, but Marie thought I was pious enough, so she let me say only my set prayers.

One day one of my teachers at the Abbey school asked me what I did on my days off when I was alone. I replied that I would go behind my bed into an empty space that was there and that was easy for me to shut off with the curtain, and there, *"I would think."* "But what do you think about?" she said. "I think about God, about life . . . about ETERNITY, I just *think! . . .*" The good nun laughed a lot at me. Later she liked to remind me of the time *when I used to think,* and asked me if I was still *thinking. . . .* I understand now that I was praying at length without knowing it, and that already God was teaching me in secret.

The three months of preparation went by quickly. Soon I was to go on retreat, and for that I was to become a full boarder at the Abbey and sleep there. I cannot tell the sweet memory that this retreat left me. Truly, if I suffered a lot by staying full time in the Abbey, I was amply repaid by the inexpressible happiness of those few days spent awaiting Jesus. . . . I don't believe that one can taste that joy elsewhere than in religious communities. Since the number of children is small, it's easy to be concerned with each one in particular, and truly our teachers poured out motherly care on us at that time. They were concerned with me even more than the others. Each night the head teacher came with her little lantern to kiss me good night as I went to my bed, showing me great affection. One night, touched by her goodness, I told her that I was going to confide in her a *secret.* Taking my *precious little book* that was under my pillow, I showed it to her, my eyes shining with joy. . . .

In the morning, I found it very nice to see all the pupils getting out of bed as soon as they had been awakened and to do as they did. But I wasn't used to getting myself ready all alone. *Marie* wasn't there to *curl my hair*, so I found myself obliged to go and timidly present my comb to the mistress of the dressing room. She laughed when she saw a big girl, eleven years old, who didn't know how to take care of herself. However, she combed my hair, but not as *gently* as Marie. Nonetheless, I didn't dare to *cry out*, something that I used to do every day under the *gentle* hand of my *godmother*. . . .

I had the experience during my retreat of being a child who was fussed over and watched over like few· people on earth, especially among children who have been deprived of their mother. . . . Every day Marie and Léonie used to come to see me with Papa, who spoiled me a great deal, so I didn't suffer the privation of being away from the family, and nothing came to obscure the beautiful heaven of my retreat.

I listened with a great deal of attention to the instructions that Fr. Domin gave us, and I even wrote down a summary of them. As far as my *thoughts* were concerned, I didn't want to write any of them down, saying that I would remember them well, which was true. . . .

For me it was a great happiness to go with the nuns to all the services. I made myself noticed among my classmates due to a *big Crucifix* that Léonie had given me and that I would place on my belt the way missionaries do. This Crucifix was the envy of the nuns, who thought that by wearing it I wanted to imitate my

Carmelite sister. . . . Oh! It really was toward her that my thoughts would go. I knew that *my Pauline* was on retreat like me, not so that Jesus would give Himself to her, but to give herself to Jesus. So this solitude spent waiting was doubly precious to me. . . .

I remember that one morning they had me go to the infirmary because I was coughing a lot. (Since my illness the teachers used to pay a lot of attention to me. For a slight headache, or if they saw that I was more pale than usual, they would send me to get some air or to rest in the infirmary.) I saw my *beloved Céline* come in. She had obtained permission to come see me in spite of the retreat, in order to offer me a picture that gave me a lot of pleasure. It was *"The Divine Prisoner's Little Flower."* Oh! how sweet it was to receive this memento from the hand of *Céline!* . . . How many thoughts of love I had because of her! . . .

The day before the big day I received absolution for the second time. My general confession left me with great peace in my soul, and God didn't allow the slightest cloud to come and trouble it. In the afternoon I asked for forgiveness of *the whole family* who came to see me, but I could speak only by my tears—I was too moved. . . . Pauline wasn't there, but I nonetheless felt that she was near me in heart. She had sent me a *beautiful picture* through Marie. I never got tired of admiring it and having everyone else admire it, too! . . .

I had written to the good Fr. Pichon to commend myself to his prayers, telling him that soon I would be a Carmelite and then he would be my spiritual director. (That is in fact what happened four years later, since it

was at Carmel that I opened my soul to him. . . .) Marie
gave me a *letter from him,* and truly I was too happy! . . .
All this happiness came to me at once. What pleased me
the most in his letter was this sentence: "Tomorrow I will
go up to the Holy Altar for you and your Pauline!"
Pauline and Thérèse became more and more united on
the eighth of May, since Jesus seemed to mingle them
together by flooding them with His graces. . . .

The "beautiful day of days" arrived at last. What
indescribable memories have left in my soul the *slightest
details* of this day from heaven! . . . The joyous waking
at first light, the *respectful* and tender hugs of the
teachers and the older classmates. . . . The big room
filled with *snow-white garments* that each child in turn
saw herself clothed with. Above all the entrance into
the chapel and the *morning* singing of the beautiful
hymn, "O Holy Altar surrounded by Angels!"

But I don't want to enter into the details. Just as there
are things that lose their sweet scent as soon as they are
exposed to the air, there are also *thoughts of the soul*
that cannot be interpreted in the language of the earth
without losing their intimate and heavenly feeling.
They are like that white stone that will be given to
those who are victorious and on which is written a new
name that no one *knows other than the one* who
receives it [cf. Rev. 2:17].

Oh! How sweet was the first kiss of Jesus on my soul!
. . . It was a kiss of *love.* I *felt myself loved,* and I also
said, "I love You, I give myself to You forever." There
were no demands, no struggles, no sacrifices. For a long
time Jesus and poor little Thérèse had been *looking at*

each other and understanding each other. . . . That day it was no longer a *look,* but *a fusion.* They were no longer *two;* Thérèse had disappeared, like a drop of water that disappears into the ocean. Jesus alone remained; He was the master, the King. Hadn't Thérèse asked Him to take away her *freedom, for her freedom* made her afraid? She felt herself to be so weak, so fragile, that forever she wanted to unite herself with the Divine Strength! . . .

Her joy was too great, too deep for her to be able to contain it. Delicious tears soon flooded her, to the great surprise of her friends, who later said to one another, "So, why did she cry? Wasn't there something that was bothering her? . . ." "No, it was rather that she wasn't able to have her mother near her, or her sister that she loves so much, the one who is a Carmelite." They didn't understand that when the joy of heaven comes into a heart, that *exiled* heart can't bear it without shedding tears. . . .

Oh! No, Mama's absence didn't cause me pain on the day of my first Communion. Wasn't heaven in my soul, and hadn't Mama taken her place there [in heaven] a long time ago? So on receiving Jesus' visit, I was also receiving that of my beloved mother, who was blessing me and rejoicing at my happiness. . . .

I wasn't grieving over Pauline's not being there; no doubt I would have been happy to see her at my side, but for a long time my sacrifice had been accepted. That day, joy alone filled my heart. I was uniting myself with Pauline, who was giving herself irrevocably to the One who was giving Himself so lovingly to me! . . .

In the afternoon I was the one who pronounced the act of consecration to the Blessed Virgin. It was quite just that I should *speak* in the name of my classmates to the Mother in heaven, I who had been deprived so young of my earthly mother. I put my whole heart into *speaking to her,* to consecrating myself to her, like a child who throws herself into her mother's arms and asks her to watch over her. It seems to me that the Blessed Virgin must have gazed at her little flower and *smiled* at her. Wasn't she the one whom she had cured with a *visible smile?* . . . Hadn't she placed, into the chalice of her little flower, her Jesus, the Flower of the Fields, the Lily of the Valley? . . .

On the evening of that beautiful day, I joined my earthly family again. Already the morning after the Mass, I had hugged *Papa* and all my dear relatives, but then it was the real reunion, with Papa taking the hand of his little queen and heading toward the *Carmelite convent.* Then I saw my *Pauline,* who had become Jesus' bride [by taking the nun's veil]; I saw her with her white veil like mine, and her crown of roses. . . . Oh! My joy knew no bitterness: I hoped to join her soon and with her to await *heaven!*

I was not insensitive to the family celebration that took place on the evening of my first Communion. The beautiful watch that my king gave me, gave me great pleasure. But my joy was tranquil, and nothing came to trouble my inner peace.

Marie took me with her the night that followed that beautiful day, for the most radiant days are followed by the shadows of night. Only the day of the first, the only, the eternal Communion in heaven will be without a sunset! . . .

The day after my first Communion was again a beautiful day, but it was stamped with melancholy. The beautiful outfit that Marie had bought me, all the presents that I had received, these were not filling my heart. It was only Jesus who could satisfy me. I longed for the moment when I could receive Him a second time.

About a month after my first Communion I went to confession for Ascension, and I dared to ask permission to receive Holy Communion. Against all hope, the priest allowed me to do so, and I had the happiness of going to kneel at the Holy Table between Papa and Marie. What a sweet memory I retained of that second visit of Jesus! My tears flowed again with an inexpressible sweetness. I kept repeating unceasingly to myself the words of St. Paul, "I no longer live, but Christ lives in me! [Gal. 2:20] . . ."

After that Communion, my desire to receive God became greater and greater, and I obtained permission to receive it on all the principal feast days. The day before those happy days Marie would take me in the evening on her lap and prepare me as she had done for my first Communion. I remember that once she talked to me about suffering, telling me that I would probably not walk on that path, but that God would always carry me like a child. . . .

The day after my Communion, Marie's words came back to my thoughts. I felt arising in my heart a *great desire* for *suffering* and at the same time the intimate assurance that Jesus was reserving for me a great number of crosses. I felt myself flooded with such great *consolations* that I see them as one of the *greatest* graces of my life. Suffering became my attraction; it had charms that delighted me without my being really familiar with them. Until then I had suffered without *loving* suffering. Since that day I've felt a veritable love of it. I also felt the desire to love only God, to find joy only in Him.

Often during my Communions, I would repeat these words from the *Imitation of Christ:* "O Jesus, inexpressible *sweetness,* change for me into *bitterness,* all the consolations of the earth. . . ." This prayer came out of my lips without effort, without constraint. It seemed to me that I was repeating it, not by my will, but like a child who repeats the words that a friend inspires in her. . . . Later I will tell you, beloved Mother, how Jesus was pleased to make my desire come true, how He was always, He alone, my inexpressible *sweetness.* If I were to talk to you about this right away I would be obliged to anticipate the time of my life as an adolescent, yet I still have many details to give you about my life as a child.

A short time after my first Communion, I went on retreat again for my Confirmation. I had prepared myself with great care to receive the visit of the Holy Spirit. I didn't understand why great attention wasn't paid to receiving this sacrament of Love. Ordinarily only one day of retreat was spent in preparation for Confirmation, but since the Bishop wasn't able to come on the appointed day, I had the consolation of having two days of solitude. To keep us occupied our teacher took us to Mount Cassin, and there I picked handfuls of *big daisies* for Corpus Christi [the Feast Day on the Thursday after Trinity Sunday, celebrating the institution of the Eucharist]. Oh! How joyful my soul was. Like the apostles, I was happily awaiting the visit of the Holy Spirit [Acts 2:1–4]. . . . I was full of joy at the thought that soon I would be a complete Christian, and especially at the thought that forever I would have on my forehead the mysterious cross that the Bishop would mark there when bestowing the sacrament. . . .

Finally the happy moment came. I didn't feel a violent wind at the moment of the coming down of the Holy Spirit, but rather that *gentle breeze* the murmur of which Elijah heard on Mount Horeb [1 Kings 19:11-12]. . . . On that day I received the strength to *suffer,* for soon afterward the martyrdom of my soul was to begin. . . . It was dear Léonie who served as my sponsor [just as Marie had been my sponsor at my baptism]. She was so moved that she couldn't stop her tears from flowing the whole time of the ceremony. With me she received Holy Communion, for once again I had the happiness of uniting myself to Jesus on that beautiful day.

After these delightful and unforgettable festivities, my life went back to being *ordinary.* That is, I had to go back to the life of a boarding schoolgirl that was so painful to me. At the time of my first Communion I loved that existence with children of my age, all full of good will, having made, like me, the resolution to practice virtue seriously. But I had to get back into contact with very different students, self-indulgent, not wanting to follow the rules, and that made me very unhappy. I was of a cheerful nature, but I didn't know how to give myself over to the games of my age.

Often during recess I would lean against a tree, and there I would contemplate the *evil eye,* giving myself over to serious reflections! I had invented a game I liked. It consisted in burying the poor little birds that we used to find dead under the trees. Lots of students wanted to help me, so our cemetery became very pretty, planted with trees and flowers proportionate to the size of our little feathered friends.

Furthermore, I liked to tell stories that I made up as they came to my mind. My classmates would surround me eagerly, and sometimes older students would mix with the listeners. The same story lasted for several days, because I liked to make it more and more interesting according to how I saw the impressions that it produced and that manifested themselves on the faces of my classmates. But soon the teacher forbade me to continue my career as an orator, preferring to see us play and *run* rather than to *make speeches.*

I would easily retain the meaning of the things that I learned, but I had trouble learning word for word. So for the catechism, almost every day during the year that preceded my first Communion, I asked for permission to learn it during recess. My efforts were always crowned with success, and I was always at the head of the class. If by chance, due to a *single forgotten word,* I lost my place, my sorrow manifested itself by bitter tears that Fr. Domin didn't know how to soothe. He was quite happy with me (not because I used to cry) and used to call me his *little doctor,* because of my

name of Thérèse [since Thérèse is the French equivalent
of the Spanish "Teresa," referring to St. Teresa of Avila,
a Doctor of the Church].

One time the student who came after me didn't know
how to ask her classmate the question about the catechism. Father went around to all the students in turn
before coming back to me and saying that he was going
to see if I was worthy of my place at the head of the class.
In my *profound humility,* that's all I was waiting for.
Standing up with assurance I said what was asked of me
without making a single mistake, to the great surprise of
everybody. . . . After my first Communion, my enthusiasm for the catechism continued until I left school.

I had great success with my studies—I was nearly
always first in the class. My greatest successes were history and writing. All my teachers regarded me as a very
intelligent student. It wasn't the same at my uncle's,
where I was considered to be a little know-nothing, good
and sweet, with upright judgment, but incapable and
awkward. . . . I'm not surprised at this opinion that my
aunt and uncle had and no doubt still have of me. Since
I was very timid, I almost never talked, and when I
wrote, my *cat's scrawl* and my spelling, which is nothing
less than natural, were not too *attractive.* . . .

In the little jobs of sewing, embroidery, etc., I was a
success, it's true, in the opinion of my teachers, but
the *gauche* and awkward manner in which I *held my
work* justified the rather poor opinion that they had of
me. I look at that as a grace. Since God wanted my
heart for Himself alone, He granted my prayer by
"changing into bitterness the consolations of this

world." I needed this much more than I would have if I hadn't been sensitive to praise. Often in front of me people would brag about the intelligence of others, but never about mine. So I concluded that I didn't have any, and I resigned myself to seeing myself as being deprived of it. . . .

My sensitive and loving heart would have easily given itself away if it had found another heart capable of understanding it. . . . I tried to link up with other little girls my age, especially with two of them. I loved them, and for their part they loved me as much as they were *capable* of loving. But alas! How *narrow and flighty* is the heart of created beings!!! . . . Soon I saw that my love wasn't understood.

One of my girlfriends, who had been obliged to go back home to her family, came back several months later. During her absence I had *thought about* her, carefully guarding a little ring that she had given me. My joy was great when I saw my friend again, but alas! All I got was an indifferent look. . . .

When I saw that Céline *loved* one of our teachers, I wanted to do as she did, but since I didn't *know* how to gain the good graces of others, I was unable to succeed. Oh happy ignorance! How many great ills it caused me to avoid! . . . How I thank Jesus for making me find only "bitterness in the friendships of this world." With a heart like mine, I would have let myself be taken and my wings clipped, and then how would I have been able to "fly away and find rest"? How can a heart that is given over to the affection of created beings be intimately united with God? . . . I feel that

that is not possible. Without having drunk from the poisoned cup of the too-ardent love of created things, *I feel* that I cannot be deceived.

I have seen so many souls, seduced by that *false light,* flying like poor butterflies and burning their wings, then coming back toward the true, the sweet light of *love* that gave them new wings, more brilliant and light, so that they might fly toward Jesus, that Divine Fire "who burns without consuming." Oh! I feel it: Jesus knew I was too weak to be exposed to temptation. Perhaps I would have let myself be burned up completely by the *deceitful light* if I had seen it shining before my eyes. . . .

But that is not how it was. I encountered only bitterness where stronger souls encounter joy and detach themselves from it out of faithfulness. So I have no merit in not having given myself over to the love of created things, since I was preserved from this only by God's great mercy! . . . I recognize that without Him, I would have fallen as low as Mary Magdalene did, and the profound words of Our Lord to Simon echo with great sweetness in my soul. . . . I know, "Whoever has been forgiven little, loves little" [Lk. 7:47], but I also know that Jesus has *forgiven me more* than He did for *Mary Magdalene,* since He forgave me *in advance,* keeping me from falling. Oh! How I would like to be able to explain what I'm feeling! . . .

Here's an example that will interpret my thoughts a little: Suppose that the son of a capable doctor encounters on the road a rock that makes him fall, and that as a result of this fall he breaks a limb. Immediately his father comes to him, picks him up lovingly, takes care of his wounds, and in so doing uses all the resources of his art, and soon his son, now completely healed, bears witness to his gratitude. Without any doubt, this son is quite right to love his father! But I'm going to make still another supposition. The father, knowing that on the road his son was taking there was a rock, hurries to go before him and removes it (without anybody seeing him). Certainly, this son, the object of the father's prevenient tenderness, not KNOWING the misfortune from which he's been delivered by his father, won't bear witness of his gratitude, and *will love him less* than if he had been cured by him. . . . But if he comes to know the danger that he has just escaped, *will he not love him more?*

Well, I am this child who is the object of the anticipatory love of a Father who sent His Word not to redeem the *righteous* but *sinners*. He wants me to *love Him* because He has *forgiven* me, not much, but *everything*. He didn't wait for me to *love Him much* like Mary Magdalene, but He wanted ME TO KNOW how much He loved me with an inexpressible anticipation, so that now I might love Him *to distraction!* . . . I've heard it said that there is no pure soul that can be found who loves more than a repentant soul. Oh! how I would like to belie that saying! . . .

I perceive that I've strayed far from my subject, so I'll hasten to come back to it. The year that followed my first Communion was spent almost entirely without any interior trials for my soul. But it was during my retreat before my second Communion that I saw myself assailed by the terrible illness of scruples [excessive fear of having sinned]. . . . You would have to pass through that martyrdom in order to understand it well. It would be impossible for me to say what I suffered for *a year and a half.* . . .

All my thoughts and my simplest actions became a subject of trouble for me. I had no rest except when I told them to Marie, and that cost me a lot, because I thought I was obliged to tell her the extravagant thoughts that I had about her. Immediately after my burden was laid down, I enjoyed an instant of peace, but that peace passed like a flash of lightning, and soon my martyrdom started up again.

What patience didn't my dear Marie have to have, to listen to me without ever showing annoyance! . . . Scarcely had I come back from the Abbey when she began to curl my hair for the next day (because every day in order to please Papa the little queen had her hair curled, to the great surprise of her classmates and, above all, of her teachers, who never saw students who were made so much of by their family). While my hair was being curled I couldn't stop crying as I told all my scruples.

At the end of the year Céline, who had finished her studies, came back home, and poor Thérèse, who had to go back by herself, wasn't long in getting sick. The only charm that had kept her in school was to live with her inseparable Céline. Without her, "her little girl" could never stay there. . . .

So I left the abbey school at the age of thirteen, and I continued my education by taking several lessons each week at "Mrs. Papinau's." She was a very good person who was *well educated,* who had somewhat the ways of the spinster. She lived with her mother. It was charming to see the little home that the *three* of them had together (because her *cat* was a member of the *family,* and I had to put up with her purring over my notebooks and even admire her pretty coat). I had the advantage of living intimately with the family; since Les Buissonnets was too far for the somewhat elderly legs of my teacher, she asked me to come to my lessons in her home. When I arrived, all I would usually find was the elderly Mrs. Cochain, who would look at me "with her big, bright eyes," and then she would call out with her calm and sententious voice, *"Mrs. Pa-apinau . . .* Miz Thé . . .rèse is here! . . ."* Her daughter would promptly reply with a *childish* voice, "Here I am, *Mother."* And soon the lesson would begin.

These lessons had the advantage (besides the instruction that I received) of making me familiar with the world. . . . Who would have believed it! In that room furnished in antique style, surrounded by books and notebooks, I often witnessed visits of all types— priests, ladies, girls, etc. Mrs. Cochain carried on the conversation as much as possible in order to let her daughter teach me my lesson, but on those days I didn't learn much.

With my nose in a book, I heard everything that was being said, and even what it would have been better for me not to hear: Vanity slips so easily into the heart! . . . One lady said that I had beautiful hair. . . . As another was leaving, thinking that I couldn't hear her, she asked who this girl was who was so pretty, and these words, which were so much more flattering because they weren't said in front of me, left on my soul an impression of pleasure that showed me clearly how full of self-love I was.

Oh! How much compassion I feel for souls who are becoming lost! . . . It's so easy to wander off onto the flowery paths of the world. . . . No doubt, for a soul that's a bit haughty, the sweetness that it offers is mixed with bitterness and the *immense emptiness of the desires* could never be filled by the praises of a moment. . . . But if my heart hadn't been *lifted toward God beginning with its awakening,* if the world had smiled on me beginning with my entrance into life, what would have become of me? . . .

Oh, beloved Mother, with what gratitude do I sing of the mercies of the Lord! . . . Wasn't I, according to these words of Wisdom, "taken away, lest wickedness should alter my understanding, or deceit beguile my soul" [cf. Wis. 4:11]? . . . The Blessed Virgin also was watching over her little flower, and not wanting her to be faded by contact with the things of the earth, she withdrew her onto *her mountain* before she had fully opened. . . . While awaiting that happy moment, little Thérèse was growing in the love of her Heavenly Mother. To prove her love for her, she did *an act* that *cost her a great deal* and that I'm going to tell in a few words, despite its *length.* . . .

Almost immediately after my entrance into the abbey school, I had been received into the Association of the Holy Angels. I very much liked the devotional practices that it required, having a most particular attraction for praying to the Blessed Spirits from Heaven, and particularly to the one [my guardian angel] whom God had given me to be my companion in my exile on earth.

A short time after my first Communion, the ribbon of the candidate for the Children of Mary replaced the one for the Holy Angels, but I left the Abbey without having been received into the Association of the Blessed Virgin. Having left before finishing my studies, I didn't have permission to enter the Association as a graduate. I admit that this privilege didn't excite my desire, but thinking that all my sisters had been "Children of Mary," I was afraid of being less than they the child of my Heavenly Mother. So I went very humbly (in spite of what it cost me to do so) to ask for permission to be received into the Association of the Blessed Virgin at the Abbey. The head teacher didn't want to refuse, but she placed on me the condition that I would have to come back for two afternoons a week so I could show that I was worthy of being admitted.

Far from bringing me pleasure, this permission was extremely costly for me. I didn't have, like the other former students, a *teacher friend* with whom I could go spend several hours. So I had to content myself with going and greeting the teacher, and then I would work in silence until the end of the lesson. Nobody paid attention to me, so I went up to the gallery of the chapel and I remained before the Blessed Sacrament until the time when Papa would come get me. This was my only comfort: Wasn't Jesus my *only friend?* . . . I knew how to speak to Him alone. Conversations with created beings, even pious conversations, tired out my soul. . . . I felt that it was better to talk to God rather than to talk about God, because so much pride gets mixed into spiritual conversations! . . . Oh! It really was for the Blessed Virgin alone that I was coming to the Abbey. . . .

Sometimes I felt that I was *alone,* quite alone. As during the days of my life as a resident in the boarding school, when I would walk, sad and ill, in the big courtyard, I would repeat these words that always brought peace again and strength in my heart: "Life is your ship and not your dwelling! . . ." Even when I was quite little these words used to give me courage. And still, now, in spite of the years that have caused so many impressions of childish piety to disappear, the picture of the ship still charms my soul and helps it endure exile. . . .

Doesn't Wisdom also say that "Life is like a vessel that ploughs through the troubled waves and leaves after it no trace of its rapid passage" [cf. Wis. 5:10]? When I think about these things, my soul plunges into infinity and seems to me already to touch the everlasting shore. . . . It seems to me to receive Jesus' embraces. . . . I think I see my Heavenly Mother coming to meet me with Papa . . . Mama . . . the four little angels. . . . I think I'm finally enjoying forever the true, the everlasting life with my family. . . .

Before seeing the family reunited in the *Father's home* in heaven, I would still have to go through many separations. The year when I was received as a Child of the Blessed Virgin, she took away my dear Marie, the only support of my soul. . . . Marie it was who guided me, comforted me, helped me practice virtue: She was my sole oracle.

Without a doubt, Pauline had remained right in the forefront of my heart, but Pauline was far, very far from me! . . . I had suffered martyrdom in order to become accustomed to living without her, in order to see between her and me unscalable walls, but finally I had wound up recognizing the sad reality: Pauline was lost for me, almost in the same way as if she had died. She still loved me and prayed for me, but in my eyes, *my beloved Pauline* had become a Saint, who must no longer understand the things of earth, and, if she had known them, the miseries of her poor Thérèse would have surprised her and prevented her from loving her so much. . . . Besides, even though I would have liked to confide my thoughts to her, as at Les Buissonnets, I wouldn't have been able to; the meetings at the convent parlor were only for Marie. Céline and I didn't have permission to go to them until the end, just in order to have the time to have our hearts wrung. . . .

So in reality I had only Marie. For me she was, so to speak, indispensable. She was the only one to whom I told my scruples, and I was so obedient that my confessor never knew my wretched illness. All I told him was the number of sins that Marie allowed me to confess to him, not one more, so I would have passed for being the least scrupulous soul on earth, in spite of the fact that I was one to the nth degree. . . . So Marie knew everything that was going on in my soul. She also knew my desire to enter Carmel, and I loved her so much that I couldn't live without her.

My aunt used to invite us every year to come one after the other to her home in Trouville. I would have liked to go there, only with Marie. When I didn't have her I was bored to death. However, one time I experienced pleasure in Trouville. This was the year of Papa's trip to Constantinople. In order to take our minds off of it a little (because we were quite distressed that Papa was so far away), Marie sent Céline and me to spend two weeks by the sea. I had a great time there because I had my Céline. My aunt secured every possible pleasure for us: donkey rides, fishing for eels, etc. I was still a child in spite of being twelve and a half. I remember what joy I felt when I put on pretty sky-blue ribbons that my aunt gave me for my hair. And I also remember going to confession at Trouville to confess even that childish pleasure that seemed to me to be a sin. . . .

One night I had an experience that surprised me a lot. Marie Guérin [my cousin], who was always sick, often used to *whimper like a baby.* So my aunt would sweet-talk her and call her by the most tender of names, and my dear little cousin would continue nonetheless to bawl that she had a headache. I also had a headache nearly every day and didn't complain about it, but one night I tried to copy Marie. So I took it upon myself to start sniveling in an armchair in a corner of the living room. Soon Jeanne [my other cousin] and my aunt rushed around me and asked what was wrong. I replied, like Marie, "I have a headache." It seems that it wasn't befitting for me to complain. I never was able to convince them that the headache made me cry.

Instead of sweet-talking me, they spoke to me like a grownup, and Jeanne scolded me for my lack of trust in my aunt, because she thought that I had something troubling my conscience. . . .

In the end I was no better off for all my trouble and was quite resolved not to copy others. And I understood the fable of "The donkey and the little dog." *I was the donkey* who, seeing how *the little dog* was petted, came and put his heavy hoof on the table so he could receive his share of the petting. But alas! If I wasn't beaten like that poor animal, I received my just desserts, and those desserts cured me for life of the desire to attract attention. The only time I tried to do that it cost me too much! . . .

The next year was the one when my dear godmother [Marie] left [for Carmel]. My aunt invited me to come again, but alone this time, and I was so out of my element that after two or three days I fell sick and they had to take me back to Lisieux. My sickness, which they were afraid was serious, was only homesickness for Les Buissonnets. Hardly had I set foot there when my health returned. . . . And it was from that very child that God was going to tear away the only support that attached her to life! . . . As soon as I learned about Marie's determination, I resolved no longer to take any pleasure on earth. . . .

Since I had left school, I had moved into *Pauline's* former painting room, and I had arranged it according to my taste. It was a real hodge-podge, an assemblage of piety and curios, a garden and an aviary. . . . Accordingly at the end there stood out from the wall a *big cross* made of black wood, without a Christ figure, along with a few drawings that I liked.

On another wall, there was a hamper decorated with muslin and pink ribbons with herbs and flowers. Finally, on the last wall a portrait of *Pauline* at the age of ten was enthroned alone. Underneath that portrait I had a table on which was placed a *big cage,* housing a *great* number of birds whose melodious chirping deafened the ears of my visitors, but not those of their little mistress, who appreciated them very much. . . .

In addition there was yet the "little white piece of furniture" full of my school books, notebooks, etc. On that piece of furniture was placed a statue of the Blessed Virgin, with vases always full of natural flowers and candles. All around them there were a large number of little statues of Saints, little baskets decorated with shells, boxes made of Bristol board, etc.! Finally, my garden was *suspended* in front of the window. In it I raised pots of flowers (the rarest that I could find).

I had one more plant stand in the inner part of "my museum," and there I put my most privileged plant. . . . In front of the window stood my table, covered with a green rug, and on that rug I had placed, in the center, an *hourglass,* a little statue of St. Joseph, a watch stand, baskets of flowers, an inkwell, etc. . . . A few *rickety* chairs and *Pauline's* delightful doll bed completed my furnishings. This poor little attic room was truly a world for me, and, like Mr. de Maistre, I could compose a book entitled *A Journey Around My Room.* [A book by this name, by Xavier de Maistre, was published in 1795.] It was in this room that I loved to stay by myself for hours on end to study and meditate before the beautiful view that stretched out before my eyes. . . .

When I learned about Marie's leaving, my *room* lost all its charms for me. I didn't want to leave, even for a single moment, the beloved sister who was to fly away soon. . . . How many acts of patience I caused her to practice! *Each time* I passed in front of her bedroom door, I knocked until she opened the door for me, and I hugged her with my whole heart. I wanted to store up hugs for all the time that I would be without them.

A month before she entered Carmel, Papa took us to Alençon, but that trip was far from being like the first one, because everything there for me was sadness and bitterness. I couldn't say how many tears I shed over Mama's grave, because I had forgotten to bring a bouquet of cornflowers that I had picked for her. I really had trouble over *everything*. It was the opposite of now, because God has given me the grace not to be downhearted over any passing thing.

When I remember the past, my soul overflows with gratitude on seeing the favors that I've received from heaven. Such a change has come over me that I'm not recognizable. . . . It's true that I desired the grace "to have absolute control over my actions, to be the master and not the slave." These words from the *Imitation of Christ* touched me deeply, but I had, so to speak, to purchase, by my desires, that inestimable grace. I was still only a child who seemed to have no other will than that of other people, which made people at Alençon say that I had a weak character. . . .

It was during that trip that Léonie tried out at the order of St. Clare. I was quite put out at her *extraordinary* entrance into that order, because I loved her a lot and I hadn't been able to give her a hug and a kiss before she left.

I'll never forget the goodness and the perplexity of that poor dear priest when he came to announce to us that Léonie had already taken the habit of a nun of the Poor Clares. . . . Like us, he found that quite odd, but he didn't want to say anything when he saw how unhappy Marie was. He took us to the convent, and there I felt *heart pangs* as I have never felt at the sight of a convent. It produced on me the opposite effect of Carmel, where everything gladdened my soul. . . . Neither did the sight of the nuns enchant me, and I wasn't tempted to remain with them. Poor Léonie was nonetheless quite nice in her new outfit. She told us to look deeply into her eyes, because we were to see them no longer (since the Poor Clares always lower their eyes when they are seen). But God was content with two months of sacrifice, and Léonie came back to show us her blue eyes that were often wet with tears. . . .

When we left Alençon, I thought she would stay with the Poor Clares, so it was with a very heavy heart that I went away from the sad street of the half moon. Now there were only three of us, and soon our dear Marie was to leave us. . . .

The fifteenth of October was the separation day! Of the joyful, large family that lived at Les Buissonnets, only the last two children were left. . . . The doves had flown away from the father's nest. Those who remained would have liked to fly away and follow the others, but their wings were still too weak for them to be able to take flight. . . .

God, who wanted to call to Himself the littlest and weakest of all, hastened to develop her wings. He who is pleased to show His goodness and His power by using the least worthy instruments, wanted to call me before Céline, who without a doubt was the one rather than I who was worthy of that favor. But Jesus knew how weak I was, and it was for that reason that He hid me first in the cleft in the rock [Ex. 33:22; see also Song 2:14 and 1 Cor. 1:26–29].

When Marie entered Carmel, I was still excessively scrupulous [concerned with whether I had sinned]. No longer being able to confide in her, I turned toward heaven. It was to the four little angels who had gone up there before me that I spoke, because I thought that those innocent souls who had never known trouble or fear must surely have pity on their poor little sister, who was suffering on earth. I talked to them with the simplicity of a child, pointing out to them that since I was the last child in the family, I had always been the most loved, the most showered with tenderness by my sisters, and that if they had remained on earth, they would no doubt also have given me proofs of their affection. . . . Their leaving for heaven didn't seem to me to be a reason for them to forget me. On the contrary, now that they were where they could make withdrawals straight from the Divine treasure house, they ought to withdraw *peace* for me and show me, as well as heaven, that they still know how to love! . . .

The answer wasn't long in coming. Soon peace came and flooded my soul with its delicious waves, and I understood that if I was loved on earth, I also was loved in heaven. . . . Since that moment my devotion has grown for my little brothers and sisters, and I love to talk often with them, to speak to them about the sadnesses of exile . . . and about my desire to go soon to be with them in the Homeland! . . .

CHAPTER 5

After the Grace of Christmas
1886–1887

The blood of Jesus
Pranzini, my first child
The Imitation of Christ and Arminjon
Desire to enter Carmel
Confiding in my father
Sudden change in my uncle
Opposition by the Superior
Visit to Bayeux

If heaven was pouring out graces on me, it wasn't because I deserved them. I was still quite imperfect. It's true that I had a great desire to practice virtue, but I undertook it in a funny way. Here's one example: Since I was the youngest, I wasn't used to taking care of myself. Céline cleaned the room where we slept together, and I never did any housework. After Marie entered Carmel, it happened to me sometimes to please God by trying to make the bed, or, in Pauline's absence, to bring in her pots of flowers at night. As I said, it was *for God alone* that I did these things. So I shouldn't have been waiting for a *thank you* from created beings. Alas! It was completely otherwise. If Céline had the misfortune not to look happy and surprised at my little services, I wasn't happy, and I proved it by my tears. . . .

I was really unbearable due to my overly great sensitivity. So if it happened that I involuntarily gave a slight amount of trouble to a person I loved, instead of taking the high road and *not crying*, I increased my fault, instead of reducing it, by *crying* like a baby. And when I started to become comforted by the thing itself, I *cried because I had cried*. . . . All this reasoning was useless, and I couldn't manage to correct this wicked fault. I don't know how I could soothe myself with the sweet thought of entering Carmel, seeing that I was still in *baby diapers!* . . .

It was necessary for God to do a small miracle in order to make me *grow up* in one moment, and He did that miracle on the unforgettable day of Christmas. On that radiant night that sheds light on the delights of the Holy Trinity, Jesus the sweet *little* Child, just one hour old, changed the night of my soul into torrents of light [Ps. 139:12]. . . . On that *night when* He made Himself *weak* and suffering out of love for me, He made me *strong* and courageous. He put his armor on me [Eph. 6:11], and since that blessed night I was never defeated in combat. On the contrary, I marched from victory to victory, and I began, so to speak, to run a champion's course [Ps. 19:5]. The fount of my tears was dried up, and since that time it opened only rarely and with difficulty, justifying this word that had been said to me: "You cry so much in your childhood that later you won't have any more tears to shed!"

It was on December 25th, 1886, that I received the grace to leave my childhood—in a word, the grace of my complete conversion: We were coming back from Midnight Mass, where I'd had the happiness of receiving the *strong* and *powerful* God [Ps. 24:8]. Upon arriving at Les Buissonnets, I was rejoicing at going to get my shoes [on which my Christmas presents had been placed] from the fireplace. This traditional practice had caused us so much joy during our childhood that Céline wanted to continue to treat me like a baby, since I was the youngest in the family. . . . Papa loved to see how happy I was, to hear my shouts of joy as I took out each surprise from my *magic shoes,* and the gaiety of my dear king increased my happiness even more.

But Jesus, who wanted to show me that I needed to undo these childish shortcomings, also took away these innocent joys from me. He allowed Papa, who was tired from the Midnight Mass, to feel annoyed at seeing my shoes on the fireplace, and for him to say these words that pierced me to the heart: "Well, fortunately this is the last year." I then ran up the stairs to take off my hat. Céline, who knew how sensitive I was, saw the tears shining in my eyes; she also felt like crying, because she loved me a lot and understood my grief. "Oh, Thérèse," she said, "don't go back down. It will hurt you too much to look in your shoes right away."

But Thérèse wasn't the same any longer; Jesus had changed her heart! Forcing back my tears, I ran quickly back down the stairs, and, restraining my pounding heart, I took my shoes, and, placing them in front of

Papa, *joyously* I took out all the objects, looking happy as a queen. Papa was laughing. He had also become joyful again, and Céline thought she was dreaming! . . . Fortunately, it was a sweet reality. Little Thérèse had regained the strength of soul that she had lost at the age of four and a half, and she was to keep it forever! . . .

On that *night of light* the third period of my life began, the most beautiful of them all, the most filled with graces from heaven. . . . In an instant, the work that I hadn't been able to do in ten years—Jesus did it, being content with the *good will* that I had no shortage of. Like His apostles, I could say, "Lord, I fished all night without catching anything" [cf. Lk. 5:5–10]. Then, more merciful toward me than He was toward His disciples, Jesus *Himself took* the net, threw it out, and brought it back in, full of fish. . . . He made me into a fisher *of souls* [Mk. 1:17]. I felt a great desire to work for the conversion of sinners, a desire that I had never felt so strongly. . . . In a word, I felt *charity* enter into my heart, the need to forget myself in order to please others, and ever afterward I was happy! . . .

One Sunday, as I was looking at a photograph showing Our Lord on the Cross, I was struck by the blood that was falling from one of His Divine hands. I felt great pain at the thought that this blood was falling to the ground without anyone hurrying to collect it, and I resolved to keep myself in spirit at the foot of the Cross in order to receive the Divine dew that was flowing down from it, understanding that I must then spread it over souls. . . . Jesus' cry on the Cross also resounded continually in my heart: *"I am thirsty!"* [Jn. 19:28].

These words set on fire within me a keen fervor that I hadn't known before. . . . I wanted to give something to drink to my Beloved, and I felt myself consumed with *thirst* for *souls*. . . . It was no longer the souls of priests that attracted me, but those of *great sinners*. I *was burning* with the desire to snatch them from the everlasting flames. . . .

In order to stir up my fervor, God showed me that my desires were pleasing to Him. I heard about a terrible criminal who had just been condemned to death for some horrible crimes. Everything would lead one to believe that he would die without repenting. I wanted at all cost to prevent him from going to hell. In order to do that I used every imaginable means: Sensing that in myself I could do nothing, I offered to God all the infinite merits of Our Lord and the treasures of the Holy Church. Finally I begged Céline to have a Mass said for my intentions, not daring to ask myself, for fear that I would be obliged to admit that it was for Pranzini, the terrible criminal. I didn't want to tell Céline, either, but she put such tender and such pressing questions to me that I confided my secret in her.

Far from making fun of me, she asked to help me convert *my sinner*. I accepted with gratitude, because I would have wanted every creature to unite with me in imploring for grace for the guilty one. Deep in my heart I felt *certainty* that our desires would be granted, but in order to give myself courage to continue to pray for sinners, I told God that I was quite sure that He would forgive poor miserable Pranzini, and that I would believe this even if he *did not confess* and showed *no sign of repentance,* so much did I have confidence in Jesus' infinite mercy, but I asked Him only for *"a sign"* of repentance simply for my consolation. . . .

My prayer was granted to the letter! Despite Papa's having forbidden us to read any newspaper, I didn't believe that I was disobeying him by reading the articles that talked about Pranzini. The day after his execution [on September 1st, 1887] I put my hand on the newspaper *La Croix.* I opened it hurriedly, and what did I see? . . . Oh! My tears betrayed my emotion, and I was obliged to go hide. . . . Pranzini had not confessed; he had climbed up onto the scaffold and was getting ready to put his head into the ominous opening in the guillotine, when suddenly, gripped with a sudden inspiration, he turned back, grabbed a *Crucifix* that the priest was holding up to him, and *kissed its sacred wounds three times!* . . . Then his soul went to receive the *merciful* judgment of the One who declares that in heaven there will be more joy for a single sinner who repents than for ninety-nine righteous persons who have no need for repentance! [Lk. 15:7] . . .

I had obtained "the sign" that I had asked for, and that sign was the faithful reproduction of the graces that Jesus had granted in order to draw me to pray for sinners. Wasn't it when I was facing *Jesus' wounds,* seeing His Divine *blood* flow, that the thirst for souls had entered into my heart? I wanted to give them to drink this *immaculate blood* that must cleanse them from their stains, and the lips of "my *first child"* were pressed upon the sacred wounds!!! . . . What an expressibly sweet reply! . . .

Oh! Since that unique grace, my desire to save souls has been growing every day. It seems to me that I can hear Jesus tell me, as He did to the Samaritan woman, "Give me a drink!" [cf. Jn. 4:6–15]. This was a true exchange of love: To souls I gave the *blood* of Jesus; to Jesus I offered these same souls, refreshed by His *Divine dew.* In that way it seemed to me that I was quenching His thirst, and the more I gave Him to *drink,* the more my poor little soul's thirst increased. And it was this burning thirst that He gave me as the most delicious beverage of His love. . . .

In a short time God had managed to pull me out of the narrow circle in which I was spinning without knowing how to get out. When I see the road that He had me travel, my gratitude is great. But I must admit that if the biggest step was taken, I still had many things to get rid of. Freed from its scruples and its excessive sensitivity, my spirit developed.

I had always loved great and beautiful things, but at that time I was seized with an extreme desire *for knowledge.* Not content with the lessons and homework that my teacher gave me, I applied myself all alone to special studies of *history* and *science.* The other studies left me indifferent, but these two subjects attracted my entire attention. The result was that in a few months I acquired more knowledge than during my years of study. Oh! That was nothing but a meaningless chasing after the wind [Eccl. 2:11]. . . .

The chapter in the *Imitation of Christ* that talks about *knowledge* would often come to my thoughts, but I found the means to continue anyway, telling myself that since I was of school age, there was no harm in doing it. I don't think I offended God (although I recognize that I spent some useless time in doing this) because I spent only a certain number of hours studying and didn't want to go beyond that amount of time in order to mortify my overly keen desire for knowledge. . . .

I was at the most dangerous age for girls, but God did for me what Ezekiel reports in his prophecies: Passing close to me, Jesus saw that the time had come for me to be *loved* [cf. Ezek. 16:8–14]. So He made an alliance with me and I became *His*. . . . He spread His mantle over me, He washed me with precious perfume, clothed me with embroidered garments, giving me priceless necklaces and jewelry. . . . He nourished me with the finest of wheat, honey, and oil *in abundance*. . . . Then I became beautiful in His sight, and He made me into a powerful queen! . . .

Yes, Jesus did all that for me. I could go back over each word that I've just written and prove that it became real in my favor, but the graces that I wrote about earlier are proof enough of that. So I'm only going to talk about the food that He poured out on me *"in abundance."* For a long time I had been nourishing myself on the "finest of wheat" contained in the *Imitation of Christ*. This was the only book that did me good, because I hadn't yet found the treasures hidden in the Gospels [Is. 45:3]. I knew by heart almost all the chapters of my dear *Imitation*. This little book never left me: In summer, I carried it in my pocket, in winter, in my muff, so it had become traditional. At my aunt's they found this quite amusing, and opening it at random they had me recite the chapter that they found before their eyes.

At the age of fourteen, with my desire for knowledge, God found that it was necessary to join "to the finest wheat," "honey and oil in abundance." This honey and this oil, He had me find in Fr. Arminjon's lectures about the present world and the mysteries of the future life. This book had been lent to Papa by my dear Carmelites, so, contrary to my usual habit (because I didn't read Papa's books), I asked to read it. This reading was again one of the great graces of my life. I read it at the window of my study room, and the impression that I felt from it is too intimate and too sweet for me to be able to tell you about it. . . .

All the great truths of religion, the mysteries of eternity, plunged my soul into a happiness that was not of earth [1 Cor. 2:9]. . . . I was already feeling what God reserves for those who love Him (not with the human eye, but with that of the heart), and seeing that eternal rewards have no proportion to the slight sacrifices of life [2 Cor. 4:17], I wanted to *love, love* Jesus with *passion,* give Him a thousand signs of love while I could still do it. . . . I copied several passages about perfect love and about the reception that God will give to His elect at the time when He *Himself* will become their great and eternal reward. I repeated unceasingly these words of love that had inflamed my heart. . . .

Céline had become the intimate confidante of my thoughts. Since Christmas we had been able to understand each other. The difference in age no longer existed, since I had grown big in size and especially in grace

[2 Pet. 3:18]. . . . Before that time I often used to complain about not knowing Céline's secrets. She used to tell me that I was too little, that I would have to grow "to the height of a stool" in order for her to be able to trust me. . . . I used to love to climb up on that precious stool when I was at her side, and I used to tell her to speak intimately to me, but my industriousness was useless—a distance still separated us! . . .

Jesus, who wanted us to go forward together, formed in our hearts links that are stronger than those of blood. He made us become *soul sisters*. These words of St. John of the Cross became a reality in us (speaking to the Bridegroom, the bride cries out): "Following your traces, the girls crossed the path lightly. The touching of the spark, the spiced wine, caused them to produce aspirations that were divinely perfumed." Yes, it was quite *lightly* that we followed Jesus' traces. The sparks of love that He sowed bountifully into our souls, the delicious and strong wine that He gave us to drink, caused passing things to disappear before our eyes, and from our lips there came out aspirations of love inspired by Him.

How sweet were the conversations that we used to have each evening in the belvedere! Our gaze fixed on faraway things, we would consider the white moon that was gently rising behind the big trees. . . . The silvery reflections that it would spread over sleeping nature, the brilliant stars shimmering in the infinite heavens . . . the light puff of the evening breeze making the snow-laden clouds float in the sky—all these things would lift our souls toward heaven, that beautiful heaven of which we were still contemplating only "the translucent *reverse* side." ["Sky" and "heaven" are the same word in French, thus the metaphor: the sky is the reverse side of heaven.]

I don't know if I'm wrong, but it seems to me that the outpouring of our souls was like that of St. Monica with her son [St. Augustine], when at the port of Ostia they remained lost in ecstasy at the sight of the marvels of the Creator! . . . It seems to me that we were receiving graces on as high an order as those granted to the great saints. As the *Imitation* says, God sometimes communicates Himself amidst great splendor, and sometimes "gently veiled, in the form of shadows and figures." It was in this manner that He deigned to manifest Himself to our souls. But how *transparent* and *light* was the veil that hid Jesus from our eyes! . . . Doubt was impossible; already Faith and Hope were no longer necessary; *love* made us find on earth the One that we were seeking [1 Cor. 13]. "Having found Him alone, He had given us His kiss, to the end that henceforth no one might be able to deride us."

Graces as great as these must not remain fruitless, therefore their fruits were abundant. The practice of virtue became sweet and natural to us. At the beginning my face often betrayed the struggle, but little by little that impression disappeared, and renouncement became easy for me, even at the start. Jesus said, "For those who have will be given more, and they will have an abundance" [Mt. 25:29]. For one grace faithfully received He granted me a multitude of others. . . .

He gave Himself to me in Holy Communion more often than I would have dared to hope. I had taken as a rule of conduct to receive, without missing a single one, the Communions that my confessor would give me, but to let him set the number of them without ever asking him to do so. In those days I didn't have the *audacity* that I now possess. Without that I would have behaved differently, because I'm quite sure that a soul ought to tell her confessor the attraction that she feels toward receiving her God. It isn't to remain in the golden ciborium [the covered receptacle that holds the consecrated Communion wafers] that He comes down *every day* from heaven. It's to find another heaven that is infinitely dearer to Him than the first one, the heaven of our soul, made in His image, the living temple of the adorable Trinity! [1 Cor. 3:16] . . .

Jesus, seeing my desire and the uprightness of my heart, permitted that during the month of May, my confessor told me to receive Holy Communion four times per week, and once that beautiful month had passed, he added a fifth time each time there was a feast day. The sweetest tears fell down my cheeks when I left the confessional. It seemed to me that it was Jesus Himself who wanted to give Himself to me, because I spent only a short time in the confessional. I would never say a word about my inner feelings. The road on which I was marching was so straight, so shining, that no other guide was needed for me than Jesus. . . . I used to compare spiritual directors to faithful mirrors who reflected Jesus into souls, and I used to say that for me God didn't use an intermediary, but He would act directly! . . .

When a gardener pours out attention on a fruit that he wants to mature before its season, it's never to leave it hanging from the tree, but in order to serve it on a brilliantly set table. It was with such an intention that Jesus poured out His graces on His little flower. . . . The One who cried out during the days of His mortal life, transported by joy, "I praise you, Father, . . . because you have hidden these things from the wise and learned, and revealed them to little children" [Lk. 10:21], wanted to make His mercy blaze within me. Because I was small and weak, He bent down to me and instructed me in secret about the *things* of His *love.* Oh! If the wise who have spent their lives studying had come to come ask me, no doubt they would have been astonished to see a child of fourteen understand the secrets of perfection, secrets that all their knowledge could not reveal to them, since to possess it you have to be poor in spirit! [Mt. 5:3] . . .

As St. John of the Cross put it in his canticle, "I had neither guide, nor light, except the one that was shining in my heart. That light guided me more surely than that of noonday to the place where the One was waiting for me who knows me perfectly." That place was Carmel. Before resting in the shade of the One whom I desired [Song 2:3], I was to pass through many trials, but the Divine call was so pressing that even if I had had to *pass through flames,* I would have done so in order to be faithful to Jesus. . . .

To encourage me in my vocation, I found only one *single soul,* and that was that of my *dear Mother* [my sister Pauline]. . . . My heart found in hers a faithful echo, and without her I would no doubt not have arrived at the blessed shore that had received her five years earlier on its ground imbued with the heavenly dew. . . . Yes, for five years I had been separated from you, *dear Mother.* I had thought that I had lost you, but at the time of trial it was your hand that showed me the road that I needed to follow. . . .

I needed this relief, because my times at the parlor at Carmel had become more and more painful for me. I couldn't talk about my desire to enter the Convent without feeling myself being pushed away. Marie, who thought that I was too young, did everything in her power to prevent me from entering. You yourself, Mother, in order to test me, tried sometimes to slow down my enthusiasm. In short, if I hadn't truly had the vocation, I would have stopped at the beginning, because I encountered obstacles as soon as I began to respond to Jesus' call.

I didn't want to tell Céline about my desire to enter Carmel so young, and that made me suffer more, because it was very hard for me to hide anything from her. . . . That suffering didn't last long. Soon my dear sister [Céline] learned about my determination, and far from trying to turn me away from it, she accepted with admirable courage the sacrifice that God was asking of her.

To understand how great that sacrifice was, you would have to know how united we were. . . . It was so to speak the same soul that made us live. For a few months we had been enjoying together the sweetest life that girls could dream of. Everything around us responded to our desires, the greatest freedom was given to us, to the point where I used to say that our life on earth was the *ideal* of *happiness.* . . .

Hardly had we had the time to enjoy this *ideal* of *happiness* when we had to turn away from it freely, and my dear Céline didn't rebel for an instant. However, she wasn't the one whom Jesus called first, therefore she could have complained. . . . Having the same vocation as I, it was up to her to depart! . . . But in the time of the martyrs, those who remained in prison joyously gave the kiss of peace to their brothers who were the first to leave for the combat in the arena, comforting themselves with the thought that perhaps they were reserved for even greater combats: That's how *Céline* let her Thérèse go away, and she remained alone for the glorious and bloody combat [the lonely task of caring for Papa during his long illness] to which Jesus destined her as the *privileged one* of His *love*. . . .

So Céline became the confidante of my struggles and my sufferings. She took the same part in it as if it had been a question of her own vocation. From her I had no fear of opposition, but I didn't know what means to take to announce it to Papa. . . . How was I to talk to him about letting go of his queen, he who had just sacrificed his three oldest ones? . . . Oh! What inner struggles I suffered before feeling the courage to talk about it! . . . However, I had to come to a decision.

I was about to turn fourteen and a half. Only six months still separated me from that beautiful *Christmas night* when I had resolved to enter [Carmel], at the very time when the year before I had received "my grace." In order to make my great revelation I chose the day of *Pentecost*. All day long I pleaded with the Holy Apostles to pray for me, to inspire in me the

words that I was going to have to say. . . . Weren't they
the ones in fact who had to help the timid child that
God was destining to become the apostle of apostles
through prayer and sacrifice? [Carmelites have a special
mission to pray for priests, and thus are "apostles" to
the "apostles" (priests).] . . .

It was only in the afternoon when, coming back from
Vespers [the late afternoon church service], I found the
opportunity to talk to my dear father. He had gone to
sit at the edge of the cistern, and there, with hands
clasped together, he was contemplating the marvels of
nature. The sun, whose fiery rays had lost their ardor,
was tingeing with gold the tops of the tall trees, in
which the little birds were joyfully singing their evening
prayer. Papa's beautiful face had a heavenly expression.
I was feeling that peace was flooding his heart. Without
saying a single word I went and sat beside him, with my
eyes already wet with tears. He looked at me tenderly,
and, taking my head, he pressed it against his heart,
and said, "What's the matter, my little queen? . . . Tell
me all about it. . . ." Then, standing up, as if to hide his
own emotion, he walked slowly, still holding my head
against his heart.

Through my tears I confided in him my desire to
enter Carmel. Then his tears began mingling with my
own, but he didn't say a word to turn me away from
my vocation, being simply content to point out that I
was still quite young to make such a serious determination. But I defended my cause so well, that with Papa's
simple and upright nature, he was soon convinced that
my desire was that of God Himself, and in his deep

faith he cried out that God was giving him a great honor to ask him for his children in this way.

We continued our walk for a long time. My heart, relieved by the goodness with which my incomparable father had greeted these confidences, poured itself out gently into his. Papa seemed to enjoy the tranquil joy that sacrifice, once accomplished, brings. He talked to me like a Saint, and I would like to remember his words in order to write them here, but I have retained only a memory that is too sweet to be able to write it down. What I do remember perfectly was the *symbolic* act that my beloved king accomplished without knowing it. Approaching a low wall, he showed me some *little white flowers* that looked like miniature lilies, and taking one of those flowers, he gave it to me, explaining to me with what care God had caused it to grow and had preserved it until that day. And hearing him talk, I thought I was listening to my story, so much resemblance there was between what Jesus had done for the *little flower* and *little Thérèse*. . . .

I received that little flower as if it were a Saint's relic, and I saw that by trying to pick it Papa had pulled up all its *roots* without breaking them. It seemed destined to live on in another piece of ground, more fertile than the tender moss in which its first mornings had been spent. . . . It was truly that same action that Papa had just done for me a few moments earlier, by allowing me to climb the mountain of Carmel and to leave the sweet valley that had witnessed my first steps in life.

I placed my little white flower in my copy of the *Imitation*, in the chapter entitled "On loving Jesus above all things." It's still there, only the stem has broken near the root, and God seems to be saying to me by that that He will soon break His little flower's bonds and will not leave her to fade on earth!

After I obtained Papa's consent, I thought I would be able to fly without fear to Carmel. But many sorrowful trials were still to test my vocation. It was only with trembling that I confided to my uncle [Isidore Guérin, Mama's brother] the resolve that I had taken. He showered upon me every sign of tenderness possible, but nonetheless, he didn't give me permission to leave. On the contrary, he forbade me from talking about my vocation before the age of seventeen. It was contrary to human prudence, he said, to allow the entrance into Carmel of a fifteen-year-old child. Since this life of a Carmelite was, in the eyes of the world, the life of a philosopher, it would be doing a great wrong to the religious life to let an inexperienced child embrace it. . . . Everybody would be talking about it. . . . etc. . . . etc. . . . He even said that to make him decide to let me leave, it would take a *miracle*.

I saw clearly that all reasoning would be useless. So I withdrew, my heart plunged into the deepest bitterness. My only comfort was prayer. I begged Jesus to do the *miracle* my uncle was requiring, since only at that cost would I be able to respond to His call.

A rather long time passed before I dared to talk about this again to my uncle. It cost me dearly to go see him. For his part, he no longer seemed to be thinking about my vocation, but I found out later that my great sadness influenced him a great deal in my favor. Before shining a ray of hope on my soul, God wanted to send me a most sorrowful martyrdom that lasted for *three days*. Oh! I have never understood so well as during that time of trial, the sorrow of the Blessed Virgin and St. Joseph as they were searching for the divine Child Jesus [Lk. 2:41–50]. . . .

I was in a sad desert, or rather my soul was like a fragile skiff with no pilot at the mercy of the storm-tossed waves. . . . I know, Jesus was there, asleep on my dinghy [Mk. 4:35–41], but the night was so dark that it was impossible for me to see Him. Nothing gave me light; not a single flash of lightning came to pierce the dark clouds. . . . Doubtless, lightning gives off quite a sad glimmer, but at least, if the storm had burst into the open, I would have been able to catch sight of Jesus for an instant. . . . It was *night*, the deep night of the soul. . . . Like Jesus in the agony in the garden [Lk. 22:39–46] I felt *alone*, finding comfort neither on earth nor on behalf of heaven. God seemed to have forsaken me!!! [Mt. 27:46] . . .

Nature seemed to have taken part in my bitter sadness. During those three days, the sun didn't shine a single one of its rays, and rain fell in torrents. (I've noticed that during the serious circumstances of my life, nature was the image of my soul. On days of tears, the sky wept with me; on days of joy, the sun sent its gleeful rays in profusion, and not one single cloud obscured the sky. . . .)

Finally, the fourth day arrived. It was a *Saturday*, the day dedicated to the sweet Queen of Heaven, when I went to see my uncle. What was my surprise when I saw him look at me and invite me into his office, without my having shown the desire to do so! . . . He began by reproaching me gently for seeming to be afraid of him, and then he told me that it wasn't necessary to ask for a *miracle*. He had only prayed to God to give him a "simple inclination of heart," and it had been granted. . . .

Oh! I wasn't tempted to plead for a miracle, because for me the *miracle had been granted*. My uncle was no longer the same. Without making any illusion to "human prudence," he told me that I was a little flower that God wanted to pick, and he would no longer be opposed to it! . . .

That definitive answer was truly worthy of him. For the third time that Christian from another age allowed one of the daughters whom his heart had adopted, to go bury herself far from the world. My aunt [Céline Guérin] as well was admirable for her tenderness and prudence. I don't remember that during my trial she said a word to me that might have increased it. I saw that she had great pity upon her poor little Thérèse. So when I obtained my dear uncle's consent, she gave me hers, but not without proving to me in a thousand ways that my leaving would cause her pain. . . .

Alas! At that moment our dear relatives were far from expecting that they would have to renew the same sacrifice two more times. . . . But by holding out His *hand* to continue to ask, God didn't present it *empty*. His dearest friends were able to draw from it, in abundance, the strength and courage that they needed so much. . . . [Their own daughter Marie would enter Carmel as well.] But my heart carries me quite far from my subject. I return to it almost regretfully.

After my uncle's response, you understand, Mother, with what happiness I took the road back to Les Buissonnets, under *"the beautiful sky,* whose clouds had completely dissipated"! . . . In my soul as well, the night had ended. Jesus, upon waking, had given joy back to me. The roar of the waves had subsided. Instead of the wind of the trial, a light breeze filled my sail, and I thought I would soon arrive on the blessed *shore* that I was seeing so close to me. It was in fact quite close to my dinghy, but *more than one storm* was still to crop up, and, concealing the sight of its bright beacon light, cause it to fear being tossed, without any return, far away from the shore that it so fervently desired to reach. . . .

A few days after I obtained my uncle's consent, I went to see you, beloved Mother [Pauline], and I told you about my joy that now my trials had passed. But how surprised and disappointed I was at hearing you tell me that the Superior would not consent to my entrance before the age of twenty-one.

No one had thought about that opposition, the most invincible of all. However, without losing courage, I went myself with Papa and Céline to visit the priest, in order to try to touch him by showing him that I really did have the vocation for Carmel. He greeted us very coldly. In vain did my *incomparable* dear father join his pleas with mine: Nothing would change his mind. He told me that there was no peril remaining at home, that I could live the life of a Carmelite at home, that if I didn't take on the discipline everything wouldn't be wasted . . . etc., etc. Finally he ended by adding that he was only the *bishop's delegate,* and that if the bishop wanted to let me enter Carmel, he himself would have nothing more to say. . . .

I left the rectory filled with *tears.* Fortunately, my umbrella hid me, because the *rain* was falling in torrents. Papa didn't know how to comfort me. . . . He promised to take me to [see Bishop Hugonin in] Bayeux as soon as I showed the desire to do so, because I was resolved *to take this as far as necessary.* I even said that I would go to the *Holy Father,* [Pope Leo XIII himself,] if the bishop didn't want to allow me to enter Carmel at the age of fifteen. . . .

Many events happened before my trip to Bayeux. On the outside my life seemed the same. I studied, I took drawing lessons with Céline, and my capable teacher found me well suited to her art. Above all, I was growing in the love of God. In my heart I felt upward impulses that I had not known until then. Sometimes I was truly transported by love.

One night, not knowing how to tell Jesus that I loved Him and how much I desired that He be everywhere loved and glorified, I was thinking with sorrow that He could never receive in hell a single act of love. So I told God that to please Him I would willingly consent to find myself plunged into hell, so that He might be eternally loved in that place of blasphemy. . . . I knew that that couldn't glorify Him, since He desires only our happiness, but when one loves, one experiences the need to say a thousand foolish things. If I spoke that way, it wasn't because heaven excited my desire, but that my personal heaven was none other than Love, and I felt like St. Paul that nothing could separate me from the divine object that had stolen my heart! [Rom. 8:35–39]. . . .

Before I left the world, [that is, before I entered Carmel,] God gave me the comfort of contemplating closely some *children's souls.* Since I was the youngest in the family, I had never had that pleasure. Here are the sad circumstances that brought this about: A poor woman, a relative of our maid, died in the flower of young age, leaving three very small children. During her illness we took into our home the two little girls, the elder of whom was not yet six years old. I took care of them all day long, and it was a great pleasure for me to see with what openness they believed everything that I told them. Holy Baptism must place into souls a very deep seed of the virtues of faith, hope, and charity, since from childhood they're already in evidence, and the hope of future good things is enough to cause them to accept sacrifices.

When I wanted to see my two little girls being considerate one to the other, instead of promising toys and candy to the one who would give in to her sister, I talked to them about the everlasting rewards that the little Jesus would give in heaven to good little children. The elder, whose reason was beginning to develop, looked at me with her eyes shining with joy, asking me a thousand charming questions about little Jesus and His beautiful heaven. She promised me enthusiastically that she would always prefer her sister, and said that never in her life would she forget "the great young lady," because that's what she called me. . . .

When I saw these innocent souls up close, I under-stood what an unfortunate thing it is not to teach them well as soon as their hearts awaken, while they are like soft wax on which virtues can be imprinted, but also vices. . . . I understood what Jesus said in the Gospel: "It would be better for you to be thrown into the sea . . . than for you to cause one of these little ones to stumble" [Lk. 17:2]. Oh! How many souls would reach holiness, if they were well directed! . . .

I know, God doesn't need anyone to do His work, but just as He allows an able gardener to raise rare and delicate plants, and for that He gives him the knowledge he needs, but reserves for Himself the care to make the plants grow—this is how Jesus wants to be helped in his Divine cultivation of souls.

What would happen if a clumsy gardener didn't graft his bushes well? What if he didn't know how to recognize the nature of each one, and wanted to make roses bloom on a peach tree? . . . That would kill the tree, which even so was good and was capable of producing fruit.

That is how one must know how to recognize, begin-ning in childhood, what God asks of souls, and how to second the action of His grace, without ever speeding it up or slowing it down.

Just as little birds learn to *sing* by listening to their parents, in the same way children learn the knowledge of virtues, the sublime *song* of Divine Love, alongside souls that have been charged with forming them in life.

I remember that among my birds, I had a canary that sang delightfully. I also had a little linnet on which I poured out my *motherly* cares, having adopted it before it had been able to enjoy the happiness of its freedom. That poor little prisoner had no parents to teach it to sing, but hearing from morning to night its canary companion making joyful vocal flourishes, it wanted to imitate it. . . . This undertaking was difficult for a linnet, so its sweet voice had a great deal of trouble harmonizing with the vibrant voice of its music teacher. It was charming to see the efforts of the poor linnet, but they were at last crowned with success, for its song, while preserving a much greater sweetness, was absolutely the same as that of the canary.

Beloved Mother! You're the one who taught me to sing. . . . It was your voice that charmed me from childhood, and now I have the comfort of hearing that I'm like you! I know how far I am from being that, but I hope, in spite of my weakness, to repeat forever the same song as you! . . .

Before my entrance into Carmel, I had many more experiences with life and the wretchedness of the world, but those details would carry me too far away, so I'm going to go back to the story of my vocation.

October 31st [All Saints' Eve] was the day appointed for my trip to Bayeux. I left by myself with Papa, my heart full of hope, but also quite moved by the thought of presenting myself at the bishop's residence. For the first time in my life, I was going on a visit without being accompanied by my sisters, and that visit was to a *bishop!* I, who never needed to speak except to answer questions that were put to me, I was going to have to explain all by myself the purpose of my visit, and

develop the reasons that caused me to petition for entry
into Carmel—in a word, I needed to show how solid
my vocation was.

Oh! What it cost me to make that trip! God had to
grant me a very special grace in order for me to be able
to overcome my great timidness. . . . It's also quite true
that "Love never meets with impossibilities, because it
believes that everything is possible and everything is
permitted." It was truly love for Jesus alone that could
have made me overcome these difficulties and those that
followed it, because it pleased Him to make me gain my
vocation through very great trials. . . .

Now that I enjoy the solitude of Carmel (resting in
the shade of the One whom I so fervently desired)
[Song 2:3], I find that I gained my vocation at very little
cost, and I would be ready to endure much greater trials
to acquire it if I still didn't have it!

It was *pouring* rain when we arrived in Bayeux. Papa
didn't want to see his little queen enter the bishop's residence with her *beautiful outfit* all wet, so he had her
climb into a carriage and drive to the cathedral. There
my troubles began. His Excellency the bishop and all
his clergy were attending a great funeral. The church
was filled with ladies in mourning, all dressed in black,
and everyone stared at me with my bright dress and my
white hat. I would have wanted to leave the church but
there was no thinking of it, because of the rain. And to
humiliate me more, God allowed Papa with his patriar-
chal simplicity to bring me to the front of the cathedral.
Not wanting to cause him pain, I carried myself with
good grace and provided that distraction to the good

citizens of Bayeux, whom I would have wished that I had never met. . . .

Finally I was able to breathe more easily in a chapel that stood behind the high altar, and I stayed there for a long time, praying fervently while waiting, that the rain would stop and let us leave. As we went back down, Papa had me admire the beauty of the building that seemed much bigger since it was deserted. But one single thought was on my mind, and I couldn't take pleasure in anything.

We went directly to see Fr. Révérony [the bishop's grand vicar, or representative], who had been instructed about our arrival, since he himself had set the date of the trip. But he wasn't home, so we had to wander in the streets, which seemed to me to be *quite sad.* Finally we arrived near the bishop's residence, and Papa had me enter into a beautiful hotel, where I didn't do honor to the capable cook. Poor dear Papa had an almost unbelievable tenderness toward me. He told me not to be vexed, that of course His Excellency was going to grant my request.

After resting, we returned to the home of Fr. Révérony. A gentleman arrived at the same time, but the grand vicar asked him politely to wait and had us enter first into his office. (The poor gentleman had the time to become bored, because the visit was long.) Fr. Révérony showed himself to be very pleasant, but I think that the purpose of this visit surprised him a great deal. After looking at me smilingly and asking a few questions, he told us, "I'm going to introduce you to His Excellency. Would you be so kind as to follow me." Seeing tears welling up in my eyes, he added, "Oh, I see some diamonds. . . . You mustn't show them to His Excellency! . . ."

He had us cross several very vast rooms, lined with bishops' portraits. Seeing myself in these great rooms had the effect on me of feeling like a poor little ant, and I wondered what I was going to dare to say to His Excellency. He [the bishop] was walking between two priests in a gallery. I saw Fr. Révérony say several words to him and come back with him. We were waiting for him in his office. There, three enormous armchairs were placed in front of the fireplace, in which a roaring fire was crackling.

Seeing His Excellency enter the room, Papa got down on his knees beside me to receive his blessing. Then His Excellency had Papa sit in one of the armchairs and sat across from him. Fr. Révérony tried to have me take the middle seat. I politely refused, but he insisted, telling me to show whether I was capable of being obedient. Immediately I sat down without thinking, and I was embarrassed to see him taking a chair while I was buried in an armchair in which four people like me would have been at ease (more at ease than I was, because I was far from being so! . . .).

I was hoping that Papa was going to speak, but he told me to explain to His Excellency myself the purpose of our visit. I did so, as *eloquently* as possible. His Excellency, who was used to *eloquence,* didn't seem very touched by my reasons. Instead of them one word from my parish priest would have served me well. Unfortunately, I didn't have it, and his opposition didn't plead in my favor at all. . . .

His Excellency asked me if I had wanted for a long time to enter Carmel. "Oh, yes! Your Excellency. . . ." "Let's see," began Fr. Révérony, laughing, "you can't say that you've had this desire for *fifteen years.*" "That's true," I replied, smiling as well, "but there aren't many years to subtract, because I've wanted to become a nun beginning with my reaching the age of reason, and I desired to enter Carmel as soon as I got to know it well, because in that order I found that all the aspirations of my soul would be fulfilled." I don't know, Mother, if these are my exact words. I think I said them more poorly than that, but that's the gist of what I said.

His Excellency, thinking that he was being kind to Papa, tried to make me stay a few more years with him. So he was not a little *surprised* and *edified* to see him stand up for me, interceding for me to obtain the permission to leave the nest at the age of fifteen. However, it was all of no use. He said that before he made a decision a meeting with *the Superior of Carmel* was absolutely necessary. I couldn't have heard anything that would have given me greater suffering, because I knew about the total opposition of our rector. So without taking into account Fr. Révérony's admonition, I did more than *show diamonds* to His Excellency: I *gave* him some. . . . I saw clearly that he was touched by this. Grasping me by the neck, he leaned my head onto his shoulder and patted me, in a way, it would seem, that no one had ever been greeted by him.

He told me that everything was not lost, that he was quite happy for me to take the trip to Rome in order to

affirm my vocation, and that instead of crying I ought
to be joyful. He added that the next week, since he had
to go to Lisieux, he would speak about me to the rector of St. James [our parish church], and that certainly
I would receive his reply in Italy. I understood that it
was useless to lodge more protests. Besides, I had nothing
more to say, having exhausted all the resources of my
eloquence.

His Excellency led us out as far as the garden. Papa
amused him a lot by telling him that in order to look
older I'd had my hair put up. (This wasn't wasted,
because His Excellency never talks about "his little
girl" without telling the story of her hair. . . .) Fr.
Révérony wanted to go with us as far as the end of the
bishop's garden. He told Papa that such a thing had
never been seen before: "A father who was in as much
a hurry to give his child to God as that child is to offer
herself!"

Papa asked him for several explanations about the
pilgrimage. Among them was how one should dress
for an appearance before the Holy Father. I can still see
him turn about in front of Fr. Révérony, asking him,
"Do I look all right like this? . . ." He had also told His
Excellency that if he didn't allow me to enter Carmel,
I would ask that grace of the Supreme Pontiff [the
Pope]. He was quite simple in his words and his manners, my beloved king, but he was so *handsome.* . . .
He had a most natural distinction that must have
pleased His Excellency a lot, accustomed as he was to
being surrounded by persons who were acquainted
with all the rules of etiquette of fine salons, but not the

king of France and *Navarre* in *person* with his *little queen.* . . .

When I found myself in the street my tears began to flow again, not so much because of my disappointment, but rather on seeing my dear beloved father, who had just made a futile trip. . . . He, who had been imagining the joy of sending a dispatch to Carmel, announcing His Excellency's happy reply, was obliged to come back without having one. . . . Oh! What suffering I felt! . . . It seemed that my future was broken forever. The closer I came to the end, the more my affairs were becoming entangled. My soul was plunged into bitterness, but also into peace, because I was seeking only the will of God.

As soon as I arrived in Lisieux, I went to seek consolation at Carmel, and I found it at your side, beloved Mother. Oh, no! I will never forget all that you suffered because of me. If I wasn't afraid to profane them by using them, I could say the words that Jesus spoke to His apostles, on the night of His Passion: "*You* are those who have stood by me in my trials" [Lk. 22:28]. . . . *My beloved* sisters also offered me the *sweetest consolations.* . . .

CHAPTER 6

The Trip to Rome
1887

Paris: Notre-Dame-des-Victoires [Our Lady of Victories]
Switzerland
Milan, Venice, Bologna, Loretto
The Coliseum and the catacombs
Audience with Leo XIII
Naples, Assisi, return to France
Three months of waiting

Three days after the trip to Bayeux, I was to make a much longer one, one to the Eternal City. . . . Oh! What a trip that was! . . . All by itself it taught me more than long years of studies. It showed me the vanity of every passing thing, and that everything is a meaningless chasing after the wind under the sun [Eccl. 2:11]. . . . However, I saw many beautiful things, I contemplated all the marvels of art and religion, and above all I set foot on the same ground as the Holy Apostles, the ground drenched with the blood of the Martyrs, and my soul grew on contact with these holy things. . . .

I'm very happy to have been in Rome, but I understand the persons of the world who thought that Papa had me take that long trip in order to change my ideas about the religious life. There was in fact sufficient means to unsettle a vocation that wasn't quite firm.

Never having lived among the upper classes, Céline and I found ourselves among the nobility who almost exclusively comprised the pilgrimage. Oh! Far from dazzling us, all those titles and all those names with "de" in them [showing nobility] seemed to us only so much smoke. . . . Seen from afar, all that had sometimes thrown a bit of powder in my eyes, but up close, I saw that "all that glitters is not gold," and I understood this word from the *Imitation*: "Do not pursue that mirage that is called a great name; desire neither numerous entanglements, nor the particular friendship of any person."

I understood that true greatness is found in the *soul* and not in the *name,* since, as Isaiah said, ". . . you will be called by a new name that the mouth of the LORD will bestow" (Isa. 62:2), and St. John also said, "To those who are victorious, I will give some of the hidden manna. I will also give each of them a white stone with a *new name* written on it, known only to the one who receives it" (Rev. 2:17). So it's in heaven that we will know what our titles of nobility are. Then each person will receive from God the praise that he merits, and the one who on earth attempted to be the poorest, the most forgotten for the love of Jesus, will be the first, the *noblest,* and the richest! . . .

The second experience that I had concerns the priests. Never having lived close to them, I couldn't understand the principal goal of the Carmelite reform [to pray for priests]. To pray for sinners delighted me, but to pray for the souls of priests, whom I thought of as purer than crystal, seemed astonishing to me. . . .

Oh! I understood *my vocation in Italy* was not to go looking too far for such a useful acquaintance. . . .

For a month I lived with many *holy priests,* and I saw that if their sublime dignity raises them above the angels, they are nonetheless weak and fragile men. . . . If *holy priests* whom Jesus calls in the Gospel "the salt of the earth" show in their behavior that they have an extreme need of prayers, what can one say about the ones who are lukewarm? Didn't Jesus add, "But if the salt loses its saltiness, how can it be made salty again?" [Mt. 5:13]?

Oh, Mother! How beautiful is the vocation that has as its object to *preserve the salt* that is destined for souls! That vocation is Carmel's, since the only objective of our prayers and our sacrifices is to be *the apostle of the apostles,* praying for them while they evangelize souls through their words and especially by their examples. . . . I have to stop; if I were to continue to talk about this subject I would never finish! . . .

Beloved Mother, I'm going to tell you about my trip giving some details. Forgive me if I give you too many of them. I don't reflect before writing, and I do it at so many different times, because of my having very little free time, that my tale will perhaps seem boring to you. . . . What comforts me is to think that in heaven I'll talk to you again about the graces that I received, and that I will be able to do so then in pleasant and charming terms. . . . Nothing more will come and interrupt our intimate outpourings, and in a single glance you will have understood everything. . . . Alas! Since I still have to use the language of the sad earth, I'm going to try to do so with the simplicity of a little child who knows the love of her Mother! . . .

It was the seventh of November that the pilgrimage left Paris, but Papa took us to that city several days beforehand in order to have us visit it.

One morning at 3 AM I passed through a still-sleeping Lisieux. Many impressions swirled through my soul at that time. I felt that I was going toward the unknown, and that great things were awaiting me there. . . . Papa was filled with joy; when the train got under way, he sang the old refrain, "Roll on, roll on, stagecoach, here we are on the big highway."

We arrived in Paris in the morning and immediately began to visit it. Poor dear Father got very tired in order to give us pleasure, so we had soon seen all the marvels of the capital. As for me, I found *only one* that delighted me, and that marvel was Notre-Dame-des-Victoires [Our Lady of Victories, a center of devotion to the Immaculate Heart of Mary]. Oh! What I felt at her feet I wouldn't be able to say. . . . The graces that she granted me moved me so deeply that only my tears betrayed my happiness, as on the day of my first Communion. . . .

The Blessed Virgin made me feel that it was *truly she who had smiled at me* and *had healed me.* I understood that she was watching over me, that I was *her* child, so that I could no longer call her anything but *Mama,* because that name seemed even more tender than that of Mother. . . . With what fervor I prayed to her to guard and keep me always, to soon realize my dream by hiding me *in the shadow of her virgin's mantle!* . . . Oh! That was one of my first desires as a child. . . . As

I was growing up I had understood that it was at Carmel that it would be possible for me to truly find the mantle of the Blessed Virgin, and it was toward that fertile mountain that all my desires leaned. . . .

I once again pleaded with Our Lady of Victories to remove far away from me everything that might have been able to tarnish my purity. I was not unaware that on a trip like the one to Italy, I would encounter many things that were capable of troubling me. Especially because, not being acquainted with evil, I was afraid of uncovering it, not having experienced that for the pure, everything is pure [Titus 1:15], and that the simple and upright soul doesn't see evil in anything, because in fact evil exists only in impure souls and not in inanimate objects. . . .

I also prayed to St. Joseph to watch over me. Since childhood I had had for him a devotion that mingled with my love for the Blessed Virgin. Every day I used to recite the prayer "St. Joseph, Father and protector of virgins," so it was without fear that I undertook my trip to distant places. I was so well protected that it seemed impossible to me to be afraid.

After consecrating ourselves to the Sacred Heart of Jesus in the Sacré-Cœur [Sacred Heart] basilica in the Montmartre district—we left Paris on the morning of Monday the seventh. Soon we had met the persons who were going on the pilgrimage. I was so timid that ordinarily I hardly dared to speak, but I found myself completely rid of that troubling fault. To my great surprise I spoke freely with all the great ladies, the priests, and even His Excellency the Bishop of Coutances. It seemed to me that I had always lived in that world [of the privileged classes].

We were, I believe, well liked by everyone, and Papa was proud of his two daughters. But if he was proud of us, we were equally proud of him, because in all the pilgrimage that was no other gentleman who was more handsome or more distinguished than my dear king. He loved to be seen between Céline and me. Often when we were not in our carriage and I was some distance from him, he would call me so that I would give him my arm as in Lisieux. . . .

The Reverend Father Révérony was examining our actions carefully. I often saw him watching us from a distance. At mealtimes, when I wasn't facing him, he found the means to lean over me to see me and hear what I was saying. No doubt he wanted to get to know me to find out if I was truly capable of being a Carmelite. I think that he must have been satisfied with his examination, because at the end of *the trip* he seemed well disposed toward me. But in Rome he was far from being favorable to me, as I'm going to tell about later.

Before we arrived in the Eternal City, the objective of our pilgrimage, it was given to us to contemplate many marvels. First it was Switzerland, with its mountains with their summits lost in the clouds, its graceful waterfalls gushing in a thousand different ways, its deep valleys full of giant ferns and pink briars. Oh! Beloved Mother, how these beauties of nature, spread out *in profusion*, did good to my soul! How they lifted it up toward the One who was pleased to toss such masterpieces onto a land of exile that must last only a day. . . .

I didn't have eyes enough to look at it. Standing at the carriage door I almost lost my breath. I would have liked to be on both sides of the carriage at once, because as I turned from side to side, I saw countrysides of an enchanting aspect that were completely different from the ones that stretched out before me.

Sometimes we found ourselves on a mountain peak. At our feet there were sheer drops, whose aspect couldn't reveal their depth, that seemed ready to swallow us up. Or there was a delightful little village with its graceful chalets and its bell tower, above which softly hovered a few dazzling-white clouds. . . .

Farther on there was a vast lake that the last rays of the sun tinged with gold. The calm and pure waves, borrowing from the deep blue tint of the sky that mixed with the fires of the setting sun, presented to our marveling eyes the most poetic and most enchanting spectacle that could ever be seen. . . .

At the end of the vast horizon we could see the mountains, whose indistinct contours would have escaped our eyes if their snowy peaks made dazzling by the sun hadn't come to add one more charm to the beautiful lake that delighted us. . . .

As I looked at all these beauties, very deep thoughts arose in my soul. It seemed to me that I understood already the greatness of God and the marvels of heaven. . . . The religious life appeared to me *as it is* with its *obligations,* its little sacrifices accomplished in the shadows. I understood how easy it is to become fixated on oneself, to forget the sublime objective of one's vocation, and I said to myself, "Later, in the time of testing, when I'm a prisoner [a cloistered nun] in Carmel, I'll be able to contemplate only a little corner of the starry sky, and I'll remember what I'm seeing today. That thought will give me courage. I'll easily forget my petty little interests by seeing the grandeur and the power of God whom alone I want to love. I won't have the misfortune of becoming attached to *straw,* now that my *heart* has *seen* 'these things God has prepared for those who love him!' [1 Cor. 2:9] . . ."

After admiring God's power, I could still admire that which He has given to His creatures. The first city in Italy that we visited was Milan. Its cathedral all of white marble with its statues that were numerous enough to comprise a nearly countless people, we visited in all its smallest details. Céline and I were plucky, and were always the first to follow His Excellency directly in order to see everything concerning the relics of the Saints and to hear the explanations well. So while he was offering the Holy Sacrifice [saying Mass] on St. Charles's tomb, we were with Papa behind the altar, our heads leaning against the reliquary that houses the body of the Saint, dressed in its pontifical garments.

And that's how it was everywhere. . . . Except when it was a question of climbing up to where the dignity of a Bishop wouldn't allow, because then we knew quite well how to leave His Excellency behind. . . . Leaving the timid ladies hiding their faces in their hands after climbing up the first pinnacle turrets that ringed the cathedral, we followed the hardiest pilgrims and arrived at the peak of the *last* marble turret. There we had the pleasure to see at our feet the city of Milan, whose numerous inhabitants looked like a little *swarm of ants.* . . . Coming back down from our pedestal, we began our tours by carriage that were to last a month, and that would quench for good my desire to *keep moving* indefatigably!

The *campo santo*—the cemetery—delighted us even more than the cathedral, with all its white marble statues that a genius's chisel seemed to have brought to life. These statues are placed on the vast field of the dead in a sort of haphazard fashion that for me increases their charm. . . . One would be tempted to comfort the ideal personages who surround you. Their expression is so true, their sorrow so calm and so resigned, that one can't help recognizing the thoughts of immortality that must fill the hearts of the artists as they're executing these masterpieces. Here a child is tossing flowers on the tomb of its parents; the marble seems to have lost its weight, and the delicate petals seem to slide among the child's fingers. The wind seems already to disperse them, and it seems also to ruffle the light veils of the widows and the ribbons that adorn the girls' hair.

Papa was as delighted as we were. In Switzerland he'd been tired, but then his gaiety had reappeared, and I enjoyed the spectacle that we were contemplating. His artist's soul was revealed in the expressions of faith and admiration that appeared on his handsome countenance.

An elderly French gentleman, who no doubt didn't have as poetic a soul as we, was watching out of the

corner of his eye, and he said, with ill humor, all the
while looking as if he regretted not being able to share
our admiration, "Oh! How enthusiastic the French
are!" I think that this poor gentleman would have done
better to stay at home, because he didn't seem to me to
be happy with his trip. He was often near us, and
always there were complaints coming out of his mouth.
He was unhappy with the carriages, with the hotels,
with the people, with the cities—in short, with everything. . . . Papa, with his customary greatness of soul,
tried to comfort him, offered him his seat, etc. In
short, he was always at ease everywhere, being of a
character that was diametrically opposed to that of his
disagreeable neighbor. . . . Ah! How many different
personalities we saw! How interesting it is to study the
world when one is close to leaving it [in order to enter
the religious life]! . . .

In Venice the scene changed completely. Instead of
the noise of the great cities there was heard amidst the
silence only the shouts of the gondoliers and the murmur
of the waves stirred up by the oars. Venice is not without its charms, but I find that city sad. The Doges'
palace is splendid; however it, too, is sad with its vast
apartments in which are arranged gold, wood, the most
precious marbles, and the paintings of the greatest
masters. For a long time its resonant vaults have ceased
to hear the voices of the governors who once pronounced judgments of life and death in the rooms that
we crossed through. . . . They have ceased to suffer,
those unfortunate prisoners who were locked up by the
Doges in the cells and underground dungeons. . . .

When I visited those awful prisons, I thought I was back in the time of the Martyrs, and I would have liked to be able to stay there in order to imitate them! . . . But we had to leave promptly and pass over the Bridge of Sighs, so called because of the sighs of relief that the condemned prisoners heaved when they saw that they had been delivered from the horror of the dungeons, to which they preferred death. . . .

After Venice, we went to Padua, where we venerated the tongue of St. Anthony, then to Bologna where we saw St. Catherine, who retains the mark of the Child Jesus' kiss. There are many interesting details that I could give about each city and about the thousand little particular circumstances of our trip, but I would never finish, so I'm going to write down only the principal details.

It was with joy that I left Bologna [the site of a famous university]. That city had become intolerable for me because of the university students who filled it. They formed a hedge when we had the misfortune of setting out on foot, and especially because of the little adventure that happened to me with one of them, I was happy to take the road to Loretto.

I'm not surprised that the Blessed Virgin chose that place to transport her blessed home. [Loretto was the site of the *Santa Casa* (the "holy home"), thought to be Jesus' home in Nazareth, transported miraculously to Italy.] Peace, joy, and poverty reign supreme there. Everything is simple and primitive. The women have preserved their graceful Italian costume and have not, like the women of other cities, adopted *Paris fashion*. In short, Loretto charmed me!

What can I say about the blessed home? . . . Oh! My emotion was deep when I found myself under the same roof as the Holy Family, contemplating the walls on which Jesus had fixed His divine eyes, walking the ground that St. Joseph had watered with sweat, the place where Mary had carried Jesus in her arms, after carrying Him in her virgin's womb. . . . I saw the little room in which the angel came down to the Blessed Virgin. . . . I placed my rosary beads into the Child Jesus' little bowl. . . . How delightful are those memories! . . .

But our greatest consolation was to receive *Jesus Himself* in His *home* and to be His living temple [1 Cor. 3:16] in the very place that He had honored with His presence. Following a custom in Italy, the Blessed Sacrament is preserved in each church only on an altar, and only there can one receive Holy Communion. That altar was in the very basilica in which the blessed home stood, enclosed like a precious diamond in a jewel case of white marble. That didn't make our happiness! It was in the *diamond* itself and not in the *jewel case* that we wanted to receive Communion. . . .

Papa, with his usual gentleness, did as everyone else did, but Céline and I went to find a priest who accompanied us everywhere and was in fact preparing to celebrate his mass in the *Santa Casa* by a special privilege. He asked for *two small hosts* that he placed on his paten [the gold or silver plate used to hold the host] with his large host, and you understand, my dear Mother, our delight that *both of us* were able to receive Holy Communion in that blessed house! . . . This was quite a heavenly happiness that words are powerless to describe.

So, what will it be like when we receive Communion in the everlasting dwelling of the King of heaven? . . . Then we will no longer see our joy come to an end, there will be no more sadness on leaving, and to carry away a souvenir it won't be necessary for us to *furtively scratch* the walls that have been hallowed by the Divine presence, since His *home* will be ours for eternity. . . . He doesn't want to give us an earthly home; He's content to show it [the humble home in Loretto] to us in order to make us love poverty and the hidden life. The home that's reserved for us is His Palace of glory where we'll no longer see Him hidden under the appearance of a Child or a white host, but as He is in the brightness of His infinite splendor!!! (1 Jn. 3:2) . . .

It now remains to me to talk about Rome—Rome, the objective of our trip, the place where I thought I would meet with consolation but where I found the Cross! . . . When we arrived it was nighttime, and since we had fallen asleep, we were awakened by the train station employees who were shouting, "Roma, Roma." It wasn't a dream: I was in Rome! . . .

The first day was spent outside the walls, and this was perhaps the most delicious day, because all the monuments have preserved their feel of antiquity, unlike at the center of Rome, where you could think you were in Paris when you saw the magnificence of the hotels and stores. This walk in the Roman countryside left me with a sweet memory.

I won't talk about the places that we visited—there are enough books that describe them in all their scope

—but only about the *principal* impressions that I felt. One of the sweetest was the one that made me shudder when I saw the *Coliseum*. So I was finally seeing it, that arena in which so many Martyrs shed their blood for Jesus. I was preparing myself already to kiss the ground that they had made holy, but what a disappointment! The center is nothing but a pile of rubble that pilgrims have to be content to just look at, because a barricade prevents them from entering. Besides, no one is tempted to try to penetrate into the midst of those ruins. . . .

Must we have come to Rome without going down to the Coliseum? . . . That seemed impossible to me. I was no longer listening to the guide's explanations. One single thought was filling me: to go down into the arena. . . . Seeing a workman who was passing by with a ladder, I was on point of asking him. Fortunately I didn't put my idea into action, because he would have taken me for a madwoman. . . .

It's said in the Gospel that Mary Magdalene remained constantly near the tomb, and going down *several times* to look inside, ended up seeing two angels [Jn. 20:11-12]. Like her, while recognizing the impossibility of seeing my desires become a reality, I continued to go down toward the ruins into which I wanted to enter. In the end, I didn't see angels, but *what I was looking for.* I shouted with joy, saying to Céline, "Come quickly, we're going to be able to get in! . . ." Immediately we crossed the barrier that the rubble came up to at that spot, and there we were, climbing over the ruins, which crumbled under our footsteps.

Papa was watching us, completely surprised by our audacity. Soon he told us to come back, but the two fugitives were no longer hearing anything. In the same way as warriors who feel their courage increasing in the midst of peril, that's how our joy was growing in proportion to the trouble that we were having in reaching the object of our desires.

Céline, who was more far-sighted than I was, had listened to the guide, and remembering that he had just indicated a certain paving stone in the form of a cross as being one on which the Martyrs had fought, started looking for it. Soon, finding it and kneeling on that sacred ground, our souls joined in one single prayer. . . . My heart was pounding when my lips approached the dust that was tinged with crimson by the blood of the first Christians. I asked for the grace also to be a Martyr for Jesus, and I felt in the depths of my heart that my prayer was being granted! . . .

All this was accomplished in a very short time. After taking a few stones, we went back toward the ruined walls to begin our perilous undertaking once again. Papa, who saw that we were so happy, couldn't scold us, and I saw clearly that he was proud of our courage. . . . God protected us visibly, because the pilgrims didn't catch sight of our undertaking, since they were farther along than we were. They were no doubt busy looking at the magnificent arcades, where the guide was showing us "the little *cornices* and the *cupids* that had been placed on them," so neither he nor "my lords the priests" knew about the joy that was filling our hearts. . . .

The catacombs also left a sweet impression on me: They are just as I had imagined them to be when I read the description of them in the life of the Martyrs. After spending a part of the afternoon in them, it seemed to me that I had been there only a few moments, so much did the atmosphere that I was breathing there seem to have a lovely fragrance. . . .

I had to carry away some souvenir of the catacombs, so letting the procession go a little farther, Céline and Thérèse slipped away together into the bottom of the ancient tomb of St. Cecilia and took some of the earth that had been made holy by her presence. Before my trip to Rome I'd had no particular devotion for that Saint, but on visiting her home that had been changed into a church, the place of her martyrdom, and on learning that she had been proclaimed the queen of harmony, not because of her beautiful voice or her talent for music, but in memory of the *virgin's song* that she sang to her Heavenly Bridegroom who was hidden in the depths of her heart, I felt for her more than devotion: It was the true *tenderness of a friend*. . . . She became my favorite Saint, my intimate confidante. . . . Everything about her delighted me, especially her *abandon,* her boundless *trust* that rendered her capable of making virgins of souls who never desired any other joys than those of the present life. . . .

St. Cecilia is like the bride in the Song of Songs: In her I see "A *choir* in an army camp! . . ." Her life is none other than a melodious song in the very midst of the greatest of ordeals, and that doesn't surprise me, since "the holy Gospel *dwelt in her heart!" and in that heart dwelt* the Bridegroom of Virgins! . . .

The visit to the church of St. Agnes also was very sweet for me. She was a *childhood friend* whom I was going to visit in her home. I spoke to her for a long time about the one who bears her name so well [my sister Pauline, now Sr. Agnes of Jesus], and I made every effort to obtain one of the relics of the Angelical patron of my dear Mother in order to take it back to her. But it was impossible for us to have anything but a little red stone that came loose from a rich mosaic whose origin went back to the time of St. Agnes and that she must have often looked at. Wasn't it charming that the lovable Saint herself would give us what we were looking for and that was forbidden to us to take? . . . I've always regarded that as a nice touch, and a proof of the love with which sweet St. Agnes watches over and protects my dear Mother [Pauline]! . . .

Six days went by as we visited the principal marvels of Rome, and it was on the *seventh* that I saw the greatest of them all: [Pope] "Leo XIII." . . . That was the day I desired to see and yet feared at the same time. That was the day on which my vocation depended, because the reply that I was to receive from the Bishop had not arrived, and I had learned through a letter from you, *Mother,* that he was no longer well disposed toward me. So my only life preserver was the permission of the Holy Father. . . . But to get it, I had to ask for it. I was required, in front of everyone, *to dare to speak—"to the Pope."* That thought made me tremble.

How much I suffered before the audience, God alone knows, along with my *dear Céline.* I'll never forget the part she took in all my ordeals. It seemed as if my vocation were hers. (Our love for each another had been remarked about by the priests on the pilgrimage. One night, since there were so many of us that we didn't have enough seats, Céline took me on her lap and we looked at each other so nicely that one priest exclaimed, "How they love each other! Oh! Those two sisters will never be able to be separated!" Yes, we loved each other, but our affection was so *pure* and so strong that the thought of separation didn't trouble us, because we felt that nothing, even the ocean, could make us distant one from the other. . . . Calmly, Céline was to see my little dinghy land on the shore of Carmel. She was to resign herself to remain as long as God would desire on the stormy sea of the world, sure that she would land in turn on the bank, the object of our desires. . . .)

Sunday, the twentieth of November, after dressing according to the ceremonial requirements of the Vatican (that is, in black, with a lace mantilla as a head covering), and having decorated ourselves with a large medal of Leo XIII hanging on a blue and white ribbon, we made our entrance into the Vatican in the Supreme Pontiff's chapel. At eight o'clock our emotion was deep when we saw him enter to celebrate Holy Mass. . . . After blessing the many pilgrims gathered around him, he climbed up the steps of the Holy Altar and showed us, through his piety that was worthy of the Vicar of Jesus, that he was truly *"the Holy* Father." My heart was beating strongly, and my prayers were most fervent, while Jesus came down into the hands of His Pontiff [as he celebrated Mass]. Nevertheless, I was full of confidence.

The Gospel for that day included these delightful words: "Do not be afraid, little flock, for your Father has been pleased to give you the kingdom" [Lk. 12:32]. No, I wasn't afraid, I was hoping that the kingdom of Carmel would belong to me soon. I wasn't thinking then about these other words of Jesus, "And I confer on you a kingdom, just as my Father conferred one on me . . ." [Lk. 22:29]. That is to say, for you I'm reserving crosses and tribulation. That's how you'll be worthy of possessing that kingdom that you're longing for. Since it was necessary for Christ to suffer and through suffering enter into His glory, if you want to have a place beside Him, drink the cup that He Himself drank! . . . That cup was presented to me by the Holy Father, and my tears mingled with the bitter brew that was offered to me [Lk. 24:26, Mt. 20:21–23].

After the thanksgiving Mass that followed the one given by His Holiness, the audience began. Leo XIII was seated on a great chair. He was dressed simply in a white cassock and a cloak of the same color, and on his head he wore only a little skullcap. Around him stood cardinals, archbishops, and bishops, but I only saw them in general, since I was busy with the Holy Father. We passed before him in procession; each pilgrim knelt in turn, kissed Leo XIII's foot and hand, and received his blessing. Then two gentlemen of the Papal Guard touched the pilgrim ceremoniously, indicating by this that he should stand (the pilgrim, that is, because I'm explaining this so poorly that you might think I meant the Pope).

Before entering into the pontifical apartments I was quite resolved *to speak,* but I felt my courage weaken when I saw, at the Holy Father's right hand, "Fr.

Révérony! . . ." Almost at the same moment we were told on *his behalf* that he *forbade us to speak to* Leo XIII, since the audience was going on too long. . . . I turned toward my beloved Céline, in order to learn her opinion. "Speak," she told me.

A moment later I was at the Holy Father's feet and had kissed his slipper, and he was extending his hand out to me. But instead of kissing it, I joined my hands together and, lifting toward his face my eyes bathed in tears, I cried out, "Most Holy Father, I have a great grace to ask of you! . . ." Then the Supreme Pontiff lowered his head toward me in such a way that my face almost touched his, and I saw his *dark* and *deep eyes* fix on me and seem to pierce me to the depths of my soul. "Most Holy Father," I said to him, "in honor of your jubilee, allow me to enter Carmel at the age of fifteen! . . ."

Emotion had without a doubt made my voice tremble, so, turning around toward Fr. Révérony, who was looking at me with surprise and discontent, the Holy Father said, "I don't understand very well." If God had allowed it, it would have been easy for Fr. Révérony to obtain for me what I desired, but it was the cross and not consolation that He wanted to give me. "Most Holy Father," replied the Grand Vicar, "this is *a child* who wants to enter Carmel *at the age* of fifteen, but the superiors are examining the question right now." "Well, my child," the Holy Father continued as he looked at me kindly, "do what the superiors tell you." Then, placing my hands on his knees, I attempted one last effort, and I told him with a pleading voice, "Oh! Most Holy Father, if you were to say yes, everyone would be willing! . . ." He looked at me fixedly and pronounced these words, emphasizing each syllable: "All right. . . . All right. . . . *You will enter if it is God's will.*" (His tone of voice had something so penetrating and so convincing, that it seems to me that I can still hear it.)

The Holy Father's kindness was so encouraging that I wanted to speak to him some more, but the two gentlemen of the Papal Guard *touched me politely* to make me stand. Seeing that that wasn't sufficient, they took me by the arms, and Fr. Révérony helped them lift me up, because I was remaining there with my hands clasped together, leaning on Leo XIII's knees, and it was *by force* that they tore me away from his feet. . . . At the moment when I had been made to *stand up* in this way, the Holy Father put his hand over my lips, then raised it to bless me. Then my eyes filled with tears, and Fr. Révérony was able to contemplate at least as many *diamonds* as he had seen in Bayeux. . . . The two Papal Guards carried me so to speak as far as the door, and there, a third one gave me a Leo XIII medal.

Céline, who was following me, had witnessed the scene that had just taken place, and was almost as moved as I was. Nonetheless, she had the courage to ask the Holy Father for a blessing for Carmel. Mr. Révérony replied, in a displeased voice, "Carmel is already blessed." The good Holy Father repeated gently, "Oh, yes! It is already blessed."

Before us, Papa had come to Leo XIII's feet (with the gentlemen). Fr. Révérony had been charming to him, introducing him as the *father of two Carmelites*. The

Supreme Pontiff, in a sign of particular benevolence, placed his hand on the venerable head of my beloved king, seeming in this way to mark him with a *mysterious seal,* in the name of the One whom he truly represents. . . .

Oh! Now that he's in heaven, this *father of four Carmelites,* it's no longer the hand of the Pontiff that rests on his forehead, prophesying martyrdom for him. . . . It's the *hand* of the Bridegroom of Virgins, the King of Glory, who makes the head of his Faithful Servant shine, and that adored hand will never again cease to rest on the forehead that it has glorified! . . .

My dear papa was very troubled to find me all in tears when I left the audience. He did everything he could to comfort me, but in vain. . . . In the depths of my heart I felt a great peace, since I had done absolutely everything that was in my power to do in order to respond to what God was asking of me. But that *peace* was in the *depths,* and bitterness *was filling* my soul, for Jesus was silent. He seemed to be absent; nothing was revealing His presence to me. . . . That day again the sun didn't dare to shine, and the beautiful blue sky of Italy, laden with dark clouds, didn't stop weeping with me. . . .

Oh! It was over. My trip no longer had any charm in my eyes, since its objective had been thwarted. However, the Holy Father's last words should have comforted me. Weren't they a veritable prophecy? Despite all the obstacles, what *God willed* had been accomplished. He did *not allow* creatures to do what they willed, but *His own will.* . . .

For some time I had offered myself to the Child Jesus to be his *little toy.* I had told Him not to use me like a valuable toy that children are happy to look at without daring to touch it, but like a little ball of no value that He could throw on the ground, kick around, *pierce,* leave in a corner or press to His heart if that pleased Him. In a word, I wanted to *entertain* the *little* Jesus and please Him. I wanted to give myself over to His *childish whims.* . . . He had granted my prayer. . . .

In Rome Jesus *pierced* His little toy. He wanted to see what was inside it, and then, having seen it, content with His discovery, He dropped his little ball and went to sleep. . . . What did He do during His sweet sleep, and what became of the little abandoned ball? . . . Jesus dreamed that He was still *entertaining Himself* with His toy, leaving it and taking it back up in turn, and then, after making it roll far away, He was pressing it to His heart, never letting it get far from His little hand again. . . .

You understand, beloved Mother, how sad the little ball was to see itself *on the ground.* . . . Nevertheless I didn't stop hoping against all hope [Rom. 4:18].

A few days after the audience with the Holy Father, Papa, who had gone to see the good Brother Simeon, met there none other than Fr. Révérony, who was very pleasant. Papa reproached him lightly for not having helped me in my *difficult undertaking,* and then he told the story of his *queen* to Brother Simeon. The venerable old man listed to his story with a great deal of interest, even taking notes on it, and said, with emotion, "We don't see that in Italy!" I think that this meeting made a very good impression on Fr. Révérony. Afterward he never stopped proving to me that he was *finally* convinced of my vocation.

The day after the memorable day, we had to leave in the morning for Naples and Pompeii. In our honor Vesuvius rumbled the whole day, letting off, with its *cannon blasts,* a thick column of smoke. The traces that it has left on the ruins of Pompeii are frightening. They show the power of God, ". . . who looks on the earth, and it trembles, who touches the mountains, and they smoke!" [Ps. 104:32]. I would have liked to walk alone amidst the ruins, to dream about the fragility of human things, but the throngs of travelers took away a large part of the melancholic charm of the destroyed city. . . .

In Naples it was the opposite. The *great number* of two-horse carriages made our ride magnificent as we went to the monastery of San Martino, placed on a high hill dominating the whole city. Unfortunately, the horses that were pulling us were constantly taking the bit between their teeth, and more than once I thought I had reached the last hour of my life. In vain did the coachman constantly repeat the magic word used by Italian drivers, "Appippo, appippo. . . ." The poor horses tried to overturn our carriage, but finally, thanks to the help of our guardian angels, we arrived at our magnificent hotel.

During the whole trip, we had been placed in princely hotels. I had never been surrounded with so much luxury. It's quite the case that money doesn't buy happiness, because I would have been happier under a thatched roof with the hope of entering Carmel, than surrounded by gilded paneling, with white marble staircases, and silk carpets, with bitterness in my heart.

. . . Oh! I felt it so well: Joy isn't found in the objects that surround us; it's found in the innermost recesses of the soul. One can possess it as well in a prison as in a palace. The proof is that I'm happier at Carmel, even in the midst of inward and outward hardships, than in the world surrounded by the comfortable things of life and *above all* of the joys of my father's home! . . .

My soul was plunged into sadness. On the outside, however, I was the same, because I thought the request that I had made of the Holy Father was hidden. Soon I was able to convince myself to the contrary, when, having remained alone in the train with Céline (the other pilgrims having gotten off and gone to a buffet during the few minutes of the train stop), I saw Mr. Legoux, the vicar-general of Coutances, open the carriage door. Looking at me, smiling, he said, "Well, how is our little Carmelite doing? . . ." I understood then that the whole pilgrimage knew my secret. Fortunately, no one talked to me about it, but I saw by the sympathetic way in which they looked at me, that my request had not produced a bad effect—on the contrary. . . .

At the little city of Assisi, I had the opportunity to go into Fr. Révérony's carriage, a favor that was not granted *to any lady* during the whole trip. Here's how I obtained that privilege:

After visiting the places made fragrant by the virtues of St. Francis and St. Clare, we ended up at the convent of St. Agnes, St. Clare's sister. I had contemplated the Saint's head for as long as I liked, when, as I was among the last to leave, I noticed that I had lost my belt. I *looked for* it in the midst of the crowd. A priest took pity on me and helped me, but after finding it for me I saw him walk away, and I stayed alone *searching,* because I did have the belt, but it was impossible to put it on since the buckle was missing. . . . Finally I saw it shining in a corner and didn't take long to grab it and adjust its ribbon.

But the preceding work had taken a long time, so I was greatly surprised to find myself alone in the church. All the many coaches had disappeared, with the exception of that of Fr. Révérony. What course should I take? Should I run after the coaches, which I couldn't see any longer, expose myself to missing the train, and cause my dear papa to worry, or should I ask for a ride in Fr. Révérony's coach? . . . I decided to take the latter course. With my most gracious look, and the least *embarrassed* possible despite my extreme *embarrassment,* I exposed to him my critical situation and put him into an *embarrassing situation* himself, because his coach was filled with the most distinguished *gentlemen* of the pilgrimage, and there was no means of finding one more place. But a very gallant gentleman hastened to get off, had me climb into his place, and sat modestly next to the coachman.

I looked like a squirrel caught in a trap, and I was far from being at ease, surrounded as I was by all those great persons, and especially by the most *redoubtable* one [Fr. Révérony], across from whom I was seated. . . . However, he was very pleasant to me, from time to time interrupting his conversation with these gentlemen to talk to me about *Carmel.* Before arriving at the train station all these *great persons* took out their *big* wallets in order to give some money to the coachman (who had already been paid). I did as they did and took out my *very little* wallet. But Fr. Révérony wouldn't consent for me to take out some pretty *little* coins. He preferred to give one *big one* for us both.

Another time I found myself beside him on the trolley. He was even more pleasant, and promised to do everything he could in order for me to enter Carmel. . . . While putting a little salve on my wounds, these little encounters didn't keep the return trip from being much less pleasant than the original trip, because I no longer had the hope of "the Holy Father." I found no help on earth, which seemed to me to be a dry and parched desert [Ps. 63:1]. All my hope was in God *alone*. . . . I had just had the experience that it is better to have recourse to Him than to His Saints. . . .

The sadness of my soul didn't stop me from taking great interest in the holy places that we were visiting. In Florence I was happy to contemplate St. Magdalene di Pazzi in the midst of the choir of Carmelite nuns who opened their big grille for us. Since we didn't know how to take advantage of that privilege, many persons wanted to have their rosaries touch the Saint's tomb. I was the only one who could pass my hand through the grille that separated us, so everyone brought me their rosaries, and I was quite proud of my function. . . .

I always had to find the means to *touch everything*, so in the Church of the Holy Cross in Jerusalem (in Rome) we were able to venerate several pieces of the true Cross, two thorns and one of the sacred nails that were enclosed in a magnificent reliquary of wrought gold, but *without glass.* So I found a way, while venerating the precious relic, of slipping my *little finger* into one of the openings in the reliquary, and I *was able to touch* the nail that was bathed in the blood of Jesus. . . . I really was too daring! . . . Fortunately, God, who sees into the depths of the heart, knows that my intention was pure, and that for nothing in the world would I have wanted to displease Him. I acted toward Him like a *child* who thinks that everything is allowed her, and who regards her Father's treasures as her own [Lk. 15:31].

I still can't understand why women are so easily excommunicated in Italy. At every moment we were told, "Don't come in here. . . ." "Don't go in there, you would be excommunicated! . . ." Oh! Poor women, how they are disparaged! . . . However, they love God in much greater numbers than men, and during the Passion of Our Lord, the women had more courage than the apostles [Lk. 23:27] since they braved the insults of the soldiers and dared to wipe the adorable Face of Jesus. . . . It's no doubt for that reason that He allows scorn to be their lot on earth, since He chose that for Himself. . . . In heaven He'll know how to show that His thoughts are not man's thoughts [Isa. 55:8-9], because then the *last* will be the *first* [Mt. 20:16]. . . .

More than once during the trip, I didn't have the patience to wait for heaven in order to be the first. . . . One day when we were visiting a monastery of Carmelite monks, not content to follow the pilgrims in the *outer* galleries, I continued on walking into the *inner* cloisters. . . . Suddenly I saw a good elderly monk who from afar was signaling me to go away, but instead of leaving, I went up to him and, pointing to the paintings in the cloister, I made a sign to him that they were pretty. He recognized no doubt by my hair hanging down my back and my youthful look that I was a child, so he smiled at me kindly and went away, seeing that he didn't have an enemy in front of him. If I had been able to speak Italian to him, I would have told him that I was a future Carmelite nun, but because of the builders of the tower of Babel, that was impossible for me [Gen. 11:9].

After visits to Pisa and Genoa, we returned to France. On the trip the view was magnificent. At times we were traveling along the coast, and the train was so close to the sea that it seemed to me that the waves were going to come right up to us. (That spectacle was caused by a storm. It was nighttime, which made the scene even more imposing.) At other times we traveled through plains covered with orange trees bearing ripe fruit, green olive trees with light foliage, and graceful palm trees. . . . At nightfall we saw numerous little seaports lit up with a multitude of lights, while in the sky the first *stars* were shimmering. . . .

Oh! Such poetry was filling my soul at the sight of all those things that I was looking at for the first and last time in my life! . . . It was without regret that I saw them vanish into the distance; my heart was aspiring toward other marvels. It had had enough of contemplating *the beauties* of the *earth; the beauties* of *heaven* were the object of its desires, and in order to give them to *souls,* I wanted to become a *prisoner!* [That is, a cloistered nun.] . . . Before I saw opening before me the gates of the blessed prison after which I was longing, I still had to struggle and suffer. I felt that as I was returning to France. However, my confidence was so great that I didn't stop hoping that I would be allowed to enter on the twenty-fifth of December. . . .

Scarcely had we arrived in Lisieux, when our first visit was to the Carmelite convent. What a discussion that was! . . . We had so many things to tell each other, after a month of separation, a month that seemed longer to me and during which I learned more than during several years. . . .

Oh, my dear Mother! How sweet it was for me to see you again, to open up to you my poor wounded soul. To you who knew so well how to understand me, to whom one word, one glance were enough to guess everything! I gave myself up completely. I had done everything that depended on me, everything, even so far as speaking to the Holy Father, so I didn't know what I still should do.

You told me to write to His Excellency and to remind him about his promise. I did that immediately, as best as possible, but in terms that my uncle found a little too simple, so he redid my letter. At the moment when I was going to send it, I received one from you, telling me not to write, to wait for a few days. I obeyed immediately, because I was sure that this was the best way not to do the wrong thing. Finally, ten days before Christmas, my letter went on its way. Quite convinced that the reply wouldn't be long in coming, every morning after Mass I went to the post office with Papa, thinking that I would find the permission to fly away [to

Carmel], but each morning brought a new disappointment that nonetheless didn't shake my faith. . . .

I asked Jesus to loose my bonds [Ps. 116:16]. He broke them, but in a very different way from the one I was expecting. . . . The beautiful celebration of Christmas came, and Jesus didn't wake up. . . . He left His little ball on the ground, without even glancing at it. . . .

My heart was broken as I went to the Midnight Mass. I had been counting so much on going to it behind the grille at the Carmelite convent! . . . This ordeal was very great for my faith, but the One whose heart is awake as He sleeps [Song 5:2], made me understand that to those whose faith is as *small as a mustard seed* [Lk. 17:6], He grants *miracles* and makes mountains move [Mt. 21:21], in order to strengthen that faith, which is so tiny. But for His *cherished* ones, for His *Mother,* He doesn't do miracles *until He has tested their faith.* Didn't He let Lazarus die, even though Martha and Mary had told Him that he was sick? [Jn. 11:3]. . . . At the wedding at Cana, when the Blessed Virgin asked Jesus to help His hosts, didn't He answer her that His hour had not yet come? [Jn. 2:1–11]. . . . But after that testing, what a reward! Water changes into wine . . . Lazarus is raised from the dead! . . . That's how Jesus acts toward His little Thérèse: After testing her for a *long time,* He fulfills all the desires of her heart. . . .

Having spent the afternoon of that dazzling celebration in tears, I went to see the Carmelites; great was my surprise to see, when they opened the grille, the delightful little Jesus holding in His hand a ball with my name written on it: The Carmelites, in place of Jesus, who was too little to talk, sang a hymn to me that was composed by my beloved Mother. Each word spread into my soul a most sweet consolation. Never will I forget that delicate mother's heart that always poured out upon me the most exquisite tenderness. . . .

After saying thank you as I shed sweet tears, I encountered the surprise that dear Céline had given me when we came back from Midnight Mass. I had found in my room, in the middle of a charming basin, a *little* boat that was carrying the *little* Jesus sleeping with a *little* ball next to Him. On the white sail Céline had written these words, "I'm sleeping, but my heart is awake" [cf. Song 5:2], and on the vessel this single word: "Abandonment!" Oh! If Jesus wasn't still speaking to His little bride, if His divine eyes were remaining closed, at least He was revealing Himself to me by means of souls who understood all the tenderness and love of His heart. . . .

The first day of the year 1888, Jesus made me another present of His Cross, but this time I was alone in carrying it, because it was all the more sorrowful since I couldn't understand it. . . . A *letter from Pauline* [now Sr. Agnes of Jesus] arrived, letting me know that His Excellency the bishop's reply had arrived on December 28th, the feast day of the Holy *Innocents,* but that she hadn't let me know about it, having decided that my entrance would not take place *until after Lent.* I couldn't hold back my tears at the thought of such a long delay.

For me this trial had a most particular character. I was seeing my *bonds broken* from the point of view of the world, and this time it was the blessed ark that was refusing entrance to the poor little dove [Gen. 8:6–12] . . . . I'm willing to believe that I must have seemed unreasonable in not accepting joyfully my three months of exile, but I also believe that, without it appearing to be so, this was a *very great* hardship, and it made me *grow* a great deal in abandonment and in the other virtues.

How did these *three months* go by, these months that were so rich in graces for my soul? At first the thought came to me of not bothering to live as strict a life as I was used to doing. But soon I understood the value of the time that was being offered to me, and I resolved to give myself over more than ever to a *serious* and *mortified* life.

When I say mortified, this is not to make you believe that I was always doing penances. Alas! I *never did a single one*. Far from being like those beautiful souls who from childhood practiced every kind of mortifications, I felt no attraction for them. Without a doubt this came from my cowardice, because I could, like Céline, have found a thousand little ways to make myself suffer. Instead of that I let myself always be coddled in cotton and fattened up like a little bird that has no need of doing penance. . . . My mortifications consisted in breaking my will, which was always ready to impose itself; in holding my tongue instead of answering back; in doing little things for others without hoping to get anything in return; in not slumping back when I was sitting down; etc., etc. . . .

It was through the practice of these *little nothings* that I prepared myself to become Jesus' bride, and I can't tell you how much that period of waiting left sweet memories for me. . . . Three months passed by very quickly, and finally the moment that I had so fervently longed for arrived.

CHAPTER 7

First Years at Carmel
1888–1890

Confession to Fr. Pichon
Thérèse and her Superiors
The Holy Face
Taking the habit
Papa's illness
Small virtues

Monday, the ninth of April, the day when Carmel celebrated the feast day of the Annunciation [when the angel Gabriel announced to the Virgin Mary that she would conceive a Child by the Holy Spirit, normally celebrated on the twenty-fifth of March, but]—delayed until then because of Lent—was chosen for my entrance. The day beforehand, the whole family was gathered around the table at which I was to sit one last time. Oh! How wrenching are these intimate family meetings! . . . Whereas you would wish to see yourself forgotten, the hugs, the tenderest of words are offered and make you feel the sacrifice of the separation. . . .

My dear king didn't say much of anything, but his gaze was fixed on me with love. . . . My aunt was crying from time to time, and my uncle gave me a thousand affectionate compliments. Jeanne and Marie [my cousins] were also full of tenderness toward me, especially Marie, who, taking me aside, asked my forgiveness for the troubles she thought she had caused me. Finally my dear Léonie, having come back from the Visitation convent a few months before, covered me even more with kisses and hugs. There remains only Céline that I haven't talked about, but you may guess, my dear Mother, how the last night was spent when we slept together in the same bed. . . .

The morning of the big day, after casting one last look about Les Buissonnets, that graceful nest of my childhood that I was not to see again, I left on the arm of my dear king to climb the mountain of Carmel. . . . As on the previous day, the whole family found itself gathered to attend Holy Mass and to receive Communion.

Immediately after Jesus had come down into the hearts of my beloved relatives, all I heard around me was sobs. I was the only one who wasn't shedding tears, but I felt my heart pound with *such violence* that it seemed impossible to me to go forward when someone came to beckon us to come to the convent door. I went forward nonetheless, wondering all the while if I wasn't going to die because the pounding of my heart was so strong. . . . Oh! What a moment that was; you would have had to go through it to know what it is. . . .

My emotions didn't show on the outside. After embracing all the members of my beloved family, I knelt before my incomparable father, asking for his blessing. In order to give it to me he *knelt as well* and blessed me while weeping. . . . This was a sight that ought make the angels smile, that of this elderly man presenting his daughter to the Lord in the springtime of her life! . . . A few moments later, the doors of the blessed ark closed on me [Gen. 7:16], and there I received the welcoming embraces of the *dear sisters* [Marie and Pauline] who had served me as *mothers,* and whom I was henceforth going to take as the models for my actions. . . . Finally my desires had been accomplished, and my soul felt such sweet and such deep PEACE that it would be impossible for me to express it. And for seven and a half years that inner peace has remained my lot; it hasn't abandoned me amidst the greatest trials.

Like all postulants, I was led to the choir immediately after my entrance. It was dark because the Blessed Sacrament was exposed there. What struck my glance immediately were the eyes of our holy Mother Geneviève [the co-foundress of the convent] that were fixed on me. I remained for a moment on my knees at her feet, thanking God for the grace that He was granting me to meet a Saint, and then I followed Mother Marie de Gonzague [the prioress of the convent] into the different places in the community. Everything seemed delightful to me—I thought I had been transported into a desert [a place of calm meditation, as enjoyed by the Desert Fathers and Mothers in the early centuries of the Church]. Our little cell was especially charming to me, but the joy that I felt there was *calm;* the slightest summer breeze didn't come to make ripples on the tranquil waters on which my little dinghy was sailing. Not a single cloud was covering my deep-blue sky. Oh! I was fully rewarded for all my trials! With what deep joy did I repeat these words, "It's forever, forever that I'm here!"

This happiness wasn't fleeting. It wasn't to fly away with "the illusions of the first days." As for the *illusions,* God gave me the grace *not to have* ANY as I entered Carmel. I found the religious life to be as I had conceived it. No sacrifice surprised me, despite the fact that, as you know, dear Mother, my first steps met with more thorns than roses! . . . Yes, suffering held out its arms to me, and I threw myself into those arms with love. . . .

What I was coming to do at Carmel, I declared at the feet of Jesus in the Host, in the examination that preceded my taking of vows: "I came to save souls and above all in order to pray for priests." When you want to reach a goal, you must use every means to do so. Jesus made me understand that it was by the Cross that He wanted to give me souls, and my drawing toward suffering grew in proportion to the suffering that was increasing. For five years that path was mine, but outwardly, nothing betrayed my suffering, which was all the more sorrowful because I was the only one to be acquainted with it. Oh! What a surprise we will have at the end of the world when we read the story of souls! . . . How astounded people will be when they see the way by which mine has been led! . . .

It's true that, two months after my entrance, when Fr. Pichon came for the profession of Sr. Marie of the Sacred Heart [my sister Marie], he was surprised to see what God was doing in my soul. He told me that the previous day, as he had watched me praying in the choir, he had thought my fervor was quite childish and my path quite easy.

My meeting with the good Father was a very great comfort for me, but it was bathed in tears because of the difficulty I had in opening my soul. Nonetheless I made a general confession, as I had never done before. At the end Father spoke these words to me, the most comforting that had ever sounded in the ear of my soul: "In the presence of God, of the Blessed Virgin, and all the Saints, *I declare that you have never committed a single mortal sin.*" Then he added, "Thank God for what He's doing for you, because if He were to abandon you, instead of being a little angel, you would become a little demon."

Oh! I had no trouble believing him. I felt how weak and imperfect I was, but gratitude was filling my soul. I had such a great fear of soiling my baptismal robe, that such an assurance from the mouth of a spiritual director, as our Holy Mother Teresa [of Avila] desired, that is, joining *knowledge with virtue,* seemed to me to have issued from the very mouth of Jesus. . . .

The good Father continued on, saying these words that are sweetly engraved on my heart: "My child, may Our Lord always be your Superior and your Novice Master." In fact, He was, and He was also "my spiritual director." It's not that I mean by this that my soul was closed to my Superiors in the convent, oh! far from that. I have always tried to make my soul an *open book* to them. But our Superior [Mother Marie de Gonzague], who was often ill, had little time to be busy with me. I know that she loved me a great deal and said the best things possible about me, but nonetheless God permitted that, *without her knowing it,* she was VERY STRICT. I couldn't meet her without kissing the ground. It was the same in the rare meetings for spiritual direction that I had with her. . . . What an inestimable grace! . . . How *visibly* God was acting in the one who stood in His place! . . .

What would have become of me if, as persons of the world believed, I had been the "little doll" of the community? . . . Perhaps instead of seeing Our Lord in my Superiors I would have considered only the persons, and my heart, which had been so *well guarded* when I was in the outside world, would have become humanly attached when in the cloister. . . . Fortunately, I was preserved from that misfortune. Without a doubt *I loved* our Mother *very much,* but with a pure affection that lifted me up toward the Bridegroom of my soul. . . .

Our Novice Mistress was a *real saint,* the archetype of the first Carmelites. All day long I was with her, because she taught me to work. Her kindness toward me knew no bounds. And yet, my soul wasn't opening up. . . . It was only with effort that it was possible for me to participate in my spiritual direction. Not being used to talking about my soul, I didn't know how to express what was happening in it.

A kindly old nun understood what I was feeling: She told me one day during our recreation period, "Little girl, it seems to me that you must not have much to say to your superiors." "Why do you say that, Mother?" "Because your soul is extremely *simple,* but when you become perfect, you will be *even simpler;* the closer we come to God, the simpler we become." The good nun was right. However, the difficulty that I was having in opening up my soul while coming out of my simpleness was a real ordeal. I recognize this now, because without ceasing to be simple, I express my thoughts with very great ease.

I said that Jesus had been "my spiritual Director."
When I entered Carmel I met with the person [the priest
assigned to be my spiritual director] who was to serve me
in this capacity, but hardly had he admitted me among his
spiritual children when he left for exile [in Canada]. . . .
So I had met him only to have him immediately taken
away. . . . I was reduced to receiving from him one letter
per year compared to the twelve that I wrote to him, so
my heart turned quite quickly toward the Director of
directors: He it was who taught me in that knowledge
that is hidden to the knowledgeable and the wise [Lk.
10:21], that He deigns to reveal to the *smallest ones*. . . .

The little flower that was transplanted onto the
mountain of Carmel was destined to open in the shadow
of the Cross. The tears and the blood of Jesus became
the dew that watered it, and its Sun was His Adorable
Face veiled with tears. . . . Until then I hadn't plumbed
the depths of the treasures hidden in the Holy Face of
Jesus [Isa. 53:3]. It was through you, dear Mother, that
I learned to know them. Just as you had once gone
before us all to Carmel, in the same way you were the
first to penetrate the mysteries of love hidden in the
Countenance of our Bridegroom. Then you called me,
and I understood. . . . I understood what was the *real
glory*. The one whose kingdom is not of this world [Jn.
18:36] showed me that true wisdom consists in "wanting to be unknown and counted as nothing, in placing
one's joy in disdain for oneself." Oh! Like Jesus' face, I
wanted "My face to be truly hidden, that on earth no
one should recognize me" [cf. Isa. 52:14]. I was thirsty
for suffering and for being forgotten. . . .

How merciful is the path along which God has always led me. He *never* made me desire anything without giving it to me, so His bitter cup seemed delicious to me. . . .

After the radiant celebrations of the month of May, celebrations of the taking of vows by Marie, *the eldest* of the family that *the youngest* had the happiness of crowning on the day of her becoming Jesus' bride, hardship had to come visit us. . . . The previous year in the month of May, Papa had been struck by an attack of paralysis in his legs. We were quite worried then, but the strong temperament of my dear king soon took the upper hand, and our fears disappeared. However, more than once during the trip to Rome, we had noticed that he would tire easily, and wasn't as jolly as usual. . . .

What I noticed the most was the progress that Papa was making in perfection. Following the example of St. Francis de Sales, he had reached the point of mastering his natural exuberance to the point where he seemed to have the gentlest nature in the world. . . . The things of earth seemed scarcely to graze him. He easily took the high road in the contrary things of this life. In short, God *flooded him with consolations.* During his daily visits to the Blessed Sacrament, his eyes would often fill with tears, and his face would breathe a heavenly bliss. . . . When Léonie left the Visitation convent [after a health crisis], he wasn't afflicted by this. He didn't reproach God for not having granted the prayers that he had prayed to Him to obtain a vocation for his dear daughter. It was even with a certain joy that he went to get her. . . .

With what faith Papa accepted his separation from his little queen: He announced it in these terms to his friends from Alençon: "My dear friends, Thérèse, my little queen, entered Carmel yesterday! . . . God alone can require such a sacrifice. . . . Do not feel sorry for me, because my heart is overflowing with joy."

It was time for such a faithful servant to receive the reward for his work [Mt. 25:21]. It was proper that his payment should be like the one that God gave to the King of heaven, His only Son. . . . Papa had just offered an *Altar* to God, and he was the victim chosen to be offered on it with the spotless Lamb. You know, my dear Mother, how bitter was the month of June, and especially the twenty-fourth in the year *1888* [when it was discovered that Papa had disappeared on the twenty-third and was found miles away at Le Havre on the twenty-seventh]. Those memories are too deeply engraved on the depths of our hearts for it to be necessary to write them. . . . Oh, Mother! How we suffered! . . . And this was only the *beginning* of our ordeal. . . .

However, the time of my taking of the habit had arrived. I was welcomed by the chapter [the vowed community], but how could I think about celebrating? Already they were talking about giving me the blessed habit without making me come out, when they decided to wait. Against all hope, our dear father recovered from the second attack, and His Excellency fixed the date of the ceremony on the tenth of January. The wait was long, but also, what a beautiful celebration! . . . Nothing was missing, nothing, not even *snow*. . . .

I don't know if I've already talked to you about my

love of snow. . . . When I was quite little, its whiteness used to delight me. One of my greatest pleasures was to go walking in the midst of falling snowflakes. Where did I get this liking of snow? . . . Perhaps from the fact that being a *little winter flower,* [having been born in January,] the first covering with which my child's eyes saw nature embellished must have been its white coat. . . . But then, I have always wanted that on the day of my taking of the habit [wearing the white color of Novices], nature would be, like me, decked out in white. The day before that beautiful day I sadly watched the gray sky from which a fine rain was escaping from time to time, and the temperature was so warm that I was no longer hoping for snow.

The next morning the sky hadn't changed, but nonetheless, the celebration was delightful. And the most beautiful, the most delightful flower was my beloved king. Never had he been so handsome, so *dignified.* . . . He was the admiration of everyone. This was the day of his *triumph,* his last celebration here on earth. He had given *all* his children to God, for when Céline had confided in him that she also had a vocation, he had had *wept for joy* and had gone with her to thank the One who "was honoring him by taking all his children."

At the end of the ceremony, His Excellency intoned the *Te Deum.* A priest tried to point out that this hymn was chanted only at Professions, but the impulse had been given, and the hymn *of thanksgiving* continued to the end. Wasn't it necessary for the celebration to be *complete* since it joined all the others into one? . . .

After hugging my beloved king one last time, I went back into the enclosure. The first thing that I caught sight of under the cloister was "my little pink Jesus" smiling at me among the flowers and the lights, and then immediately my eyes fell on *snowflakes*. . . . The meadow was white, like me. What a tender touch from Jesus! Foreseeing the desires of His little bride, He was giving her snow. . . .

Snow! What mortal is so strong that he can cause snow to fall from heaven to charm his beloved? . . . Perhaps the persons of the world have asked themselves that question, but what is certain is that the snow at my taking of the habit seemed like a small miracle to them and the whole town was astonished at it. They thought that I had a curious taste in my love for snow. . . . Well and good, that brings out even more *the incomprehensible condescendence* of the Bridegroom of virgins . . . of the One who cherishes *lilies* that are *white* as SNOW! . . .

His Excellency entered after the ceremony. He had a most fatherly tenderness toward me. I quite think that he was proud to see that I'd succeeded. He told everyone that I was *"his* little girl." Each time he came back after that beautiful celebration, His Excellency was always most kind toward me. I especially remember his visit at the occasion of the commemoration of our father St. John of the Cross [the previous December 14th]. He took my face in his hands and gave me all kinds of signs of endearment. Never had I been so honored! At the same time God made me think about the signs of endearment that He wanted to shower on me before the angels and the Saints, and of which He was giving me a pale image even on earth. So the comfort that I felt was very great. . . .

As I have just said, the day of the tenth of January was the triumph of my king. I compare it to Jesus' entrance into Jerusalem on Palm Sunday [Mt. 21:1–11]. Like that of Our Divine Master, Papa's glory *for one day* was followed by a sorrowful passion, and that passion wasn't for him alone. Just as Jesus' suffering pierced with a sword the heart of His Divine Mother [Lk. 2:35], our own hearts felt the sufferings of the one whom we cherished the most tenderly on earth. . . .

I remember that in the month of June, 1888, at the moment of our first ordeals [when Papa disappeared for four days and turned up miles away], I said, "I'm suffering a lot, but I feel that I can endure even greater trials." I wasn't thinking then about the ones that were reserved for me. . . . I didn't know that on the twelfth of February, one month after my taking the habit, our beloved father would drink the *bitterest,* the *most humiliating* of all cups [by being obliged to enter the Bon Sauveur mental hospital in Caen]. . . .

Oh! That day I didn't say that I would be able to suffer more!!! . . . Words can't express our anguish, so I'm not going to try to describe it. One day in heaven we will love to talk to each other about our *glorious* times of trial—are we not already happy to have suffered them? . . . Yes, the three years of Papa's martyrdom seemed to me to be the most pleasant, the most fruitful of our entire life. I wouldn't give them in exchange for all the ecstasies and revelations of the Saints. My heart is overflowing with gratitude when I think about this inestimable *treasure* that must cause holy jealousy among the Angels of the heavenly court. . . .

My desire for suffering was gratified. However, my attraction for it didn't diminish, so my soul soon shared the sufferings of my heart. Dryness was my daily bread. Deprived of all consolation, I was nevertheless the happiest of creatures, since all my desires had been satisfied. . . .

Oh, my dear Mother! How sweet was our great time of trial, since from all our hearts there issued only sighs of love and gratitude! . . . We were no longer walking in the paths of perfection, all five of us were flying. The two poor little exiles in Caen [Céline and Léonie], though they were still in the world, were no longer of the world. . . . Oh! What marvelous things this ordeal did in the soul of my beloved Céline! . . . All the letters that she wrote at that time bear the imprint of acceptance and love. . . .

And what can we say about the meetings we used to have together? . . . Oh! Far from separating us, the grille of Carmel united our souls more strongly. We had the same thoughts, the same desires, the same *love for Jesus* and for *souls*. . . . When Céline and Thérèse talked together, never one word of the things of the earth came into their conversations, which were already completely in heaven [Phil. 3:20]. Just as once was the case in the *belvedere,* they dreamed about the things of *eternity,* and in order to enjoy right away that happiness without end, they chose here on earth, as their unique portion, "suffering and contempt."

That is how the time of my preparation for becoming Jesus' bride was spent. . . . It was very long for poor little Thérèse! At the end of my year [the usual length of the time as a Novice], our Mother [Marie de Gonzague] told me not to think about asking to make my Profession, that certainly the Reverend Father Superior would reject my request, so I had to wait another eight months. . . . At first it was very difficult for me to accept that great sacrifice, but soon light flooded my soul. I then meditated on *The Foundations of the Spiritual Life* by Fr. Surin [based on the *Imitation of Christ*, the Jesuit Jean-Joseph Surin's book by this name was published in 1667].

One day during prayers I understood that my keen desire to make my profession was tinged with great self-love. Since I had *given myself to* Jesus in order to please Him and comfort Him, I must not oblige Him to do *my will* instead of His. I understood further that a bride ought to be adorned for the day of her wedding, and I had done nothing toward that end. . . . Then I told Jesus, "Oh, my God! I'm not asking of You to take my blessed vows. *I'll wait as long as You wish,* only I don't want, due to my own fault, for my union with You to be put off. So I'm going to take every care to make myself a beautiful gown adorned with precious jewels. When You find it richly ornate enough, I'm sure that every creature will not keep You from coming down to me in order for me to unite myself to You for ever, my Beloved!"

Since my taking of the habit, I had received a great deal of illumination about religious perfection, principally on the subject of the vow of Poverty. During my postulancy, I was content to have nice things for my use and to find at hand everything that I needed. *"My Director"* suffered all that patiently, for He doesn't like to show everything to souls at the same time. Ordinarily He gives His light little by little. (At the beginning of my spiritual life, around the age of thirteen or fourteen, I used to wonder what I would have to gain later, because I thought that it was impossible for me to understand perfection any better. I very quickly recognized that the more one advances on this path, the farther one believes oneself from being near the end. So now I'm resigned to seeing myself as always imperfect, and in that I find my joy. . . .)

I'll come back now to the lessons that *"my Director"* was giving me. One night after Compline [the last office of the day, held in the evening] I looked in vain for our little lamp on the boards that were reserved for that use. It was the Great Silence [the time when no one in the convent speaks until morning], so it was impossible to ask for it. . . . I understood that one nun, thinking she was taking her lamp, had taken ours. I was in very great need of it, but instead of feeling annoyed at being deprived of it, I was quite happy, feeling that poverty consists in seeing oneself deprived not only of pleasant things but also of indispensable things. So in the *outer darkness* I was enlightened within. . . .

I was taken at that time with a real love of the ugliest and least fitting objects. So it was with joy that I saw myself deprived of our cell's pretty *little pitcher* and being given in its place a *large pitcher that was all cracked*. . . .

I also took great pains not to excuse myself, something that seemed quite difficult to me, especially with our Novice Mistress, from whom I wouldn't have wanted to hide anything. Here's my first victory; it's not great, but it cost me dearly: A little vase placed behind a window was found broken. Our Mistress, thinking that I was the one who had left it behind, showed it to me, telling me to pay more attention in the future. Without saying anything I kissed the ground and then promised to be more orderly in the future. Because of my lack of virtue these little practices cost me a great deal, and I needed to think that at the Last Judgment everything will be revealed [Mt. 25:31–46], because I made this remark: When one has done her duty, never excusing herself, no one knows it. On the contrary, her imperfections appear immediately. . . .

I applied myself above all to practicing the little virtues, since I didn't have the facility for practicing the big ones. So I loved to fold the mantles that had been forgotten by the Sisters, and to do all the little services for them that I could.

The love of mortification was also given to me. It was even greater since nothing was permitted to me to satisfy it. . . . The only little mortification in the world that I used to do, consisting of not leaning back when I was sitting down, was forbidden to me because of my propensity for vaulting out of my chair. Alas! My fervor would no doubt not have lasted long if I had been assigned many penances to do. . . . The ones that were given to me without my asking for them consisted in mortifying my self-love, which did me much more good than bodily penances. . . .

The refectory [the dining room], which was my only job immediately after I took the habit, furnished me with more than one opportunity to put my self-love in its place, that is, under foot. . . . It's true that I took great consolation in being in the same job assignment as you, dear Mother, and to be able to contemplate your virtues up close, but being close to you was a subject of suffering. I didn't feel as *I used to,* free to tell you everything. There was the Rule to observe: I couldn't open up my soul to you. In short, I was at *Carmel* and no longer at *Les Buissonnets under Papa's roof!* . . .

However, the Blessed Virgin was helping prepare the garment of my soul. As soon as it was complete, the obstacles went away by themselves. His Excellency sent me the permission that I had asked for: The Community was willing to receive me, and my Profession was set for the *eighth of September* [the Blessed Virgin Mary's birthday]. . . .

Everything I have just written in a few words would require many pages of details, but those pages will never be read on earth. Soon, dear Mother, I will talk to you about all the those things *in our Father's house,* in beautiful heaven, for which our hearts are longing! . . .

My wedding gown was ready. It was made rich with the *former* jewels that my Bridegroom had given me, but that was not enough for His generosity. He wanted to give me a *new* diamond with innumerable facets. Papa's ordeal was, with all its sorrowful circumstances, the *former* jewels, and the *new one* was an ordeal that was quite small in appearance, but that made me suffer a great deal: For some time, our poor dear father, since he was feeling a little better, had been allowed to go out in a carriage. There was even a question about letting him travel by train to come see us. Naturally, Céline thought right away that it would be necessary to choose the day of my taking the veil. "So as not to tire him out," she said, "I won't have him attend the whole ceremony. Only at the end I'll go get him and I'll lead him quite gently up to the grille so that Thérèse can receive his blessing."

Oh! In this I recognize quite well the heart of dear Céline. . . . It's quite true that "Never does love find a pretext of impossibility because it believes that everything is possible and that everything is allowed. . . ." *Human prudence* on the contrary, trembles at every step and doesn't dare, so to speak, to put its foot down. So God, who wanted to test me, used human prudence as a passive instrument, and the day I took my bridal vows I was truly an orphan, no longer having a father on earth, but being able to look at heaven with confidence and to say in all truthfulness, "Our Father in heaven [Mt. 6:9]. . . ."

CHAPTER 8

From Profession to the Offering of Love
1890–1895

Taking the veil
Mother Geneviève of St. Teresa
Epidemic of influenza
Retreat of Fr. Alexis
Priorship of Mother Agnes
Papa's death
Entrance of Céline
End of Manuscript A

Before speaking to you about this ordeal, dear Mother, I should have spoken to you about the retreat that preceded my profession. It was far from bringing me consolations. The most absolute dryness and something approaching abandonment were my lot. Jesus was sleeping as always in my little dinghy. Oh! I see clearly that souls rarely let Him sleep tranquilly within them. Jesus is so tired from always serving at others' expense and from their advances that He hurries to take advantage of the rest that I offer Him [Mk. 4:37–39]. No doubt He won't wake up before my great retreat of all eternity, but instead of causing me pain, that gives me extreme pleasure. . . .

I really am far from being a Saint. That alone is proof of it. Instead of rejoicing at my dryness, I should attribute it to the smallness of my fervor and faithfulness. I ought to be extremely sorry at sleeping (for seven years) during my prayers and my *times of thanksgiving.* Well, I'm not sorry. . . . I think that *little children* please their parents as much when they're asleep as when they're awake. I think that in order to perform operations, doctors put their patients to sleep. Finally, I think that the Lord "knows how we are formed, he remembers that we are dust" [Ps. 103:14].

So my retreat before my profession was, like all the ones that followed it, a retreat of great dryness. However, God showed me clearly, without my being aware of it, the way to please Him and to practice the most sublime of virtues. I've noticed many times that Jesus doesn't want to give me *food.* He's nourishing me at every moment with a completely new nourishment; I find it within me without knowing how it got there. . . . I believe quite simply that it's Jesus Himself, hidden in the depths of my poor little heart, who is giving me the grace within to act, and He causes me to think everything that He wants me to do in the present moment.

A few days before the day of my profession, I had the happiness of receiving the blessing of the Supreme Pontiff. I had asked for it through the good Brother Simeon for *Papa* and for me, and it was a great comfort to me to be able to give back to my dear father the grace that he had obtained for me by taking me to Rome.

Finally the *beautiful day* of my becoming a bride arrived. It was cloudless, but the day before there arose in my soul a storm like one that I had never seen before. . . . Not a single doubt about my vocation had yet come to my thoughts; it was necessary for me to become acquainted with that ordeal. That night, after visiting the Stations of the Cross after Matins [the early morning church service], my vocation appeared to me as a dream, a figment of my imagination. . . . I found life at Carmel to be quite beautiful, but the devil inspired in me the *assurance* that it wasn't made for me, that I'd be deceiving the Superiors by going forward along a path to which I wasn't called. . . . My darkness was so great that I could see or understand only one thing: I didn't have the *calling!* . . .

Oh! How can I depict the anguish of my soul? . . . It seemed to me (an absurdity that shows that this temptation came from the devil) that if I told all my fears to my Novice Mistress, she was going to prevent me from pronouncing my Holy Vows. However, I wanted to do God's will and return to the world rather than remain in Carmel doing my own will. So I asked my Mistress to come out, and, *full of embarrassment and shame*, I told her the state of my soul. . . .

Fortunately she saw more clearly than I did, and she reassured me completely. Besides, the act of humility that I had done had just put to flight the devil, who was perhaps thinking that I wasn't going to be daring enough to admit my temptation. Immediately after I finished speaking, my doubts left me. Nonetheless, in order to make my act of humility complete, I wanted to go on and confide my strange temptation to our Superior, who was content to laugh at me.

On the morning of the eighth of September, I felt myself *flooded* with a river *of peace* [Isa. 66:12], and it was in that peace, "which transcends all understanding" [Phil. 4:7], that I pronounced my Holy Vows. . . . My union with Jesus was made, not amidst thunder and lightning, that is, with extraordinary graces, but in the midst of a *gentle whisper* like the one that our father Elijah heard on the mountain [1 Kings 19:11–13]. . . . What graces I asked for that day! . . . I felt myself truly the QUEEN, so I took advantage of my title of nobility to deliver captives, to obtain the favors of the King toward His ungrateful subjects—in short, I wanted to deliver all souls from purgatory and convert sinners. . . . I prayed very much for my mother, my beloved sisters . . . for the whole family, but above all for my dear father who was so sorely tried and so holy. . . . I offered myself to Jesus so that He might accomplish His *will* perfectly in me without creatures ever placing any obstacle in its path. . . .

That beautiful day passed just as the saddest ones do, since the most radiant of days has a tomorrow. But it was without any sadness that I placed my crown at the feet of the Blessed Virgin. I felt that time wouldn't take away my happiness. . . . What a beautiful feast day was the birthday of *Mary* to become Jesus' bride! It was the *little* Blessed Virgin of one day who presented her *little* flower to the *little* Jesus. . . . That day everything was little except the graces and the peace that I received, except the *peaceful* joy that I felt that evening when I watched the stars twinkling in the heavens, as I was thinking that *soon,* beautiful heaven would open to my delighted eyes and I would be able to unite myself with my Bridegroom in the midst of everlasting joy and gladness. . . .

On the twenty-fourth the ceremony took place of my taking of the *veil,* but it was completely veiled with tears. . . . Papa wasn't there to bless his queen. . . . My director was in Canada. . . . His Excellency, who was to come and dine at my uncle's, fell sick and couldn't come, either. In short, everything was sadness and bitterness. . . . Nonetheless, *peace,* always *peace,* was found in the bottom of the cup. . . . That day Jesus allowed me to be unable to hold back my tears, and my tears weren't understood. . . . In fact, I'd gone through many greater trials without crying, but then I had been helped by a powerful grace. On the contrary, on the twenty-fourth, Jesus left me to my own strength, and I showed how small it was.

A week after my taking the veil Jeanne's marriage took place. To tell you, dear Mother, how much her example taught me about the tenderness that a bride should pour out on her bridegroom would be impossible for me. I listened eagerly to everything that I could learn, because I didn't want to do less for my beloved Jesus than Jeanne for Francis, who was no doubt quite a perfect creature, but who was, after all, a *creature!* . . .

I even had fun composing a letter of invitation in order to compare it to hers. Here's how it read:

Letter of invitation to the Wedding of Sister Thérèse of the Child Jesus of the Holy Face.

Almighty God, Creator of Heaven and earth, the Supreme Governor of the World, and the Very glorious Virgin Mary, Queen of the heavenly Court, request the honor of your presence at the Marriage of their August Son, Jesus, King of kings and Lord of lords, with Miss Thérèse Martin, now Lady and Princess of the kingdoms brought by dowry by her Divine Bridegroom, namely, the Childhood of Jesus and His Passion, her titles of nobility being: of the Child Jesus and of the Holy Face.

Mr. Louis Martin, Owner and Master of the Lordships of Suffering and Humiliation, and Mrs. Martin, Princess and Lady of Honor of the Heavenly Court, request the honor of your presence at the Marriage of their Daughter Thérèse, with Jesus, the Word of God [Jn. 1:1–3], second Person of the Adorable Trinity, who through the operation of the Holy Spirit was made Man and the Son of Mary, the Queen of Heaven.

Not having been able to invite you to the Nuptial blessing that was given them on the mountain of Carmel, the eighth of September, 1890 (only the heavenly court having been admitted), you are nonetheless requested to attend the Return from the Marriage Feast that will take place tomorrow, the Day of Eternity, on which day Jesus, Son of God, will come on the Clouds from Heaven in the brightness of His Majesty, to judge the Living and the Dead [Mt. 25:31–40].

The time being still uncertain, you are invited to remain ready and to watch [Mt. 24:42–44].

Now, dear Mother, what is left for me to tell you? Oh! I thought I had finished, but I haven't told you anything yet about my happiness at having known our Holy Mother Geneviève. . . . That was an inestimable grace. Well, God, who had already given me so many graces, wanted me to live with a *Saint*, not one I couldn't imitate, but a Saint who was made holy through hidden and ordinary virtues. . . .

More than once I received great consolations from her, especially one Sunday. Heading to meet with her as usual in order make my little visit, I found two Sisters beside Mother Geneviève. I looked at her, smiling, and I was getting ready to leave since there can't be three persons at the bedside of a person who is ill, but she, looking at me with an inspired look, said to me, "Wait, my little daughter, I'm only going to tell you one little word. Each time that you come, you ask me to give you a spiritual bouquet. Well, today I'm going to give you this one: Serve God with peace and with joy. Remember, my child, that our God is the God of peace" [1 Cor. 14:33]. After thanking her simply, I left, moved to tears and convinced that God had revealed to her the state of my soul. That day I had been extremely tested, almost sad, and was in a night of soul such that I no longer knew if I was loved by God. But the joy and the comfort that I felt, you can well imagine, dear Mother! . . .

The following Sunday, I wanted to know what revelation Mother Geneviève had had. She assured me that she had not received *any*. Then my admiration was still greater, seeing to what an eminent degree Jesus was living in her and was making her act and speak. Oh!

That *holiness* seemed to me the most *true,* the most *holy,* and that's what I desire, because in it there is no illusion. . . .

On the day of my Profession I was also quite comforted to learn from the mouth of Mother Geneviève that she had gone through the same ordeal as I before taking her own vows. . . . At the moment of our *great* sufferings, do you remember, dear Mother, the consolations that we found at her side? In short, the memory that Mother Geneviève left in my heart is a fragrant remembrance. . . .

The day she departed for heaven I felt that I was particularly touched. This was the first time that I was present at a death, and truly this was a delightful sight. . . . I was placed just at the foot of the bed of the dying Saint. I could see perfectly her slightest movements. It seemed to me during the two hours that I spent in that way that my soul ought to have felt full of fervor. On the contrary, a sort of insensitivity had taken hold of me, but at the *very moment* of the birth in heaven of our saintly Mother Geneviève, my inner disposition changed. In a twinkling of an eye I felt myself filled with an unutterable joy and fervor. It was as if Mother Geneviève had given me a part of the bliss that she enjoyed, because I'm quite persuaded that she went straight to heaven. . . . While she was living I told her one day, "Oh, Mother! You won't go to purgatory! . . ." *"I hope so,"* she replied gently. . . . Oh! Of course God couldn't betray a hope so full of humility. All the favors that we received are proof of that. . . .

Each Sister hurried to claim some relic. You know, dear Mother, the one that I have the happiness of possessing. . . . During Mother Geneviève's agony, I noticed a *tear* shimmering on her eyelid, like a diamond. That *tear, the last one of all those* that she shed, didn't fall. I saw it still *shining* in the choir without anyone thinking of collecting it. Then, taking a piece of fine linen, I dared to approach her that evening without being seen and take as a *relic the last tear* of a Saint. . . . Since then I have always carried it in the little sachet that holds my vows.

I don't attach any importance to my dreams, and besides, I rarely have any symbolic ones. And I even wonder how it is that, thinking all day long about God, I'm not more concerned with Him during my sleep. . . . Usually I dream about the woods, flowers, streams, and the sea, and almost always, I see pretty little children, and I catch butterflies and birds like ones I've never seen. You see, Mother, that if my dreams have a poetic appearance, they are far from being mystical. . . .

One night after Mother Geneviève's death, I had a dream that was more comforting. I dreamed that she was making her testament, giving to each Sister one thing that had belonged to her. When my turn came, I thought I wouldn't receive anything, because she had nothing left. But standing up, she said three times with a penetrating accent, "To you, I leave my *heart.*"

A month after our Holy Mother's departure, influenza was declared to be in the community. I was the only one left standing with two other Sisters. I'll never be able to tell all that I saw, what life and everything that passes seemed like to me. . . .

The day of my nineteenth birthday was celebrated by a death, followed soon by two others. At that time I was the only one in the sacristy. The head Sister for this duty being gravely ill, I was the one who had to prepare the burials, open the grilles of the choir at the time of Mass, etc. God had given me many graces of strength at that time. I wonder now how I was able to do without fear all that I did. Death was the rule everywhere. The sickest ones were cared for by those who could hardly walk. As soon as one Sister had given up her last breath, we were obliged to leave her alone.

One morning as I got up, I had the feeling that Sr. Magdalene had died. The dormitory was in darkness, and no one was leaving the cells. Finally I decided to enter into Sr. Magdalene's cell, the door of which was open, and I saw her in fact dead, dressed and lying on her mattress, and I wasn't the least bit afraid. Seeing that she had no candle, I went to get one for her as well as a crown of roses.

The night of the death of the Sub-Prioress, I was alone with the infirmary Sister. It's impossible to describe the sad state of the community at that time. Those who were on their feet are the only ones who have any idea of it, but in the midst of all that abandonment, I felt that God was watching over us. It was without effort that the dying ones passed to a better life. Immediately after their death an expression of joy and peace spread over their features—one would have described it as a sweet sleep. It truly was one, since after the face of this world has passed away [1 Cor. 7:31], they will awaken to enjoy forever the delights reserved for the elect. . . .

The whole time that the community was tested in this way, I was able to have the indescribable consolation of receiving Holy Communion *every day*. . . . Oh! How sweet that was! . . . Jesus spoiled me for a long time, longer than His faithful brides, because He permitted me to *receive Him* without the others having the happiness of receiving Him. I was also quite happy to touch the sacred vessels, to prepare the little *linens* that were used to touch Jesus. I felt that I needed to be quite fervent, and I often remembered this word that was addressed to a holy deacon: "[B]e pure, you who carry the articles of the LORD's house" [Isa. 52:11].

I can't say that I often received consolations during my prayers of thanksgiving. This is perhaps the time when I have the least number of them. . . . I find that quite natural, since I offered myself to Jesus, not as a person who desires to receive His visit for her own consolation, but on the contrary for the pleasure of the One who gives Himself to me. I conceive of my soul as an *empty* field, and I pray to the Blessed Virgin to take away the *debris* that could prevent it from being *empty*. Then I implore her to raise up herself a vast tent worthy of *heaven*, to decorate it *with her own* finery, and then I invite all the Saints and the Angels to come make a magnificent concert. It seems to me when Jesus comes down into my heart, that He is content to find Himself so well received there, and I am also happy. . . .

All that doesn't prevent distractions and sleepiness from coming to visit me, but when I leave the time of prayers of thanksgiving, seeing that I've done them so poorly, I make the resolution to spend all the rest of the day in thanksgiving. . . . You see, dear Mother, that I'm far from being led by the way of fear. I always know how to find the means to be happy and to profit from my wretchedness. . . . No doubt that isn't displeasing to Jesus, because He seems to encourage me on that road.

One day, contrary to my usual pattern, I was a little troubled when going to Communion. It seemed to me that God wasn't happy with me, and I told myself, "Oh! If today I receive only *one half of a host,* that's going to cause me pain. I'm going to believe that Jesus is coming regretfully into my heart." I approached. . . . Oh, happiness! For the first time in my life, I saw the priest take *two hosts* that were quite separated, and give them to me! . . . You understand my joy and the sweet tears that I shed when I saw such great mercy. . . .

The year after my profession, that is, two months before the death of Mother Geneviève, I received great graces during the retreat. Ordinarily, retreats that are preached are even more sorrowful for me than those that I do all alone, but that year it was otherwise. I had made a preparatory novena [nine days of prayer] with a great deal of fervor, in spite of the inner feeling that I had. That was because it seemed to me that the preacher wouldn't be able to understand me, since he was especially destined to do good to great sinners but not to religious souls. But since God wanted to show me that He alone was the director of my soul, He in fact used that priest, who was appreciated only by me. . . .

At that time I was having great inner trials of all kinds, going as far as wondering sometimes if there was a heaven. I felt myself disposed not to say anything about my inner dispositions, not knowing how to express them. Hardly had I entered into the confessional when I felt my soul expand. After saying a few words, I was understood in a marvelous way, as if *my thoughts were being read.* . . . My soul was like a book in which the priest was reading better than I was. . . . He launched me at full sail on the waves of *trust* and *love* that drew me so strongly but on which I didn't dare to advance. . . . He told me that *my faults did not grieve* God, and that *standing in His place* he was telling me that *as far as he was concerned*, God was very happy with me. . . .

Oh! How happy I was at hearing those comforting words! . . . Never had I heard it said that faults could not grieve God. That assurance flooded me with joy and let me endure patiently the exile of life. . . . I felt clearly in the depths of my heart that it was true, because God is more tender than a mother. Well, you, dear Mother, aren't you always ready to forgive the little indelicate actions that I do to you involuntarily? . . . How many times have I had that sweet experience! . . . No reproach would have touched me as much as one of your tender gestures. I'm of a nature such that fear causes me to draw back; with *love* not only do I go forward, but I *fly.* . . .

Oh, Mother! It was especially after the blessed day of your election [as prioress, in 1893] that I flew in the paths of love. . . . That day, Pauline became my living Jesus. . . . [Now *Mother* Agnes of Jesus,] she became, for the second time, "Mama! . . ."

For what will soon be three years I've had the happiness of contemplating *the marvelous things* that Jesus is operating by means of my beloved Mother. . . . I see that *suffering alone* can give birth to souls, and more than ever these sublime words of Jesus are unveiling their depth to me: "Very truly I tell you, unless a kernel of wheat falls to the ground and dies, it remains only a single seed. But if it dies, it produces many seeds" [Jn. 12:24].

What an abundant harvest you've gathered! . . . You've sown in tears, but soon you'll see the fruit of your work. You'll come back full of joy, bearing sheaves in your hands [Ps. 126:5-6]. . . . Oh, *Mother,* among those flowery sheaves, the *little white flower* is staying hidden, but in heaven she'll have a voice to sing of the *gentleness* and the *virtues* that she sees you practice every day in the shadow and the silence of the life of exile. . . .

Yes, for three years I've well understood mysteries that had been hidden for me until then. God showed me the same mercy that He showed to King Solomon [cf. 2 Chron. 1:7–11]. He didn't want me to have a single desire that wouldn't be fulfilled, not only my desires for perfection, but even those of which *I understood* the meaninglessness without having experienced it.

Having always regarded you, my dear Mother, as my *ideal*, I wanted to be like you in everything. When I saw you make beautiful paintings and delightful poems, I used to tell myself, "Oh! How happy I would be to be able to paint, to know how to express my thoughts in verse and also to do good to souls. . . ." I wouldn't have wanted to *ask for* those natural gifts, and my desires remained *hidden* in the depths of my *heart. Jesus,* who was also *hidden* in my poor little *heart,* was also pleased to show that all is meaningless and a chasing after wind under the sun [Eccl. 1:14]. . . .

To the great surprise of my Sisters, I was told to *paint,* and God allowed me to know how to take advantage of the lessons that my dear Mother gave me. . . . He also wanted me to be able to follow her example in writing poetry, composing poems that people found quite pretty. . . . Just as Solomon, *surveying all that his hands had done and what he had toiled to achieve, saw that everything was meaningless, a chasing after the wind* [Eccl. 2:11], in the same way I recognized through EXPERIENCE that happiness consists only in staying hidden, in remaining in ignorance of created things. I understood that without *love,* all works are only nothingness, even the most dazzling, such as raising the dead or converting entire peoples [1 Cor. 13:1–3]. . . .

Instead of doing me harm, leading me to meaninglessness, the gifts that God poured out on me (without my asking Him for them) led me to *Him.* I see that He alone is *unchanging,* that He alone can fulfill my immense desires. . . .

There are still other desires of another type that Jesus was pleased to fulfill, childish desires similar to those of the snow when I took the habit.

You know, dear Mother, how much I like flowers. By making myself a prisoner [a cloistered nun] at the age of fifteen, I renounced forever the happiness of running through fields decked with the treasures of springtime. Well! Never have I possessed more flowers than since my entrance into Carmel. . . . It is a custom for men who are engaged to be married, to often offer bouquets to their fiancées. Jesus didn't forget. He sent me in profusion sheaves of cornflowers, big daisies, poppies, etc., all the flowers that delight me the most. There was even a little flower called the corn-cockle, which I haven't found since our stay at Lisieux. I wanted to see it again, that flower of *my childhood* gathered by me in the fields of Alençon. It was at Carmel that these flowers came to smile at me and show me that in the smallest things as well as in the biggest ones, God gives a hundred times as much in this present age to souls who have left everything for love of Him [Mk. 10:29-30].

But the most intimate of my desires, the greatest of all, that I thought I would never see come true, was the entrance of my beloved Céline into the same Carmel as us. . . . That *dream* seemed to me to be highly unlikely— to live under the same roof, to share the joys and the sorrows of the companion of my childhood. So I had completely made my sacrifice: I had entrusted to Jesus the future of my dear sister, being resolved to see her leave for the ends of the earth if necessary. The only thing that I couldn't accept was for her not to be the bride of Jesus, because, since she loved Him as much as I did, it was impossible for me to see her give her heart to a mortal. I'd already suffered by knowing that she'd been exposed in the world to dangers that I hadn't known. I can say that my affection for Céline was, since my entrance into Carmel, as much a motherly love as a sisterly one. . . .

One day when she was to go out to an evening affair, that gave me so much pain that I begged God to *prevent* her from *dancing* and even (contrary to my custom), I shed a torrent of tears. Jesus deigned to grant my request: He didn't allow His little bride *to be able to dance* that night (although she wasn't embarrassed to do so graciously when it was necessary). Though she'd been invited without being able to refuse, her escort found himself totally unable to get her to *dance;* to his great confusion, he was condemned to simply *walk* in order to take her back to her place. Then he slipped away and didn't reappear all evening. This adventure, unique in its kind, made me grow in trust and in love for the One who, having placed *His sign* on my forehead, had at the same time stamped it on the forehead of my beloved Céline. . . .

On the twenty-ninth of July last year, God, breaking the bonds of His incomparable servant, [Papa,] and calling him to his eternal reward, at the same time broke the bonds that held His beloved bride [Céline] to the world. She had fulfilled her first mission: Charged with *representing all of us* at the side of our father, who was so tenderly loved, she had accomplished that mission like an angel. . . . And angels don't stay on earth. When they've accomplished God's will, they immediately return to Him—that's why they have wings. . . .

Our angel as well shook her white wings. She was ready to fly *very far* in order to find Jesus, but Jesus made her fly *very near.* . . . She was content with accepting the great sacrifice that was very *sorrowful* for little Thérèse. . . . For *two years* her Céline had hidden

a secret from her. . . . Oh! How she also had suffered!
. . . Finally, from up above in heaven, my dear king,
who on earth never liked to go slow, hurried to arrange
the quite entangled affaires of his Céline, and the fourteenth of September [the Feast Day of the Exaltation of
the Holy Cross], she joined us! . . .

One day when the difficulties seemed insurmountable,
I told Jesus during my prayers of thanksgiving: "You
know, my God, how much I desire to know if Papa went
straight to heaven. I'm not asking You to speak to me,
but give me a sign. If Sr. Aimée of Jesus consents to
Céline's entrance or sets no obstacle to it, that will be
the answer that Papa went *straight to You.*" That Sister,
as you know, dear Mother, found that three of us [in the
same convent] were too many, and consequently didn't
want to admit one more, but God, who holds in His
hand the hearts of creatures and channels it as He wishes
[Prov. 21:1], changed the attitude of that Sister. The first
person that I met after my time of thanksgiving prayers
was she, who called me with a kind attitude, told me to
go up to see you, and spoke to me about *Céline* with
tears in her eyes. . . .

Oh! How many subjects I have to thank Jesus for,
Jesus who knew how to fulfill all my desires! . . .

Now I no longer have any desire, unless it's to *love*
Jesus passionately. . . . My childish desires have all
flown away. Undoubtedly, I still love to decorate with
flowers the altar of the Little Jesus, but since He gave
me the *Flower* that I desired, my *beloved Céline,* I no
longer desire any other. It's she that I am offering as my
most delightful bouquet. . . .

I don't desire suffering or death, either, and yet I love both of them. But it is *love* alone that draws me. . . . For a long time I desired them both. I possessed suffering, and I thought I was touching the shores of heaven. I thought that the little flower would be gathered in its springtime. . . . Now it's abandonment alone that guides me—I have no other compass! . . .

I can ask for nothing fervently any more except the perfect accomplishment of God's will in my soul [Mt. 6:10], without created things being able to place any obstacle in its path. I can say these words from the spiritual canticle of our father St. John of the Cross: "In the interior cell of my Beloved, I drank, and when I went out, in all that plain I no longer was familiar with anything, and I lost the flock that I had previously been following. . . . My soul was fully engaged with all its resources at its service. I no longer keep watch over a flock, I no longer have any other office, because now my entire practice is *to Love!* . . ." Or another passage: "Since I have experienced it, love is so powerful in works that it knows how *to profit from everything,* from the good and from the *bad* that it finds in me, and to transform my soul into LOVE ITSELF."

Oh, beloved Mother! How sweet is the path of *love.* No doubt, one can fall down, one can commit unfaithful acts, but love, knowing how *to profit from everything,* quickly consumes *everything* that can be displeasing to Jesus, leaving only a humble and profound peace in the depths of the heart. . . .

Oh! How much enlightenment I have plumbed in the works of our father St. John of the Cross! . . . At the age of seventeen and eighteen I had no other spiritual nourishment, but later all books left me in dryness, and I'm still in that state. If I open a book written by a spiritual author (even the most beautiful, the most touching), right away I feel my heart constrict, and I read, so to speak, without understanding, or if I understand, my mind stops without being able to meditate. . . . In that state of impotence, *Holy Scripture* and the *Imitation of Christ* come to my aid. In them I find nourishment that is solid and completely *pure*. But above all it is the *Gospels* that keep me fed during my times of prayer. In them I find everything that is necessary to my poor little soul. In them I always discover new illuminations, hidden and mysterious meanings. . . .

I understand and I know by experience that "the kingdom of God is in our midst" [Lk. 17:21]. Jesus has no need of books or teachers to instruct souls. As the Teacher of teachers, He teaches without the noise of words. . . . I have never heard Him speak, but I feel that He is with me. At every moment, He guides me and inspires in me what I ought to say or do. I discover, just at the moment when I need them, understandings that I hadn't yet seen. Most often it's not during my times of prayer that they're the most abundant, but rather in the midst of the occupations of my day. . . .

Oh, beloved Mother! After so many graces can I not sing with the psalmist, "For the LORD is good and his love endures forever" [Ps. 100:5]? It seems to me that if all creatures had the same graces as I, God would be feared by no one, but loved passionately, and that out of *love* and not out of trembling [in fear], no soul would ever consent to cause Him grief. . . .

I understand, however, that all souls can't look alike. There have to be some from different families in order to especially honor each of God's perfections. To me He's given His *infinite Mercy,* and it's *through it* that I contemplate and adore the other Divine perfections! . . . Then all of them appear to me radiant with love. Righteousness and Justice themselves (and perhaps even more than any other perfections) seem to me to be *clothed in love.* . . .

What sweet joy it is to think that God is *just*—that is, that He takes into account our weakness, He knows perfectly the fragility of our nature. What should I be afraid of? Oh! The infinitely just God who deigned to forgive with such kindness all the faults of the prodigal son [Lk. 15:21–24], should He not also be just toward me who am "always with him" [cf. Lk. 15:31]? . . .

This year on the ninth of June, the feast day of the Holy Trinity, I received the grace to understand more than ever how much Jesus desires to be loved.

I was thinking about the souls who offer themselves as victims to God's Justice in order to turn it aside and draw to themselves the chastisements reserved to the guilty. That offering seemed great and generous to me, but I was far from feeling myself brought to the point of doing it. "Oh, my God!" I cried in the depths of my heart, "will it only be Your Justice that will receive souls that offer themselves as sacrificial victims? . . . Doesn't Your Merciful *Love* need them as well? . . . Everywhere it is misunderstood, rejected. The hearts

into which You desire to pour it are turned toward
created things, asking them for happiness with their
wretched affection, instead of throwing themselves into
Your arms and accepting Your infinite *Love*. . . .

Oh, my God! Meeting with such contempt, is Your
Love going to remain in Your Heart? It seems to me that
if You found souls that were offering themselves as
sacrificial victims to Your Love, You would consume
them rapidly. It seems to me that You would be happy
not to dam up the waves of infinite tenderness that are
within You. . . . If Your Justice, which extends only over
the earth, likes to vent itself, how much more does Your
Merciful Love desire to *set souls on fire*, since your
Mercy rises all the way to heaven [Ps. 36:5]. . . . Oh, my
Jesus! Let *me* be that happy victim; consume your
sacrifice through the fire of Your Divine Love! . . .

Beloved Mother, you who have allowed me to offer
myself in this way to God, you know the rivers or
rather the oceans of graces that have come to flood
my soul. . . . Oh! Since that happy day, it seems to me
that *Love* penetrates and surrounds me. It seems to
me that at every moment that *Merciful Love* is renew-
ing me, purifying my soul, and leaving there no trace
of sin, so I cannot fear purgatory. . . . I know that in
myself I wouldn't be worthy even to enter that place
of expiation, since only holy souls can have access to
it, but I also know that the Fire of Love is more sanc-
tifying than that of purgatory. I know that Jesus can't
desire useless sufferings for us, and that He wouldn't
inspire in me the desires that I feel if He didn't want
to fulfill them. . . .

Oh! How sweet is the path of Love! . . . How I want to apply myself to always doing, with the greatest abandonment, the will of God! [Mt. 6:10] . . .

There, beloved Mother, is all that I can tell you about the life of your little Thérèse. You know much better yourself what she is and what Jesus has done for her. So you will forgive me for having greatly abridged the story of her religious life. . . .

How will it end, this "story of a little white flower"? . . . Perhaps the little flower will be picked in its freshness or perhaps transplanted onto other shores. . . . I don't know, but what I am certain of is that God's Goodness and Love will always follow it [Ps. 23:6], and that she will never stop blessing the beloved Mother who gave her to Jesus. Forever she will rejoice at being one of the flowers in her crown. . . . Forever she will sing with that beloved Mother the ever-new hymn of Love [Rev. 14:3]. . . .

CHAPTER 9

My Vocation, Love
1896

The secrets of Jesus
The venerable Mother Anne of Jesus
All vocations
Throwing flowers
The little bird
The divine Eagle
End of Manuscript B

Letter to Sister Marie of the Sacred Heart
[Thérèse's eldest sister, Marie]

Jesus +

Beloved sister, you're asking me to give you a memoir of my retreat, a retreat that will perhaps be the last one. . . . Since our Mother [Marie de Gonzague, who has been re-elected prioress] is allowing it, it is a joy for me to come and speak with you, who are twice my sister, with you who lent me your voice, promising in my name [when you served as my sponsor at my baptism] that I wanted to serve only Jesus, when it was not possible for me to speak. . . .

Dear Godmother, it is the child whom you offered to the Lord who is going to talk to you this evening. She it is, who loves you as a child knows how to love its mother. . . . Only in heaven will you know all the gratitude that overflows from my heart. . . . Oh, beloved sister! You would like to hear the secrets that Jesus is confiding to "your little girl." I know that He confides in you these secrets, for it is you who taught me to gather the Divine teachings. However, I am going to try to stammer out a few words, although I feel that it is impossible for the human voice to repeat things that the human heart can scarcely feel [1 Cor. 2:9]. . . .

Do not think that I am swimming in consolations. Oh, no! My consolation is in not having any consolations on earth. Without showing Himself, without making His voice heard, Jesus instructs me in secret. It is not by means of books, because I do not understand what I read, but sometimes a word like this one that I pulled out at the end of the prayer time (after remaining in silence and dryness) comes to comfort me: "Here is the teacher that I am giving you, He will teach you everything that you must do. I want to make you read in the book of life, in which is contained the knowledge of Love." The knowledge of Love, oh, yes! That word resounds sweetly in the ear of my soul. I desire only that knowledge; having given all my riches in exchange for it, I consider, as did the bride in the Song of Songs, that I have given nothing [Song 8:7]. . . .

I understand so well that only love can make us pleasing to God, and that love is the only good thing that I covet. Jesus is pleased to show me the only way that leads to that Divine furnace, and that way is the *abandonment* of the little child who falls asleep without fear in the arms of its Father. . . . "Let all who are *simple* come to my house," said the Holy Spirit through the mouth of Solomon [Prov. 9:4], and that same Spirit of Love said again that "to [one] that is little, mercy is granted" [Wis. 6:7 D-R]. In its name, the prophet Isaiah reveals to us that at the last day the Lord will tend "his flock like a shepherd: He gathers the lambs in his arms and carries them close to his heart" [Is. 40:11]. And as if all these promises were not enough, the same prophet, whose inspired glance already plumbed into the eternal depths, cried out in the name of the Lord, ". . . you will nurse and be carried on her arm and dandled on her knees. As a mother comforts her child, so will I comfort you" [Isa. 66:12-13]. Oh, beloved Godmother! After such language, all we can do is keep silence and weep out of gratitude and love. . . .

Oh! If all weak and imperfect souls felt what the smallest of all souls feels, the soul of your little Thérèse, not a single one would despair of arriving at the top of the mountain of love, since Jesus does not ask for great actions, but only for abandonment and gratefulness. For He said, in Psalm 50[:9–13], "I have no need of a bull from your stall or of goats from your pens, for every animal of the forest is mine, and the cattle on a thousand hills. I know every bird in the mountains. . . . If I were hungry I would not tell you, for the world is mine, and all that is in it. Do I eat the flesh of bulls or drink the blood of goats?" . . .

"Offer to God a sacrifice of praise and thanksgiving" [cf. Ps. 50:14, Heb. 13:15]. This, then, is what Jesus requires of us. He has no need of our works, but only of our love, for this same God who declares that He has no need to tell us if He is hungry, was not afraid to *beg* for a little water from the Samaritan woman. He was thirsty. . . . But in saying, "Will you give me a drink"? [Jn. 4:7], it was the *love* of His poor creature that the Creator of the universe was asking for. He was thirsty for love. . . . Oh! I feel more than ever that Jesus is *thirsty*. He meets only ungrateful and indifferent people among the disciples of the world, and among His *own disciples,* He finds, alas! few hearts that give themselves to Him without reserve, who understand all the tenderness of His infinite Love.

Dear sister, how happy we are to understand the intimate secrets of our Bridegroom. Oh! If you wanted to write down all that you know about them, we would have beautiful pages to read, but I know, you prefer to keep in the depths of your heart "the secret of a King." To me you say, "how honorable to reveal and confess the works of God" [Tob. 12:7 D-R]. I find that you are right to keep silence, and it is only in order to please you that I write these lines, because I feel my powerlessness to use earthly words to tell about the secrets of heaven. And then, after having written pages and pages, I would find that I had not yet begun. . . . There are so many different horizons and so many infinitely varied nuances, that the palette of the Heavenly Painter alone, after the night of this life, will be able to furnish me with the colors that are capable of painting the marvels that He is disclosing to the eye of my soul.

My dear sister, you have asked me to write to you about my dream and "my little doctrine," as you call it. . . . I have done so in the following pages, but so poorly that it seems impossible to me for you to understand. Perhaps you are going to find my expressions to be exaggerated. Oh! Forgive me, that must come from my not-too-pleasant style. I assure you that there is no exaggeration in my *little soul,* and that there, all is calm and at rest.

(In writing, it is to Jesus that I speak. That makes it easier to express my thoughts. Which, alas! does not stop them from being poorly expressed!)

September 8th, 1896
[The celebration of the Nativity of the Blessed Virgin Mary, and the sixth anniversary of my Profession]

(To my dear Sister Marie of the Sacred Heart.)

Oh, Jesus, my Beloved! Who will be able to say with what tenderness, what sweetness, You are leading *my little soul?* How much it pleases You to make shine upon it the ray of Your grace even in the midst of the darkest storm? . . .

Jesus, the storm was roaring quite strongly in my soul after the beautiful celebration of Your triumph, the radiant feast day of Easter, when one Saturday in May, thinking about the mysterious dreams that are some-times granted to certain souls, I was telling myself that this ought to be the sweetest comfort, but I was not asking for it. That night, considering the clouds that were darkening its sky, my *little soul* was saying again that beautiful dreams were not for it, and under that storm it went to sleep. . . . The next day was the tenth of May, the second Sunday of Mary's month, perhaps the anniversary of the day when the Blessed Virgin deigned to *smile at* her little flower. . . .

At the first light of day, I found myself (in a dream) in a sort of gallery. There were several other persons, but far away. Only our Mother was at my side, when suddenly, without my having seen how they had entered, I caught sight of three Carmelite nuns dressed in their mantles and large veils. It seemed to me that they were coming for our Mother, but what I understood clearly is that they were coming from heaven. From the depths of my heart, I cried out, "Oh! How happy I would be to see the face of one of these Carmelites."

Then, as if my prayer had been heard by her, the tallest of these holy ones advanced toward me. Immediately I fell to my knees. Oh! What happiness! The Carmelite lifted her veil, or rather, raised it and covered me with it. . . . Without any hesitation I recognized the venerable Mother Anne of Jesus, foundress of the Carmelite order in France. Her face was beautiful, of an immaterial beauty. No ray of light was escaping it, and yet, in spite of the veil that was enveloping both of us, I saw that heavenly visage illuminated with an indescribably sweet light, a light that it was not receiving but that it was producing by itself. . . .

I would not know how to tell you the gladness that I felt in my soul. These things are felt and cannot be expressed. . . . Several months have passed since that sweet dream, yet the memory that it has left on my soul has lost nothing of its freshness, its heavenly charms. . . . I can still see the look and the smile *full of love* of the Venerable Mother. I think I can still feel the tender touches with which she flooded me. . . .

Seeing myself loved so tenderly, I dared to pronounce these words: "Oh, Mother! I implore you, tell me if God will leave me for a long time on earth? . . . Will He come soon to get me?" Smiling tenderly, the Saint murmured, "Yes, soon, soon. . . . I promise you." "Mother," I added, "tell me another thing, whether God is not asking me for something more than my poor little actions and my desires. Is He happy with me?" The Saint's face took on an expression that was *incomparably more tender* than the first time that she spoke to me. Her look and her caresses were the sweetest of replies. However, she told me, "God is not asking anything else from you, He is happy, very happy!" After she caressed me with more love than the most tender of mothers has ever done to her child, I saw her go away. . . . My heart was filled with joy, but I remembered my Sisters, and I wanted to ask for some graces for them, but alas! . . . I woke up!

Oh, Jesus! Now the storm was not roaring, the sky was calm and serene. . . . *I believed, I felt* that there is a heaven, and that heaven is peopled with souls who cherish me, who regard me as their child. . . . That impression remains in my heart, so much the better since, up till then, I had always been *absolutely indifferent* toward the Venerable Mother Anne of Jesus. I had never invoked her, and the thought of her never came to my mind except when I heard people talk about her, which was rare. So when I understood to what point *she loved me*, how little she was *indifferent* toward *me*, my heart melted in love and gratitude, not only for the Saint who had visited me, but also for all the Blessed ones who dwell in heaven. . . .

Oh, my Beloved! This grace was only the prelude to greater graces that You wanted to shower on me. Let me, my only Love, remind You of them today. . . . Today, the sixth anniversary of *our union*. . . . Oh! Forgive me, Jesus, if I am talking nonsense by wanting to tell about my desires and my hopes that touch on the infinite. Forgive me and heal my soul by giving it what it hopes for!!! . . .

To be Your *Bride,* Jesus, to be a *Carmelite,* to be, through my union with You, the *mother* of souls, ought to be enough for me. . . . That is not the case. . . . No doubt, those three privileges are my vocation— Carmelite, Bride, and Mother—but I feel within myself other vocations. I feel the vocation of Warrior, Priest, Apostle, Teacher, Martyr. In short, I feel the need and the desire to accomplish for You, Jesus, all the most heroic works. . . . I feel in my soul the courage of a Crusader, of a soldier in the papal army; I would like to die on a field of battle for the defense of the Church. . . .

I feel within me the vocation of *Priest.* With what love, Jesus, would I bear You in my hands when, at the sound of my voice, You would come down from heaven. . . . With what love would I give You to souls! . . . But alas! While desiring to be a Priest, I admire and I envy the humility of St. Francis of Assisi, and I feel in myself the vocation of being like him in refusing the sublime dignity of the priesthood.

Oh, Jesus! My love, my life. . . . How do I harmonize these contrasts? How can I realize the desires of my poor *little soul?* . . .

Oh! In spite of my littleness, I would like to shed light on souls like the Prophets, the Doctors. I have the vocation to be an Apostle. . . . I would like to travel across the world, preach Your name, and plant Your glorious Cross on the soil of unbelievers. But, my *Beloved,* a single mission wouldn't be enough for me. I would at the same time like to preach the gospel in the five parts of the world and as far as the remotest islands [Isa. 66:19]. . . . I would like to be a missionary, not only for a few years, but I would like to have been one since the creation of the world and be one until the end of the ages. . . . But above all, my Beloved Savior, I would like to shed my blood for You until the last drop. . . .

Martyrdom: That is the dream of my youth. That dream has grown within me under the cloisters of Carmel. . . . But there again I feel that my dream is foolishness, because I would not know how to limit myself to *one* type of martyrdom. . . . To satisfy me I would have to have *all of them.* . . .

Like You, my Beloved Bridegroom, I would like to be scourged and crucified. . . . I would like to die by being skinned alive like St. Bartholomew. . . . Like St. John, I would like to be plunged into boiling oil. I would like to undergo all the tortures inflicted on the Martyrs. . . . With St. Agnes and St. Cecilia, I would like to present my neck to the sword, and like Joan of Arc, my dear sister, I would like to be burned at the stake, murmuring your name, *Jesus.* . . .

When I think about all the torments that will be the lot of Christians at the time of the Antichrist, I feel my heart leap, and I would like for those torments to be reserved for me. . . . Jesus, Jesus, if I wanted to write down all my desires, I would have to borrow *Your book of life* [Rev. 20:12]. In it are the records of the actions of all the Saints, and those actions, I would like to have accomplished them for You. . . .

Oh, my Jesus! To all my foolishness, what are You going to reply? . . . Is there a soul that is *smaller* and more powerless than mine! . . . However, even because of my weakness, You were pleased, Lord, to fulfill my *little childish desires,* and You now want to fulfill other *desires that are bigger* than the universe. . . .

At prayer time my desires were making me suffer a true martyrdom, so I opened the letters of St. Paul in order to look for some sort of answer. Chapters 12 and 13 of the first letter to the Corinthians fell under my eyes. . . . I read in the first of those chapters, that *everyone cannot* be apostles, prophets, teachers, etc.; that the Church is composed of different members, and that the eye cannot at *the same time* be a hand [1 Cor. 12:29, 21]. . . . The answer was clear, but it did not fulfill my desires. It did not give me peace. . . .

Just as Mary Magdalene, who kept bending toward the empty tomb, ended up finding what she was looking for [Jn. 20:11–18], in the same way, abasing myself even as far as the depths of my nothingness, I raised myself so high that I was able to reach my goal. . . . Without becoming discouraged, I continued my reading, and this sentence gave me relief: "Now eagerly desire the greater gifts. And yet I will show you the most excellent way" [1 Cor. 12:31]. And the Apostle explains how the most *perfect gifts* are nothing without Love . . . and that Charity is the *excellent way* that leads surely to God. Finally I had found rest. . . .

Considering the mystical body of the Church, I had not recognized myself in any of the members described by St. Paul, or rather, I wanted to recognize myself in *all of them.* . . . Charity gave me the key to my *vocation.* I understood that if the Church had a body composed of different members [1 Cor. 12:12], it was not missing the most necessary, the most noble of all: I understood that the Church had a heart, and that this heart was *burning with Love.* I understood that Love alone can cause the members of the Church to act. If Love were to be extinguished, the Apostles would no longer preach the gospel, the Martyrs would refuse to shed their blood. . . . I understood that *Love* contains all the Vocations, that Love is all, that it embraces all times and all places . . . in a word, that it is Everlasting!

Then in the excess of my delirious joy, I cried out, "Oh, Jesus, my Love . . . I have finally found my vocation: My vocation is Love! . . .

Yes, I have found my place in the Church, and that place, my God, You have given me. . . . In the Heart of the Church, my Mother, I will be *Love* . . . That way I will be everything . . . that way my dream will become a reality!!!

Why do I speak about a delirious joy? No, that expression is not accurate. It is rather the calm and serene peace of the navigator when he sees the beacon light that will lead him into port. . . . Oh, luminous Beacon Light of love, I know how to reach You, I have found the secret of appropriating Your flame to myself.

I am only a child, powerless and weak, but it is my very weakness that gives me the boldness to offer myself as a victim to Your Love, Jesus! In ancient times only pure and spotless hosts were accepted by the God of Power and Might. To satisfy Divine *Justice,* perfect victims were required [cf. Lev. 22:18–25]. But the law of fear was succeeded by the law of Love, and Love chose me to be a sacrifice, weak and imperfect creature that I am. . . . Is that choice not worthy of Love? . . . Yes, for Love to be fully satisfied, it is necessary for it to be abased, to be abased to nothingness, and for it to transform that nothingness into *fire.* . . .

Oh, Jesus, I know, love is repaid only by love, so I sought, I found, the means to relieve my heart by rendering to You, Love for Love. "[U]se worldly wealth to gain friends for yourselves, so that when it is gone, you will be welcomed into eternal dwellings" [Lk. 16:9]. That, Lord, is the advice that You gave to Your disciples after telling them that "the people of this world are more shrewd in dealing with their own kind than are the people of the light" [Lk. 16:8]. As a child of the light, I understood that my *desires to be all things,* to embrace every vocation, were riches that could well make me unrighteous, so I used them to make friends. . . .

Remembering the prayer of Elisha to his father Elijah when he dared to ask for a *double portion of his spirit* [2 Kings 2:9], I presented myself before the Angels and the Saints, and I told them, "I am the littlest of creatures, I know my wretchedness and my weakness, but I also know how much noble and generous hearts love to do good. I beg you, then, you Blessed inhabitants of heaven, I beg you to *adopt me as your child. To you alone will be the glory* that you will cause me to acquire, but deign to grant my prayer. It is foolhardy, I know, but nonetheless I dare to ask you to obtain this for me: *a double portion of your Love.*"

Jesus, I cannot make my request any deeper. I would be afraid to find myself crushed under the weight of my impudent desires. . . . My excuse is that I am only *a child.* Children do not think of the impact of their words, but their parents, when they are placed on the throne, though they possess immense treasures, do not hesitate to content the desires of the *little beings* that they cherish as much as themselves. To give them pleasure, they even do foolish things, they go as far as *weakness.* . . .

Well! I am THE CHILD of *the Church,* and the Church is Queen since she is Your Bride, O Divine King of kings. . . . It is not riches and Glory (even the Glory of Heaven) that the heart of the little child clamors after. . . . The child understands that glory belongs by right to her brothers and sisters, the Angels, and the Saints. . . . The child's own glory will be the reflection of the one that springs from the brow of her mother. What she asks for is Love. . . . She knows only one thing, and that is to love You, Jesus. . . .

Dazzling works are forbidden to her; she cannot preach the gospel or shed her blood. . . . But what does it matter? Her brothers and sisters are working in place of her, and she, the *little child,* remains very close to the *throne* of the King and the Queen, and she loves in the place of her brothers and sisters who are going into combat. . . . But how will she bear witness to her Love, since Love is proved by works? Well, the little child will throw out *flowers,* she will use her *perfumes* to give a lovely fragrance to the royal throne, she will sing with her silvery voice the hymn of Love. . . .

Yes, my Beloved, that is how my life will be consumed. . . . I have no other means of proving my love for You than to throw flowers, that is, not to pass up any little sacrifice, any look, any word, to take advantage of all the little things and to do them out of love. . . . I want to suffer out of love and even rejoice out of love, so I will throw flowers before Your throne. I will not encounter a single one without *plucking off its leaves* for You [leaving only the pure beauty of the flower]. . . . Then, as I throw my flowers, I will sing (could a person weep while doing so joyful an action?). I will sing, even when I will have to gather my flowers among thorns, and my song will be all the more melodious as the thorns are long and piercing.

Jesus, what purpose will my flowers and my songs serve You? . . . Oh! I know well that this sweet-scented rain, these fragile petals that have no value, these songs of love of the littlest of hearts—these will charm You. Yes, these little nothings will give You pleasure. They will make the Triumphant Church [the Blessed ones in Heaven] smile. That Church will gather up my flowers whose leaves have been plucked off *by Love,* and causing them to pass through Your Divine Hands, Jesus, that Church of Heaven, wanting to play with its little child, will also throw *these flowers* that through Your divine touch have acquired an infinite value—that Church will throw them on the Suffering Church [the souls in purgatory] in order to put out its flames. It will throw them on the Church in Combat [Church Militant: the Christians still on earth] in order to make it win the victory! . . .

Oh, my Jesus! I love You, I love the Church, my Mother. I often remember that "The tiniest movement of *pure love* is more useful to it than all other works taken together." But is *pure love* at home in my heart? . . . Are not my immense desires just a foolish dream? Oh! If this is so, Jesus, let me know it: You know that I am seeking the truth. . . . If my desires are foolhardy, make them disappear, because these desires are for me the greatest of martyrdoms. . . . However, I know, Jesus, after aspiring toward the highest regions of Love, if it befalls to me not to attain them one day, I will have tasted more *sweetness in my martyrdom, in my folly,* than I will taste in the midst of the *joys of heaven,* unless by some miracle You take away the memory of my earthly hopes. So let me, during my exile, enjoy the delights of Love. Let me delight in the sweet bitterness of my martyrdom. . . .

Jesus, Jesus, if the *desire to love You* is delicious, what is it then to possess, to enjoy the fruits of Love? . . . How can a soul as imperfect as mine aspire to possess the fullness of Love? . . .

Jesus! My *first, my only Friend,* You whom ALONE *I love,* tell me, what is this mystery? Why do You not reserve these immense aspirations to great souls, to the eagles that soar in the heights? . . . I consider myself as a weak little bird covered only with a light down. I am not an eagle, I simply have an eagle's *eyes* and *heart.* For, despite my extreme smallness, I dare to fix my eyes on the Divine Sun, the Sun of Love, and my heart feels in itself all the aspirations of the eagle. . . . The little bird would like to fly toward that brilliant Sun that charms its eyes. It would like to copy the eagles, its brothers, which it sees rising up to the Divine home of the Holy Trinity. . . . Alas! All that it can do is to *lift its little* wings. But to fly away, that is not in its *little* power! What is going to become of it? Die of disappointment when it sees how powerless it is? . . .

Oh, no! The little bird is not even going to be bothered by that. With daring abandon, it wants to stay fixed on its Divine Sun. Nothing could frighten it, neither wind nor rain, and if dark clouds come to hide the Star of Love, the little bird will not change its place. It knows that above the clouds its Sun is always shining, that its brilliance will not be able to be eclipsed for one single second.

Sometimes, it is true, the little bird's heart finds itself assailed by the storm. It seems to it that it cannot believe that anything else exists than the clouds that are enveloping it. This, then, is the moment of perfect joy for the weak little being. What happiness for it to *stay there* anyway, to remain fixed on the invisible light that reveals itself to its faith!!! . . .

Jesus, up till now I understand Your love for the little bird, because it does not go far from You. . . . But I know, and You know, too, often the imperfect little creature, while remaining in its place (that is, under the rays of the Sun), lets itself become a little distracted from its only duty [Lk. 10:41–42]. It takes a little seed from the right or the left, runs after a little worm. . . . Then, encountering a little puddle, it gets its feathers *wet,* feathers that have scarcely been formed. It sees a little flower that pleases it, so its little mind becomes busy with that flower. . . . Finally, not being able to soar like the eagles, the poor little bird becomes busy again with the worthless baubles of the earth.

However, after all its misadventures, instead of going to hide in a corner to weep over its misery and die out of repentance, the little bird turns toward its beloved Sun. It presents to Its kindhearted rays its little *wet* wings. It moans like a mourning dove [Isa. 38:14], and in its sweet song it confides, it tells in detail its unfaithfulness, thinking in its daring abandonment that in this way it will acquire more of a hold, attract more fully the love of the One who came not to call the righteous but sinners [Mt. 9:13]. . . . If the Adorable Star remains deaf to the plaintive chirpings of His little creature, if He remains veiled . . . Well! The little creature stays *wet,* it accepts to be chilled to the bone with cold, and it continues to rejoice at this suffering that, after all, it deserved. . . .

Jesus! How happy Your *little bird* is to be *weak and small.* What would happen to it if it were big and great? . . . Never would it dare to appear in Your presence, to *fall asleep* in Your sight. . . . Yes, there again is a weakness of the little bird, when it wants to fix its eyes on the Divine Sun and the clouds prevent it from seeing a single ray. In spite of itself, its little eyes close, its little head hides under its little wing, and the poor little being goes to sleep, thinking that it is still fixing its gaze on its Beloved Star.

When it wakes up, it does not become depressed. It begins its office of *love* once again. It invokes the

Angels and the Saints, who rise like eagles toward the consuming Home, the object of its desire. And the eagles, taking pity on their little sister, protect it, defend it, and put to flight the vultures who would like to devour it. The vultures, images of the demons—the little bird does not fear them. It is not destined to become their *prey,* but that of *the Eagle* that it contemplates at the center of the Sun of Love.

O Divine Word [Jn. 1:1–3], You are the adored Eagle whom I love and who *draws me.* You are the One who, launching out to this world of exile, were willing to suffer and die in order to *draw* souls to the midst of the Eternal Home of the Blessed Trinity. It is You, going back up toward the unapproachable Light that will henceforth be Your dwelling place [1 Tim. 6:16], it is You still remaining in the valley of tears, hidden under the appearance of a white host. . . . Everlasting Eagle, You want to feed me with Your divine Substance, I, poor little being, who would return back into nothingness if Your divine gaze were not giving me life at each moment. . . .

Oh, Jesus! Leave me in the excess of my gratitude; let me tell You that Your love goes so far as foolishness. . . . Faced with this Foolishness, how do You want my heart not to launch out toward You? How could my trust know any limits? . . . Ah! For You, I know, the Saints also did *foolish things,* and they did great things since they were *eagles.* . . .

Jesus, I am too little to do great things. . . . My own *foolishness* is to hope that Your Love might accept me as a sacrificial victim. . . . My foolishness consists in begging my brothers the eagles to obtain for me the favor of flying toward the Sun of Love with the very wings of the Divine Eagle [Deut. 32:10-11]. . . .

As long as You wish, my Beloved, Your little bird will remain without strength and without wings. Always it will remain with its eyes fixed on You. It wants to be *fascinated* by Your divine glance. It wants to become the *prey* of Your Love. . . . I have the hope that one day, my Adored Eagle, You will come to get Your little bird, and going back up with it to the Home of Love, You will plunge it for eternity into the burning Abyss of that Love to which it has offered itself as a victim.

Jesus! If only I could tell all the *little souls* how inde-scribable is Your condescendence. . . . I feel that if by some impossibility, You were to find a weaker, smaller soul than mine, You would be pleased to pour out on it even greater favors if it abandoned itself with com-plete trust in Your infinite mercy [Lk. 10:21]. But why desire to communicate Your secrets of Love, Jesus? Is it not You alone who taught them to me, and can You not reveal them to others? . . . Yes, I know You can, and I entreat You to do this, I beg You to lower Your divine gaze on a great number of *little souls*. . . . I beg You to chose a legion of *little* victims who are worthy of Your LOVE! . . .

The very little Sister Thérèse of the Child Jesus of the Holy Face, Carmelite Nun

CHAPTER 10

The Test of Faith
1896–1897

Thérèse and her prioress
The divine elevator
First hemoptysis [coughing of blood]
The table of sinners
The call of missions
What charity is

Manuscript addressed to Sr. Marie de Gonzague [my current prioress]

June, 1897

Beloved Mother, you've shown me the desire that I'm fulfilling with you to sing the mercies of the Lord [Ps. 89:1]. I had begun that sweet song with your dear daughter Agnes of Jesus [my sister Pauline], who was the mother charged by God to guide me during the days of my childhood. So it was with her that I was to sing of the graces granted to the little flower of the Blessed Virgin, when she was in the springtime of her life.

But it's with you that I must sing of the happiness of that tiny little flower now that the timid rays of early morning have given way to the burning rays of midday. Yes, it's with you, beloved Mother; it's to respond to your desire that I'm going to repeat the feelings of my soul, my gratitude toward God, toward you who represent Him to me visibly. Wasn't it between your motherly hands that I gave myself entirely over to Him? Oh, Mother, do you remember that day [when I took my vows as a nun and you were prioress]? . . . Yes, I feel that your heart wouldn't know how to forget it. . . . For me, I must await the beauties of heaven, since here below I can't find words that are capable of interpreting what happened in my heart on that blessed day.

Beloved Mother, there was another day when my soul became even more attached to yours, if that's possible. This was the day [in March, 1896] when Jesus imposed on you once again the burden of being Superior. On that day, dear Mother, you sowed in tears, but in heaven you'll be filled with joy when you see yourself bearing precious sheaves [Ps. 126:5-6].

Oh, Mother, forgive my childish simplicity. I feel that you're allowing me to speak to you without looking for what is allowed to a young nun to say to her Prioress. Perhaps I won't always remain within the boundaries prescribed to those who are under authority, but, Mother, I dare to say it, it's your fault. I'm behaving toward you as a child because you're acting toward me not as Prioress but as Mother. . . .

Oh! I feel it well, dear Mother. It's God who always speaks to me through you. Many of the Sisters think that you've spoiled me, and that since my entrance into the holy ark [of Carmel] [Gen. 7:13], I've received from you only strokes and compliments. However, that's not the way it is. You'll see, Mother, in the notebook that contains my childhood memories [chapters one through eight, written under obedience to Mother Agnes of Jesus (Pauline) when she was prioress], what I think about the *strong* and motherly upbringing that I received from you. From the deepest part of my heart I thank you for not having spared me. Jesus knew well that His little flower needed the life-giving water of humiliation. She was too weak to take root without that help, and it's through you, Mother, that that blessing was bestowed on her.

For a year and a half Jesus has wanted to change the way to make His little flower grow. No doubt He found her *watered* enough, for now it's the *sun* that's making her grow. Jesus no longer wants for her anything other than His smile, which He continues to give her through you, beloved Mother. That sun, rather than causing the little flower to wilt, is making it grow marvelously. In the bottom of her cup she's preserving the precious drops of dew that she has received [that is, the water of humiliation], and those drops always remind her that she's small and weak. . . . All creatures can bend toward her, admire her, overwhelm her with their praises—I don't know why, but all that wouldn't know how to add one single drop of false joy to the true joy that she savors in her heart, seeing herself as what she is in the eyes of God: a poor little nothing, nothing more. . . .

I say that I don't understand why, but isn't it because she was preserved from the water of praise the whole time that her little cup wasn't full enough of the dew of humiliation? Now [that she is so ill] there is no longer any danger. On the contrary, the little flower finds the dew with which she is filled to be so delicious that she would take great care not to exchange it for the taste-less water of compliments.

I don't want to talk, dear Mother, about the love and the confidence that you show me. Don't think that your child's heart is insensitive to them, only I feel strongly that I have nothing to fear now. On the contrary I can enjoy your love and trust, bringing back to God what-ever good He has wanted to place within me. If it pleases Him to make me seem better than I am, that's not my responsibility. He's free to act as He wills. . . .

Oh, Mother, how different are the ways by which the Lord leads souls! In the lives of the Saints, we see that many are found who have wanted to leave nothing of themselves after their death—not the slightest memory, the least bit of writing. On the contrary, there are many, like our Mother St. Teresa of Avila, who have enriched the Church with their sublime revelations, not fearing to reveal the King's secrets [cf. Tob. 12:7 D-R], to the end that He may be better known, better loved by souls.

Which of these two types of Saints are the most pleasing to God? It seems to me, Mother, that they're equally pleasing to Him, since all have followed the movements of the Holy Spirit, and that the Lord has said: "Tell the righteous it will be well with them" [Isa. 3:10]. Yes, all is well, when we seek only the will of Jesus. It's for that reason that I, a poor little flower, obey Jesus by trying to give pleasure to my beloved Mother.

You know, Mother, that I've always desired to be a saint, but alas! I've always stated, when I've compared myself to the Saints, that there is between them and me the same difference that exists between a mountain the summit of which is lost in the sky, and an obscure grain of sand that is trodden under foot by passersby. Instead of becoming discouraged, I've told myself: God wouldn't know how to inspire desires that can't be realized. So despite my littleness I can aspire to sainthood. To make myself bigger is impossible; I have to put up with myself such as I am with all my imperfections. But I want to seek the means of going to heaven by a little way that is very straight, very short, a completely new little way.

We're in an age of inventions. Now there's no more need to climb the steps of a staircase. In rich homes there are elevators that replace stairs to great advantage. I would also like to find an elevator to lift me up to Jesus, because I'm too little to climb the rough staircase of perfection. So I sought in the holy books the indication of the elevator that is the object of my desire, and I read these words that come from the mouth of Eternal Wisdom: "Let all who are *simple* come to my house" [cf. Pr. 9:4]. So I came, suspecting that I had found what I was looking for, and wanting to know, God, what You would do with the simple little one who would respond to Your call.

I've continued my search, and here's what I've found: "As a mother comforts her child, so I will comfort you. . . . [Y]ou will nurse and be carried on her arm and dandled on her knees" [Isa. 66:13, 12]. Oh! Never have words more tender, more melodious, come to rejoice my soul. The elevator that must lift me up to heaven is Your arms, Jesus! For that I don't need to become big.

On the contrary, I have to stay little—may I become little, more and more.

God, You've surpassed my expectations, and I want to sing of Your mercies [Ps. 89:1]. "Since my youth, God, you have taught me, and to this day I declare your marvelous deeds. Even when I am old and gray, do not forsake me, my God" [Ps. 71:17-18]. When will be my time of being "old and gray"? It seems to me that it could be now, because 2,000 years are not more in the Lord's eyes than twenty years . . . or than a single day [Ps. 90:4]. . . .

Oh! Don't think, beloved Mother, that your child desires to leave you. . . . Don't believe that she esteems it a greater grace to die at dawn rather than at sunset. What she esteems, the only thing that she desires, is to *give pleasure* to Jesus. . . . Now that He seems to be coming near to her to draw her to the dwelling of His glory, your child is rejoicing. For a long time she has understood that God doesn't need anyone (her even less than others) to do good on earth.

Mother, forgive me if I'm making you sad. . . . Oh! I would so much like to make you happy. . . . But do you believe that if your prayers are not granted on earth, if Jesus has separated the child from her Mother *for a few days*, those prayers won't be granted in heaven? . . .

Your desire is, I know, for me to accomplish near you a very light, very easy mission. Won't I be able to complete that mission from up in heaven? . . . Just as Jesus said one day to St. Peter, you said to your child, "Feed my lambs" [Jn. 21:15] [when you asked me to assist you in forming the Novices], and I was quite surprised

at that. I told you that I was "too *little.*". . . . I pleaded
with you to feed your little lambs yourself, and to
watch over me, to feed me by grace with them. And
you, beloved Mother, responding *a little* to my just
desire, you kept the little lambs with the sheep, but at
the same time directing me to go often to feed them in
the *shade,* to show them the best and most strengthen-
ing grasses, to take care to show them the brightest
flowers that they must never touch so as not to crush
them under their feet. . . .

You weren't afraid, dear Mother, that I would cause
your little lambs to stray. My inexperience, my youth
didn't frighten you. Perhaps you remembered that often
the Lord is pleased to grant wisdom to the small, and
that one day, transported with joy, He blessed His Father
for having hidden His secrets from the wise and having
revealed them to little children [Lk. 10:21]. Mother, as
you know, rare are the souls who don't measure the
divine power according to their diminutive thoughts.
They are willing for there to be exceptions everywhere
on earth, but only God has the right to do that.

For a very long time, I know, this approach to meas-
uring experience by years has been the practice among
humans, because, in his adolescence, the holy king
David sang to the Lord, "I am very young and
despised" [Ps. 118:141 D-R (Ps. 119)]. In the same
psalm he wasn't afraid to say, however, "I have more
understanding than the elders, for I obey your precepts"
[v. 100]. . . . "Your word is a lamp to my feet and a
light for my path" [v. 105]. . . . "I will hasten and not
delay to obey your commands" [v. 60]. . . .

Beloved Mother, you weren't afraid to tell me one day that God was illuminating my soul, that He was even giving me the experience of *years*. . . . Oh, Mother! I'm *too little* to have vanity now, I'm *too little* still to turn beautiful phrases in order to make you believe that I have a great deal of humility. I prefer to concur quite simply that the Almighty has done great things in the soul of the child of His divine Mother [Lk. 1:49], and the greatest is to have shown her how *little*, how powerless she is.

Dear Mother, you know it well, God has consented to make my soul pass through many kinds of trials. I've suffered a great deal since I've been on earth, but if in my childhood I suffered with sadness, I no longer suffer that way now: It's in joy and peace. I'm truly happy to suffer. Oh, Mother, you have to know all the secrets of my soul in order not to smile when you read these lines, because is there a soul with fewer trials than mine if one were to judge by appearances? Oh! If the trial that I've been suffering for a year [my illness] were to be obvious, how surprised people would be! . . .

Beloved mother, you're familiar with that trial. However, I'm going to talk to you about it some more, because I consider it to be a great grace that I received under your blessed Priorship.

Last year, God granted me the comfort of observing the fast of Lent in all its rigor. I had never felt as strong, and that strength stayed with me till Easter. However, on Good Friday, Jesus wanted to give me the hope of going soon to see Him in heaven. . . . Oh! How sweet that memory is to me! . . . After staying at the Tomb [the chapel where the reserved Sacrament is kept between Good Friday and the Easter Vigil on Holy Saturday evening] until midnight, I went into our cell, but hardly had I had the time to place my head on the pillow when I felt something like a wave that was rising, rising, boiling up to my lips. I didn't know what it was, but I thought that perhaps I was going to die, and my soul was flooded with joy. . . . However, since our lamp was out, I told myself that I would have to wait for morning to assure myself of my happiness, because it seemed to me that it was blood that I had vomited.

The morning wasn't long in coming. When I woke up, I thought right away that I had something joyful to learn. When I went to the window I was able to confirm that I hadn't been deceived. . . . Oh! My soul was filled with great comfort. I was thoroughly persuaded that Jesus, on the day of commemoration of His death, wanted to me to hear a first call. It was like a gentle, faraway murmur that was announcing to me the arrival of the Bridegroom [Mt. 25:6]. . . .

It was with very great fervor that I attended Prime [the second church service of the day] and the chapter of faults [the service of public confession of one's faults]. I was in a hurry to see my turn come in order to be able, while asking your forgiveness, to confide in you, beloved Mother, my hope and my happiness. But I added that I wasn't suffering at all (which was quite true), and I begged you, Mother, not to give me anything in particular. And in fact I had the consolation of spending the day on Good Friday as I desired.

Never had the austerities of Carmel seemed to me as delightful. The hope of going to heaven transported me with gladness. When the evening of that blessed day arrived, I had to rest, but just as happened the night before, the good Jesus gave me the same sign that my entrance into Everlasting life was not far off [because once again I coughed up blood]. . . . I rejoiced then with a faith that was so alive, so clear, that the thought of heaven became my whole happiness. I couldn't believe that there could be unbelievers who had no faith. I thought that they were speaking against their own thoughts by denying the existence of heaven, that beautiful heaven where God Himself would like to be their everlasting reward [Gen. 15:1].

During the most joyous days of Eastertide, Jesus made me feel that there truly are souls that don't have faith, who through the abuse of graces lose that precious treasure, the source of the only pure and true joys. He allowed my soul to be invaded by the thickest darkness, and for the thought of heaven, which was so sweet to me, to be only a subject of struggle and torment. . . . This trial was not to last for several days or weeks. It was to extend only until the time fixed by God, and . . . that time has not yet come. . . . I would like to be able to express what I feel, but, alas! I feel that it's impossible. You would have to travel in that dark tunnel to understand its darkness. Nonetheless, I'm going to try to explain it through a comparison.

In this comparison, I'm supposing that I was born in a country surrounded by a thick fog. I've never contemplated the laughing aspect of nature when it's flooded and transfigured by the brilliant sun. Since my childhood, it's true, I've heard about these marvels. I know that the country where I am is not my homeland, that my home is another land toward which I must aspire without ceasing [Heb. 11:13–16]. It's not a story made up by an inhabitant of the sad country in which I find myself. It's a certain reality, because the King of the homeland of the brilliant sun came to live for thirty-three years in the land of darkness. Alas! The darkness didn't understand that this Divine King was the light of the world [Jn. 1:5, 9-10]. . . .

But Lord, Your child has understood Your divine light. She asks You for forgiveness for her brothers and sisters. She accepts to eat the bread of sorrow [Ps. 127:2] for as long as You wish, and doesn't want to rise from this table filled with bitterness, where poor sinners eat, before the day that You've appointed. . . . But also, can't she say in her name, in the name of her brothers and sisters, "Have mercy on us, Lord, for we are poor sinners. . . . Oh! Lord, send us away justified" [cf. Lk. 18:13-14]? . . .

May all those who haven't been lit with the gleaming torch of Faith finally see it glowing. . . . Oh, Jesus, if the table that has been soiled by them has to be purified by a soul who loves You, I'm willing to eat all alone the bread of trials until it pleases You to admit me into your shining Kingdom. The only grace that I ask of You is never to give You any offense! . . .

Beloved Mother, what I'm writing you has no continuation. My little story that seemed like a fairy tale has suddenly changed into a prayer. I don't know what interest you'll be able to find in reading all these confusing and poorly expressed thoughts. After all,

Mother, I'm writing, not to make a work of literature, but out of obedience. If I'm boring you, at least you will see that your child has given proof of her good will. So without becoming discouraged I'm going to continue my little comparison from the point where I left off.

I was saying that the certainty of going some day far away from the sad, dark country had been given to me beginning in my childhood. Not only did I believe according to what I heard people say, people who were more knowledgeable than I was, but even more I felt, in the depths of my heart, aspirations toward a more beautiful place. Just as the genius of Christopher Columbus caused him to feel that a new world existed, whereas no one had thought of it, in the same way I felt that another land would serve me some day as a stable dwelling place [Heb. 13:14].

But suddenly the fog that surrounds me becomes thicker. It penetrates into my soul and envelops it in such a way that it's no longer possible to find in my soul the sweet image of my Homeland. Everything has disappeared!

When I want to give rest to my heart, fatigued from the darkness that surrounds it, by remembering the luminous country toward which I aspire, my torment redoubles. It seems to me that the darkness, borrowing the voice of sinners, tells me mockingly, "You're dreaming up the light, this homeland smelling of the sweetest perfume. You're dreaming up the *everlasting* possession of the Creator of all these marvelous things. You think that someday you're going to get out of all this fog that surrounds you. Go ahead, go ahead, rejoice in death, which will give you, not what you're hoping for, but a still deeper night, the night of nothingness."

Beloved Mother, the image that I tried to give you of the darkness that obscures my soul is as imperfect as a model compared to the real thing, but I don't want to write any longer, because I would be afraid of blaspheming. . . . I'm even afraid of having said too much already. . . .

Oh! May Jesus forgive me if I've caused Him pain, but He knows well that while I don't have the enjoyment of Faith, at least I try to do its works. I believe I've done more acts of faith in the past year than during my whole life. At each new opportunity to do battle, when my enemies come and provoke me, I conduct myself bravely. Knowing that it's cowardly to fight in a duel, I turn my back on my adversary without condescending to look him in the face. But I run toward my Jesus, I tell Him that I'm ready to shed my blood even to the last drop in order to confess that there is a heaven. I tell Him that I'm happy not to enjoy that beautiful heaven on earth in order that He might open it for eternity to the poor unbelievers.

So, despite this trial that's taking away *all enjoyment*, I can nonetheless cry out, "For you make me *glad* by your deeds, LORD" [Ps. 92:4]. For, is there a greater *gladness* than that of suffering out of love for You? . . . The more private the suffering is, the less evident it is to the eyes of created beings, the more it makes You glad, God. But if, against all possibility, You Yourself were not to know of my suffering, I would still be happy to possess it, if by it I could prevent or make reparation for a single fault committed against the Faith. . . .

Beloved Mother, I may perhaps seem to you to be exaggerating my trial. In fact, if you judge according to the sentiments that I express in the little poems that I've composed this year, I must seem to you to be a soul filled with consolations and for whom the veil of faith has almost torn open, and yet . . . it's no longer a veil for me, it's a wall that rises up to heaven and covers the starry sky. . . . When I sing of the happiness of heaven, the everlasting possession of God, I feel no joy because of it, because I simply sing of what *I want to believe.* Sometimes, it's true, a tiny little ray of sunshine comes in to illumine my darkness, and so the trial stops for *an instant,* but then the memory of that ray, instead of causing me joy, makes my darkness even thicker.

Oh, Mother, never have I felt so keenly how gentle and merciful the Lord is [Ps. 103:8]. He sent me this trial only at the moment when I had the strength to endure it. I really believe that if it had come earlier, it would have plunged me into discouragement. . . . Now it takes away everything that might have been found of natural satisfaction in the desire that I had for heaven. . . . Beloved Mother, it seems to me now that nothing is preventing me from flying away, for I no longer have any great desire, if it isn't that of loving to the point of dying from love. . . . (June 9)

Dear Mother, I'm quite surprised when I see what I wrote you yesterday. What scribbling! My hand was trembling in such a way that it was impossible for me to continue, and now I'm sorry that I even tried to write. I hope that today I'm going to do it more legibly, because today I'm not in bed, but in a pretty, little, white armchair.

Oh, Mother, I'm quite aware that everything that I'm telling you has nothing to follow it, but I also feel the need, before writing you about the past, to tell you my present feelings. Later, perhaps, I will have lost the memory of them. I want to tell you first of all how touched I am by all your motherly tenderness. Oh! Believe it, beloved Mother, the heart of your child is full of gratitude—it will never forget all that it owes you. . . .

Mother, what touches me most of all is the novena [nine days of prayer] that you're making to Our Lady of Victories, and the Masses that you're having said in order to obtain my healing. I feel that all these spiritual treasures are doing great good to my soul. At the beginning of the novena, I was telling you, Mother, that the Blessed Virgin either must heal me or take me to heaven, because I found it quite sad for you and the community to have the care of a young, sick nun. Now I'm willing to be sick my whole life if that gives pleasure to God, and I consent even for my life to be very long. The only grace that I desire is for it to be broken by love.

Oh! No, I'm not afraid of living a long life. I'm not refusing the battle, because the Lord is the rock on whom I'm lifted up, who trains my hands for war, and my fingers for battle. He is my shield, I take refuge in

Him [Ps. 144:1-2]. So I've never asked God to let me die young. It's true that I've always hoped that this is His will. Often the Lord is content with the desire to work for His glory, and you know, Mother, that my desires are very great. You also know that Jesus has presented me with more than one bitter cup that He's taken away from my lips before I drank it [Lk. 22:42], but not before making me taste its bitterness.

Beloved Mother, the holy king David was right when he sang, "How good and pleasant it is when God's people live together in unity!" [Ps. 133:1]. This is true, and I've felt it quite often, but it's in the midst of sacrifices that this unity must take place on earth. It was not to live with my sisters that I came to Carmel, it was only to respond to Jesus' call. Oh! I had a strong feeling that it must be a subject of continual suffering to live with one's sisters, when one doesn't want to make any concession to nature.

How can people say that it's more perfect to go far away from one's own family? . . . Has anyone ever reproached brothers for fighting on the same field of battle? Have they ever been reproached for hurrying together to wear the palm of martyrdom? . . . No doubt, people judged rightly that they were encouraging each other mutually, but also that the martyrdom of each one became that of all. So it is in the religious life, which theologians call a martyrdom. By giving oneself to God the heart doesn't lose its natural tenderness. On the contrary, that tenderness grows by becoming more pure and more divine.

Beloved Mother, it's out of that tenderness that I love you, that I love my sisters. I'm happy to fight *as a family* for the glory of the King of Heaven, but I'm also ready to fly to another field of battle if the Divine General were to express the desire for me to do so. An order wouldn't be needed, just a glance, a simple sign.

Since my entrance into the blessed ark [of Carmel], I've always thought that if Jesus didn't take me very quickly to heaven, the fate of the Noah's little dove would be mine: One day the Lord would open the window of the ark and would tell me to fly very far, very far, toward the unfaithful shores, [to a foreign land as a missionary,] bearing with me the little olive leaf [Gen. 8:11-12].

Mother, this thought has made my soul grow. It has made me soar higher than all creation. I have understood that even at Carmel there could still be separations, that only in heaven will unity be complete and everlasting. Then I wanted my soul to live in heaven and to behold the things of earth only from afar. I accepted not only to be exiled in the midst of an unknown people, but what was *much more* bitter to me, I accepted the exile for my sisters.

I will never forget the second of August, 1896. That was the very day of the departure of the missionaries. There was a serious question about Mother Agnes of Jesus' leaving. Oh! I wouldn't have wanted to make a single movement to prevent her from leaving. Nonetheless I felt a great sadness in my heart. I found that her soul, which was so sensitive, so delicate, wasn't made to live among souls who would not know how to understand it.

A thousand other thoughts crowded into my mind, and Jesus fell silent and didn't rebuke the storm

[Mk. 4:37–39]. . . . And I would tell Him, "My God, out of love for You I accept it all: If You so desire, I'm willing to suffer to the point of dying from sorrow." Jesus was content with the acceptance.

But several months later, there was talk about the departure of Sr. Geneviève and Sr. Marie of the Trinity. Then this was another type of suffering, extremely intimate, extremely deep. I pictured all the trials, the disappointments that they would have to suffer. In short, my sky was laden with clouds. . . . Only the depths of my heart remained in calm and peace.

Beloved Mother, your good sense knew how to discover God's will, and on His behalf you forbade your Novices to think now about leaving the cradle of their religious childhood. But you understood their aspirations, since you yourself, Mother, had asked in your younger days to go to Saigon [in French Indochina]. That's often the way—the desires of mothers find an echo in the souls of their children. Oh, dear Mother, your desire to be an apostle finds in my soul, as you know, a most faithful echo. Let me confide in you why I desired and still desire, if the Blessed Virgin heals me, to go to a foreign land and leave behind the delicious oasis where I live so happily under your motherly gaze.

To live in foreign Carmelite convents, one must have, Mother (you've told me this), a very special vocation. Many souls think they are called to it without being called in fact. You also told me that I had that vocation and that only my health was an obstacle. I know well that this obstacle would disappear if God were to call me far away. So I live without being worried.

If I were required someday to leave my dear Carmel, oh! that wouldn't be without hurt. Jesus didn't give me an insensitive heart, and it's precisely because it's capable of suffering that I desire for it to give to Jesus all that it can give. *Here,* beloved Mother, I live without any encumbrance of the cares of the wretched earth. I have only to fulfill the light and easy mission that you've entrusted to me. *Here* I'm showered with your motherly attentions. I don't feel poverty, since I have never lacked anything. But above all, *here* I'm loved, by you and all the Sisters, and this affection is most sweet to me. That's why I dream about a convent where I would be unknown, where I would have to suffer poverty, lack of affection, in short, the exile of the heart.

Oh! It's not with the intention of rendering service to the convent that would be willing to receive me, that I would leave everything that is dear to me. No doubt, I would do everything that would depend on me, but I know how incapable I am, and I know that while I was doing the best I could, I wouldn't end up doing well, not having, as I was saying a short time ago, any knowledge of the things of earth. So my only goal would be to accomplish the will of God, to sacrifice myself for Him in the manner that would be pleasing to Him [cf. Mt. 6:10].

I have the strong feeling that I wouldn't be at all disappointed, because when one expects a suffering that is pure and unalloyed, the slightest joy becomes an unhoped-for surprise. And then, as you know, Mother, suffering itself becomes the greatest of joys when one seeks it as the most precious of treasures.

Oh, no! It's not with the intention of enjoying the fruit of my labors that I would like to go away. If that were my goal I wouldn't feel this sweet peace that floods me, and I would even suffer from not being able realize my vocation for faraway missions. For a long time I've no longer belonged to myself. I'm totally given over to Jesus. He's therefore free to do with me as He pleases. He gave me the attraction toward a complete exile, He made me *understand all* the *sufferings* that I would encounter there, asking me if I wanted to drain this cup to the dregs [Mt. 20:21–23]. Immediately I attempted to grasp the cup that Jesus was presenting to me, but He, pulling back His hand, gave me to understand that He was content with my accepting it.

Oh, Mother, from how many worries does one free oneself by making the vow of obedience! How happy are simple nuns. Their only compass being the will of their Superiors, they are always assured of being on the right path. They have no fear of being wrong, even if it seems certain to them that their superiors are wrong. But when one stops looking at the infallible compass, when, under the pretext of doing God's will, one steps away from the path that she says to follow and maintains that He isn't perfectly enlightening those who nonetheless stand in His place, immediately the soul goes astray into arid paths where it is soon lacking the water of grace.

Beloved Mother, you are the compass that Jesus gave me to lead me surely to the everlasting shore. How sweet it is for me to fix my gaze on you and then to accomplish the Lord's will. Since the time that He began allowing me to suffer temptations against the faith, He has greatly increased in my heart the spirit of faith that makes me see in you, not only a Mother who loves me and whom I love, but especially that makes me see Jesus living in your soul and communicating His will through you.

I well know, Mother, that you treat me [gently,] as a weak soul, as a pampered child, so I have no trouble bearing the burden of obedience. But it seems to me, according to what I feel in the depths of my heart, that I wouldn't change my behavior and that my love for you wouldn't suffer any decrease, if it pleased you to treat me severely. For I would still see that it's the will of Jesus for you to act that way for the greater good of my soul.

This year, dear Mother, God has given me the grace to understand what charity is. It's true that I understood it before, but in an imperfect way. I hadn't gone to the core of this word of Jesus, "And the second [commandment] is like it, 'Love your neighbor as yourself'" [Mt. 22:39]. I applied myself especially to loving God, and it's in loving Him that I understood that it wasn't necessary for my love to be interpreted only by words, because, "Not everyone who says to me, 'Lord, Lord,' will enter the kingdom of heaven, but only those who do the will of my Father who is in heaven" [Mt. 7:21].

That will was revealed by Jesus many times—I ought to say, almost on every page of His Gospel. But at the Last Supper, when He knew that the heart of His disciples was burning with a more ardent love for Him, who had just given Himself to them in the ineffable mystery of His Eucharist, this gentle Savior wanted to give them a new commandment. He told them with inexpressible tenderness: "A new command I give you: Love one another. As I have loved you, so you must love one another. By this everyone will know that you are my disciples, if you love one another" [Jn. 13:34-35].

How did Jesus love His disciples, and why did He love them? Oh! It wasn't their natural qualities that could have attracted Him: Between them and Him there was an infinite distance. He was knowledge and Eternal Wisdom; they were poor fishermen, ignorant and full of earthly thoughts. However, Jesus calls them His friends, His brothers. He wants to see them reign with Him in His Father's kingdom [Lk. 22:30], and in order to open this kingdom to them, He's willing to die on a cross. For He said, "Greater love has no one than this: to lay down one's life for one's friends" [Jn. 15:13].

Beloved Mother, as I meditated on these words of Jesus, I understood how much my love for my Sisters was imperfect. I saw that I wasn't loving them as God loves them. Oh! Now I understand that perfect charity consists in bearing with others' faults, in not being surprised at their weakness, in being edified by the little acts of virtue that we see them practice. But above all I understood that charity ought not to stay enclosed in the depths of the heart. Jesus said, "Neither do people light a lamp and put it under a bowl. Instead they put it on its stand, and it gives light to *everyone* in the house" [Mt. 5:15]. It seems to me that this lamp represents charity, which ought to illumine and cause to rejoice, not only those who are the dearest to me, but everyone in the house, without any exception.

When the Lord had commanded His people to love their neighbor as themselves He hadn't yet come to earth, so, knowing well to what degree we love our own selves, He couldn't ask His creatures for a greater love than love for one's neighbor [Lev. 19:18]. But when Jesus gave His apostles a new commandment, *His own commandment,* as He said later—He no longer talked about loving one's neighbor as oneself, but to love our neighbor as *Jesus loved him,* as He will love him until the end of the world. . . .

Ah! Lord, I know that You command nothing that is impossible, You know better than I my weakness, my imperfection. You know well that I would never be able to love my Sisters as You love them, if *You Yourself,* oh my Jesus, didn't continue to *love* them *in me.* It's because You wanted to grant me this grace that You gave a *new* commandment [Jn. 13:34]. Oh! How I love it because it gives me the assurance that Your will is to love *in me* all those whom You are commanding me to love! . . .

Yes, I feel it when I'm charitable: It's Jesus alone who is acting in me. The more I'm united with Him, the more also I love all my Sisters. When I want to increase this love in me, especially when the devil is trying to put before the eyes of my soul the faults of such or such a Sister whom I find the least likable, I hasten to look for her virtues, her good desires. I tell myself that if I've seen her fall one time she could well have won a great number of victories that she hides out of humility, and that even what seems to me to be a fault could very well be, because of its intent, an act of virtue.

I have no problem persuading myself of this, because one day I did a little experiment that proved to me that we must never judge. It was during a recreation period. There were two knocks at the door. We had to open the big workmen's door in order to allow the trees to be brought in for the manger scene. The recreation period wasn't cheerful, because you weren't there, dear Mother, so I was thinking that if I were sent to serve as assistant, I would be very happy. In fact, the Sub-Prioress told me to go serve, or if not me, then the Sister who was beside me. Immediately I began to undo my apron, but rather slowly so that my companion might take hers off before me, because I thought I would be pleasing her by letting her be the assistant. The Sister who was replacing the depositary watched us, laughing, and, when she saw that I had stood up last, she told me, "Oh! I had thought that you weren't the one who was going to gain a pearl in your crown. You were going too slowly. . . ."

Most certainly the whole community thought that I had acted out of my nature [since at that point they didn't consider me to be a hard worker]. Yet I couldn't tell you how much such a little thing did good to my soul and made me non-judgmental toward the weaknesses of others.

That also prevents me from having vanity when I'm judged favorably, because I tell myself this: Since they take my little acts of virtue for imperfections, they can just as well be wrong when they take as a virtue what is only imperfection. Then I say with St. Paul: "I care very little if I am judged by you or by any human court; indeed, I do not even judge myself. My conscience is clear, but that does not make me innocent. It is the Lord who judges me" [1 Cor. 4:3-4]. So, to make this judgment favorable, or rather in order not to be judged at all, I always want to have charitable thoughts, because Jesus said, "Do not judge, and you will not be judged" [Lk. 6:37].

Mother, in reading what I've just written, you could believe that the practice of charity isn't difficult for me. That's true. For several months I've no longer had to struggle to practice that beautiful virtue. I don't mean by this that it never happens that I commit faults. Oh! I'm too imperfect for that, but I don't have much trouble picking myself back up when I've fallen, because in a certain struggle I carried the victory. Therefore the heavenly Host now comes to my aid, not being able to suffer seeing me defeated after having been victorious in the glorious war that I'm going to try to describe.

There is in our community one Sister who has the talent of displeasing me in everything: Her manners, her words, her character seemed to me to be *very displeasing*. However, she's a holy nun who must be *very pleasing* to God. So, not wanting to give in to the natural dislike that I was experiencing, I told myself that charity doesn't consist in feelings but in works.

So I set about doing for this Sister what I would have done for the person that I love the most. Each time that I met her I prayed to God for her, offering Him all her virtues and her merits. I felt strongly that this was pleasing to Jesus, because there is no artist who doesn't like to receive praise for his works, and Jesus, the Artist of souls, is happy when one doesn't stop on the outside, but penetrating as far as the interior sanctuary that He has chosen for Himself as a dwelling, one admires its beauty.

I wasn't content just to pray a lot for the Sister who gave me so many struggles; I tried to render to her every possible service. And when I had the temptation to answer her in an unpleasant way, I contented myself with giving her my most pleasant smile, and I tried to turn the conversation in a different direction, because the *Imitation* says, "It is better to leave each one in his feeling than to stop to contest it."

Often, as well, when I wasn't at the recreation period (I mean during work times), having some work contact with this Sister, when my struggles were too violent, I fled away like a deserter. Since she absolutely didn't know what I was feeling toward her, she never suspected the motives of my conduct, and remains persuaded that her character is pleasing to me.

One day during the recreation period she told me something like these words, with a very happy appearance: "Would you please tell me, Sister Thérèse of the Child Jesus, what attracts you so much to me? Because every time you look at me, I see you smile." Oh! What attracted me was Jesus, hidden in the depths of her soul. . . . Jesus, who makes sweet what is the most bitter. . . . I answered her that I smiled because I was happy to see her (of course I didn't add that it was from a spiritual point of view).

Beloved Mother, as I told you, my *last means* of not being defeated in my struggles is desertion. I already used this means during my novitiate, and it has always worked perfectly for me. Mother, I want to cite you an example that I think will make you smile. During one of your bouts with bronchitis, I came one morning quite softly to put back in your room the keys to the communion grille, since I was the sacristan. Inside, I wasn't upset at having this opportunity to see you. I was even very happy, but I was very careful not to let it show.

One Sister, enlivened by a holy zeal and who nonetheless liked me a lot, seeing me enter into your room, Mother, thought that I was going to wake you up. She tried to take the keys from me, but I was too clever to give them to her and give up *my rights*. I told her as politely as possible that I desired as much as she not to wake you up, and that it was *my* job to return the keys. . . .

I understand now that it would have been much more perfect to give in to this Sister, who was young, it is true, but after all older than I was. I didn't understand that then, so, absolutely wanting to follow her in, in spite of her pushing the door to prevent me from entering, soon the misfortune that we were dreading happened: The noise that we were making caused you to open your eyes. . . . Then, Mother, everything fell on my head. The poor Sister whom I had resisted launched into quite a speech, the gist of which was this: "Sister Thérèse of the Child Jesus is the one who made noise. God, how unpleasant she is. . . . Etc." I, who was feeling quite the opposite, really felt like defending myself.

Fortunately a bright idea came to me. I told myself that certainly if I began to justify myself, I wasn't going to keep the peace of my soul. I also felt that I didn't have enough virtue to let myself be accused without saying anything. So my last escape hatch was flight. No sooner thought, than done: I left without a drum roll or a trumpet, leaving the Sister to continue her speech, which was rather like the imprecations of Camillus against Rome.

My heart was beating so strongly that it was impossible for me to go far, and I sat down on the stairs to enjoy in peace the fruits of my victory. That's not much of an example of bravery, is it, dear Mother? But I think nonetheless that it's better not to expose oneself to battle when defeat is certain.

Alas! When I think back to the time of my novitiate, I see how imperfect I was. . . . I was bothered by such small things that I can laugh about them now. Ah! How good the Lord is to have made my soul grow, to have given it wings. . . . All the nets of the hunters couldn't frighten me, for, "a net is spread in vain before the eyes of them that have wings" [Prov. 1:17 D-R]. Later, no doubt, the time in which I now find myself will seem to me to be still filled with imperfections, but now I'm no longer surprised by anything. It doesn't trouble me to see that I'm *weakness* itself. On the contrary, it's in weakness that I glory [2 Cor. 12:5], and I expect every day to discover new imperfections in myself.

Remembering that charity "covers over a multitude of sins" [1 Pet. 4:8], I draw from that bountiful mine that Jesus has opened before me. In the Gospel, the Lord explains what His new commandment consists of [Jn. 13:34-35]: He says in St. Matthew, "You have heard that it was said, 'Love your neighbor and hate your enemy.' But I tell you, love your enemies and pray for those who persecute you" [Mt. 5:43-44].

No doubt, in Carmel you won't encounter enemies, but after all there are instinctive attractions: You feel attracted to one Sister, whereas in the case of another you would make a long detour to avoid meeting up with her. So even without knowing it, she becomes a subject of persecution. Well! Jesus told me that I must love this Sister, I must pray for her, even when her behavior would lead me to believe that she doesn't like me: "If you love those who love you, what credit is that to you? Even sinners love those who love them" [Lk. 6:32].

And it isn't enough to love; you have to prove it. We're naturally happy to give a present to a friend, we even love to give surprises, but that isn't charity, because sinners do that, too. Here's what Jesus goes on to teach me: "Give to everyone who asks you, and if anyone takes what belongs to you, do not demand it back" [Lk. 6:30]. To give to all those who *ask* is less sweet than to offer oneself through the movement of one's heart.

Again, when someone asks nicely, it doesn't cost me to give, but if unfortunately they don't use delicate enough words, instantly the soul revolts if it isn't set firmly on charity. It finds a thousand reasons to refuse what is asked of it, and it's only after having convinced the asker of her lack of refinement that it finally gives *by grace* what she's asking for, or that it gives her a light service that would have required twenty times less time to fulfill than it took to lay claim to imaginary rights.

If it's difficult to give to everyone who asks, it's even more so to let someone take what belongs to you without demanding it back [Lk. 6:30]. Oh, Mother, I say that it's difficult. I ought rather to say that it *seems* difficult, because the Lord's yoke is easy and His burden is light [Mt. 11:30]. When we accept it, we instantly feel its lightness, and we cry out with the Psalmist, "I have run the way of thy commandments, when thou didst enlarge my heart" [Ps. 118:32 (Ps. 119) D-R]. Only charity can enlarge my heart, Jesus. Since that gentle flame has consumed it, I'm running with You in the way of Your *new* commandment [Jn. 13:34-35]. I want to run in it until the blessed day when, joining with the train of virgins, I will be able to follow You in the infinite spaces, singing Your *new* song [Rev. 14:3-4], which must be the song of Love.

I was saying that Jesus doesn't want me to take back what belongs to me. That ought to seem easy and natural to me, since nothing is mine. The goods of the earth—I renounced them through the vow of poverty, so I don't have the right to complain if someone takes away something that doesn't belong to me. On the contrary, I ought to rejoice, since it's my lot to feel poverty.

In the past it used to seem that I wasn't holding on to anything, but since I understood Jesus' words, I see that there are times when I'm quite imperfect. For example, when I sit down to paint, nothing belongs to me, I know that. But if, when I begin to work, I find brushes and paintings all in disorder, if a ruler or a knife has disappeared, patience is very close to abandoning me, and I have to take up my courage in both hands so as not to ask bitterly for the objects that I'm missing.

Sometimes it's necessary to ask for things we can't do without, but when we do so with humility, we're not missing out on Jesus' commandment. On the contrary, we're acting like the poor who hold out their hands in order to receive what is necessary to them. If they're refused, they're not surprised: No one owes them anything. Oh! What peace floods the soul when it rises above the responses of nature. . . .

No, there's no joy that can be compared to the one that's savored by one who is truly poor in spirit [Mt. 5:3]. If he asks with detachment for a needed thing, and not only is that thing refused to him, but an attempt is made to take what he does have, he follows Jesus' counsel: "And if any one wants to sue you and take your shirt, hand over your coat as well" [Mt. 5:40]. . . .

To give up my coat is, it seems to me, to give up my last rights, it's to consider myself as the servant, the slave of others. When I've left my coat behind, it's easier to walk, to run. So Jesus adds: "If any one forces you to go one mile, go with them two miles" [Mt. 5:41]. Therefore it's not enough to give to whoever asks me for something [Lk. 6:30]. I have to go beyond my desires and give the impression of being very obliged and very honored to be of service. And if someone takes something that I use, I mustn't give the impression of regretting it, but on the contrary I must appear to be happy to *be rid of it.* . . .

Dear mother, I'm very far from practicing what I understand, but the very desire that I have to do so gives me peace.

More than on other days I feel that I've explained myself extremely poorly. I've made a *sort* of *speech* about charity that must have tired you out reading it. Forgive me, beloved Mother, and remember that right now the nurses are practicing on my behalf what I've just written. They're not afraid to go two miles when twenty steps would suffice. So I've been able to observe charity in action! Doubtless, my soul must find this to be a sweet perfume, but as far as my mind is concerned, I admit that it has become a bit paralyzed in the face of such devotion, and my pen has lost its lightness. In order for it to be possible for me to interpret my thoughts, I have to be like a bird alone on a roof [Ps. 102:7].

That's rarely my fate. When I begin to take up my pen, here's a good Sister who passes near me, a pitchfork over her shoulder. She thinks she's entertaining me by chatting with me a little. Hay, ducks, hens, a doctor's visit, everything's on the table. To tell you the truth, that doesn't last long, but there's *more* than one *good, charitable* Sister, and suddenly another hay cutter drops some flowers in my lap, thinking that perhaps she'll inspire some poetic ideas in me. Not seeking out flowers right then, I would prefer that they remain attached to their stems.

Finally, tired of opening and closing this notorious notebook [in which I'm writing], I open a book (that doesn't want to stay open) and I say resolutely that I'm copying sayings from the Psalms and the Gospels for our Mother's birthday. That's quite true, because I'm not frugal with quotations. . . .

Dear Mother, I would amuse you, I think, by telling you all my adventures in the "thickets" at Carmel. I don't know if I've written ten lines without being disturbed. That shouldn't make me laugh or amuse me. However, for the love of God and for my Sisters (who are so charitable toward me), I try to not only to give the impression of being happy, but also to *be* happy. . . .

Look, here's one hay cutter who's leaving after saying to me in a compassionate tone, "Dear little Sister, that must tire you out to write like that all day long." "Don't worry," I answered, "I look like I'm writing a lot, but in reality I don't write much of anything." "So much the better," she said to me, looking reassured, "but all the same, I'm sure happy that we're in the middle of cuttin' hay, 'cause that always distracts you a little." In fact, it's such a great distraction for me (without counting the nurses' visits) that I'm not lying when I say I don't write much of anything.

Fortunately, I'm not easy to discourage. To show you this, Mother, I'm going to finish explaining to you what Jesus has given me to understand on the subject of charity. So far I've talked to you only from the outside. Now I'd like to confide to you how I understand purely spiritual charity. I'm quite sure that it's not going to be long before I mix one with the other, but, Mother, since you're the one I'm talking to, I'm certain that it won't be difficult for you to catch my thought and to untangle your child's yarn.

It's not always possible, at Carmel, to practice to the letter the words of the Gospel. Sometimes because of duties we're obliged to refuse to do something for someone. But when charity has cast deep roots in the soul, it shows on the outside. There's a way to refuse what one can't give, that's so gracious that the refusal gives as much pleasure as the gift. It's true that it's less bothersome to ask for help from a Sister who's always disposed to oblige. But Jesus said, "Do not turn away from the one who wants to borrow from you" [Mt. 5:42]. So, under the pretext that one would be forced to refuse, one mustn't distance oneself from the Sisters who have the habit of always asking people to do things for them.

Neither must we be obliging in order to *give the appearance* of being obliging or in the hope that some other time the Sister that we're obliging will do something for us in turn. For Our Lord said again, "And if you lend to those from whom you expect repayment, what credit is that to you? Even sinners lend to sinners, expecting to be repaid in full. But . . . do good . . . and lend . . . without expecting to get anything back. Then your reward will be great" [Lk. 6:34-35]. Oh, yes! The reward is great even on earth. . . . When we follow that road it's only the first step that costs us.

To *lend without expecting to get anything back* seems hard to our nature. We would prefer to *give,* because something we give doesn't belong to us any more. When someone comes and tell us with a convincing look, "Sister, I need your help for a few hours. But don't worry, I have permission from our Superior, and

I'll *pay back* the time that you're giving me, because I know how pressed for time you are." In truth, when we know quite well that the time we *lend* will never be paid back, we'd rather say, "I give it to you." That would make our self-love happy, because giving is a more generous act than lending, and then we make the Sister feel that we're not counting on her to do something for us. . . . Oh! How contrary Jesus' teachings are to the thoughts of nature. Without the help of His grace it would be impossible not only to put them into practice, but even more to understand them.

CHAPTER 11

Those Whom You Have Given Me
1896–1897

Mother, Jesus gave this grace to your child to make her penetrate the mysterious depths of charity. If she could express what she understands, you'd hear a melody from heaven, but alas! I only have childish stammering to share with you. . . . If the very words of Jesus didn't serve me as a support, I'd be tempted to ask you for me to be excused and to set down my pen. . . . But no, I have to continue, out of obedience, what I began out of obedience.

Beloved Mother, I was writing yesterday that since the material things found here below are not mine, I shouldn't find it difficult to never get them back if sometimes they were taken from me. The things of heaven don't belong to me any more than those of earth. They've been *lent* to me by God, who can take them away from me without my having the right to complain about it. However, the good things that come directly from God—upward risings of the mind and the heart, deep thoughts—all those things form riches to which one can become attached as much as to a material thing that no one has the right to touch. . . .

For example, if during a break someone says to a Sister some revelation received during the time of prayer, and then, a short time later, when speaking to another Sister, that Sister says the thing that had been confided in her as if she had thought of it herself, it seems as if she's taking something that isn't hers. Or if during a recreation period, someone says quietly to her neighbor an appropriate word that's full of spirit, and the second Sister repeats the word out loud without letting others know the source from which it comes, again, that seems to be stealing from the owner, who doesn't claim it but would really like to do so and seize on the first opportunity to delicately let it be known that someone has grabbed one of her thoughts.

Mother, I wouldn't be able to explain to you so well these sad reactions of nature, if I hadn't felt them in my heart. I would have liked to soothe myself with the sweet illusion that they've visited only my heart, if you hadn't asked me to listen to the temptations of your dear little Novices. I've learned a lot by fulfilling the mission that you entrusted to me. Especially, I've found myself forced to practice what I taught others. So now I can say it: Jesus has given me the grace not to be more attached to the things of the mind and the heart than to those of earth. If it happens to me to think and to say something that pleases my Sisters, I find it quite natural for them to take it over as belonging to themselves. That thought belongs to the Holy Spirit and not to me, since St. Paul said that without the Spirit of Love we can't give the name "Father" to our Father who is in heaven [Rom. 8:15]. So He's quite free to use me to give a good thought to a soul. If I believed that thought belongs to me, I would be like "the donkey bearing relics" who thought that the homage being paid to the Saints was addressed to him.

I don't spurn the deep thoughts that nourish the soul and unite it to God, but for a long time I've understood that I mustn't lean on them and make perfection consist in receiving many spiritual illuminations. The most beautiful thoughts are nothing without works. It's true that others can gain a lot of profit from them if they make themselves humble and show God their gratitude that He's allowing them to share in the feast of a soul that it pleases Him to enrich with His graces. But if this soul takes delight in her *beautiful thoughts* and prays the prayer of the Pharisee ("I thank you that I am not like other people" [Lk. 18:11]), it becomes like a person who's dying from hunger even though he's sitting in front of a table laden with food, all the while watching his guests taking an abundant meal from it and sometimes throwing a glance of envy at him, the one who possesses so many goods. Oh! There's no good possession except God alone, who knows the depths of the heart. . . .

What stunted thoughts created beings have! . . . When they see one soul that's more enlightened than others, instantly they conclude from this that Jesus loves them less than that soul and that they can't be called to the same perfection. Since when does the Lord *no longer* have the *right* to use one of His creatures to distribute, to the souls that He loves, the food that is necessary to them? In the time of Pharaoh, the Lord still had *that right,* because in Scripture He said to that ruler, "But I have raised you up for this very purpose, that I might show you my power and that my name might be proclaimed in all the earth" [Ex. 9:16]. Centuries and centuries have passed since the Most High pronounced those words, and since then, His behavior hasn't changed: He has always used His creatures as instruments for doing His work in souls.

If the canvas on which an artist paints could think and speak, certainly it wouldn't complain about being constantly touched and retouched by a *brush,* and neither would it envy the role of that instrument, because it would know that it's not to the brush but to the artist who directs it that it owes the beauty that it bears. As for the brush, it couldn't take glory in the masterpiece that it has made. It knows that artists aren't inconvenienced: They make child's play of difficulties, taking pleasure in sometimes choosing instruments that are weak and defective. . . .

Beloved Mother, I'm a little brush that Jesus has chosen to paint His image on the souls that you've entrusted to me. An artist doesn't use just one brush, he needs at least two. The first one is the most useful—

with it he gives the general colors, completely covering the canvas in a short time. The other, smaller one, he uses for the details.

Mother, you represent for me the precious brush that the hand of Jesus grasps with love when He wants to do a *big work* in the soul of your children. And I'm the *very little* one that He deigns to use afterward for the slightest details.

The first time that Jesus used His little brush was around the eighth of December, 1892 [the Feast Day of the Immaculate Conception]. I'll always remember that period as a time of graces. Dear Mother, I'm going to confide in you those sweet memories.

At the age of fifteen, when I had the happiness of entering Carmel, I found in the novitiate a classmate who had preceded me by a few months. She was eight years older than I was, but her childlike character made us forget the difference in years. Soon, you had the joy of seeing your two little postulants get along marvelously and become inseparable. In order to support that growing affection, which seemed to you would bear good fruit, you allowed us from time to time to have some little spiritual talks together. My dear classmate charmed me by her innocence and her expansive character. But on the other hand, I was surprised to see how much the affection that she had for you was different from mine. There were also many things in her behavior toward the Sisters that I would have wanted her to change. . . .

Since that period, God gave me to understand that there are souls for whom His mercy never tires of waiting, to whom He gives His light only by degrees. So I kept careful watch not to hurry His timetable, and I waited patiently for it to be pleasing Jesus to make it come.

Reflecting one day on the permission that you had given us to talk together, as it is written in our holy constitutions: "In order to inflame in us greater love for our Bridegroom," I thought sadly that our conversations weren't attaining the desired result. Then God made me feel that the time had come, and that I mustn't be afraid to speak, or I should stop these talks that were like those of friends in the world. That day was a Saturday.

The next day during my time of thanksgiving prayers, I begged God to put into my mouth sweet and convincing words, or rather for Himself to speak through me. Jesus granted my prayer. He allowed the result to fulfill my hope entirely, for those who turn their eyes on Him will be enlightened [cf. Ps. 33:6 D-R]. And in the darkness the light dawned for the upright [Ps. 112:4]. The first of these verses was addressed to me, and the second one was for my classmate, who truly was upright. . . .

The time had come that we resolved to be together, and when the poor dear Sister cast her eyes on me, she saw right away that I was no longer the same. She sat down beside me, blushing, and I, pressing her head against my heart, told her with tears in my voice *everything I thought of her,* but with such tender expressions, showing her such great affection, that soon her tears mingled with mine. She agreed with great humility that everything I was saying was true. She promised me to begin a new life, and asked me as a grace to always alert her to her faults. Finally, at the moment when we parted, our affection had become quite spiritual; it no longer had anything human about it. In us was realized this passage from Scripture: "A brother that is helped by his brother, is like a strong city" [Prov. 18:19 D-R].

What Jesus did with His little brush would soon have been erased if He hadn't acted through you, Mother, in order to accomplish His work in the soul that He wanted to be completely His. The trial seemed quite bitter to my poor classmate, but your firmness triumphed, and it was then, as I tried to comfort this one whom you had given me as a sister among all of them, that I was able to explain to her what true love consists in.

I showed her that it was *herself* that she loved and not you. I told her how I loved you and the sacrifices that I was required to make at the beginning of my religious life in order not to attach myself to you in a material fashion, like a dog that becomes attached to its master. Love is fed with sacrifices. The more the soul refuses natural satisfactions, the more its tenderness becomes strong and impartial.

I remember that when I was a postulant, I sometimes had such violent temptations to enter your room in order to satisfy myself, to find a few drops of joy, that I was obliged to pass quickly in front of the storeroom and to hang on tightly to the stair rail. There came into my mind a large number of permissions to ask of you. In short, beloved Mother, I found a thousand reasons to make my nature happy. . . .

How happy I am now to have deprived myself of this from the very beginning of my religious life! I already enjoy the reward promised to those who fight courageously. I no longer feel that it's necessary to refuse all consolations of the heart, because my soul is strengthened by the only One whom I wanted to love. I see with happiness that by loving Him, the heart becomes enlarged. I see that it can give incomparably more tenderness to those who are dear to it, than if it were to concentrate on a self-centered and unfruitful love.

Dear Mother, I reminded you about the first work that Jesus and you deigned to accomplish in me; this was only the prelude to the ones that were to be entrusted to me. When it was given to me to penetrate into the sanctuary of souls, I saw right away that the task was beyond my strength, so I placed myself in God's arms, like a little child, and, hiding my face in His hair, I told Him, "Lord, I'm too little to feed Your children. If You want to give them through me what is proper for each one, fill my little hand, and without leaving Your arms, without turning my head, I'll give Your treasures to the soul who comes to me to ask for her food. If she finds it according to her taste, I'll know that it's not to me, but to You that she owes it. On the other hand, if she complains about what I present to her and finds it bitter, my peace won't be troubled. I'll try to persuade her that this food comes from You, and I'll take care not to look for any other food for her."

Mother, since I understood that it was impossible for me to do anything by myself, the task that you imposed on me no longer seemed difficult to me. I felt that the only thing needed was to unite myself more and more to Jesus, and that all the rest would be given to me as well [Mt. 6:33]. And in fact my hope never put me to shame [Rom. 5:5]: God deigned to fill my little hand as many times as it was necessary to nourish the souls of my Sisters.

I admit to you, beloved Mother, that if I had leaned in the slightest on my own strength, I would soon have turned my weapons back in to you. . . . *From afar* all that seems quite rosy, to do good to souls, to make them love God more, in order to shape them according to one's views and personal thoughts. *From up close* it's quite the opposite. The rosiness has disappeared. . . . You feel that doing good is something almost as impossible without God's help as making the sun shine at night. . . . You feel that you must absolutely forget your own desires and personal conceptions, and guide souls along the path that Jesus has traced for them, without trying to make them walk along your own path.

But this is still not the most difficult thing. What costs me above all is to observe the faults, the slightest imperfections, and to make war to the death against them. I was going to say, "unfortunately for me"! (but no, that would be cowardice), so I say, "fortunately for my Sisters." Since I've taken my place in Jesus' arms, I'm like the watchman observing the enemy from the highest tower of a castle. Nothing escapes my sight. Often I'm surprised to see so clearly, and I find the prophet Jonah to be quite excusable for running away instead of going to announce the ruin of Nineveh [Jon. 1:2-3].

I would a thousand times prefer to receive correction than to give it to others, but I feel that it's most necessary for that to be a suffering for me, because when you act according to nature, it's impossible for the soul to whom you want to reveal her faults to understand how wrong she is. All she sees is one thing: The Sister who's in charge of directing me is angry, and everything is falling on my head—and yet I'm full of the best of intentions.

I know well that your little lambs [the Novices] find me to be strict. If they were to read these lines, they'd say that it doesn't look as if it costs me the slightest thing in the world to run after them, to talk to them in a strict way when I show them that their beautiful fleece coat is dirty or to bring them some little scrap of wool that they've allowed to become torn by thorns on the path.

The little lambs can say all they want; in the end, they feel that I love them with a true love, that I'll never be like the hired hand who, when he sees the wolf coming, abandons the flock and runs away [Jn. 10:11–13]. I'm ready to give my life for them, but my affection is so pure that I don't want them to know it. With Jesus' grace, I've never tried to draw their hearts to myself. I've understood that my mission was to draw them to God and to make them understand that here below, you were, Mother, the visible Jesus that they must love and respect.

I told you, dear Mother, that by teaching others I'd learned a great deal. I saw first of all that all souls have just about the same struggles, but they're so different from another point of view that I have no trouble understanding what Fr. Pichon said: "There's a much greater difference among souls than there is among faces." Therefore it's impossible to act with all of them in the same way. With certain souls, I feel that I have to make myself little, not being afraid to humble myself by admitting my struggles, my defeats. Seeing that I have the same weakness as they do, my dear Sisters in turn confess to me the faults that they reproach themselves for, and they rejoice that I understand them *through experience.* With others I've seen that on the contrary, in order to do them good I have to have a great deal of firmness and never take back anything once I've said it. In that case taking a low place wouldn't be humility, but weakness.

God has given me the grace not to be afraid of war; at all costs I have to do my duty. More than once I've heard this: "If you want to get anything out of me, you have to treat me gently. Come against me hard, and you'll get nothing." I know that no one is a good judge in his own case. A child that a doctor makes undergo a painful operation won't fail to cry loudly and to say that the cure is worse than the disease. However, if he finds himself cured a few days later, he's happy to be able to play and run. It's the same for souls. Soon they recognize that a little bitterness is sometimes preferable to sugar, and they're not afraid to admit it.

Sometimes I can't help smiling inside when I see what a change has taken place from one day to the next—it's enchanting. One comes and says to me, "You were right to be so strict yesterday. At first that revolted me, but afterward I remembered everything and I saw that you were very fair. . . . Listen, as I was walking away, I was thinking that it was all over. I was telling myself, 'I'm going to find our Superior and tell her that I'm not going to go anymore with Sister Thérèse of the Child Jesus.' But I felt that it was the devil who was inspiring that in me, and then it seemed to me that you were praying for me. So I stopped still, and the light began to shine. But now I need for you to explain it all to me, and that's why I'm coming." The conversation is quickly taken up, and I'm quite happy to be able to follow my heart's leading, without serving up any bitter food.

Yes, but. . . . I quickly realize that you mustn't go too far, too fast. One word can tear down the beautiful structure that was built through tears. If I have the misfortune to say a word that seems to lessen the strength of what I said the day before, I see the dear Sister try to clutch hold of the branches again, so inside I say a little prayer, and the truth always wins out. Oh! It's prayer, it's sacrifice that are entirely my strength. These are the invincible weapons that Jesus has given me. Much more than words, they can touch souls—I've very often had that experience.

There is one experience among them all that made a gentle and deep impression on me. It was during Lent. At that time I was in charge of the one single Novice who was here and whose angel [advisor] I was. She came to find me one morning, all beaming. "Oh! If only you knew," she told me, "what I dreamed about last night. I was at my sister's side, and I wanted to disengage her from all the vain things that she loves so much. To do that I explained this couplet: 'Live in love. To love You, Jesus, what a fruitful loss. All my sweet scents are Yours, no going back.' I could really feel that my words were penetrating her soul, and I was transported with joy. This morning as I was waking up, I thought that God perhaps wanted me to give Him that soul. How about if I wrote her after Lent to tell her my dream and tell her that Jesus wants her to be entirely His?"

Without thinking longer about it I told her that she might well try, but first, she needed to ask permission from our Superior. Since Lent was far from being over, you were, beloved Mother, quite surprised by a request that seemed too premature to you. And certainly, inspired by God, you answered that it wasn't through letters that Carmelites are to save souls, but through prayer.

When I learned about your decision I understood immediately that the words were from Jesus, and I told Sr. Marie of the Trinity, "We have to get to work, let's pray a lot. What a joy it would be if *at the end of Lent* our prayer were granted! . . ." Oh! Infinite mercy of the Lord, who's willing to listen to the prayer of His children. . . . At *the end of Lent,* one more soul was consecrating herself to Jesus. This was a true miracle of grace, a miracle obtained through the fervor of a humble Novice!

Therefore, how great is the power of prayer! It's like a queen's having constant free access to the king and being able to obtain all that she asks. It's not necessary in order for a prayer to be granted to read in a book a beautiful formula composed for the circumstance. If that were the case . . . alas! How I should be pitied! . . . Outside of the *Divine Office* [the services sung in Gregorian chant], which I'm *very unworthy* to recite, I don't have the courage to make a strict rule for myself to search in books for *beautiful* prayers. That gives me a headache, there are so many of them! . . . And then some are more *beautiful* than others. . . . I wouldn't know how to recite them all. Not knowing which one to choose, I do as children do who don't know how to read: I very simply tell God what I want to tell Him, without making beautiful phrases, and He always understands me. . . .

For me, prayer is an upward rising of the heart, it's a simple glance toward heaven, it's a cry of gratitude and love in the midst of trials as much as in the midst of joys. In short, it's something big, something great, something supernatural, that expands my heart and unites me to Jesus.

However, I wouldn't like you to think, beloved Mother, that the prayers we make in common in the nuns' choir, or in hermitages, I recite without devotion. On the contrary, I really love the prayers we say in common, because Jesus promised to be in the midst of those who gather together in His name [Mt. 18:19-20]. I feel then that the fervor of my Sisters adds to mine.

But when I'm all alone (I'm ashamed to admit), the recitation of the Rosary costs me more than one instrument of penance. . . . I feel that I say it so poorly. It's in vain that I attempt to meditate on the mysteries of the Rosary—I don't succeed in engaging my mind. . . . For a long time I was extremely sorry for this lack of devotion that surprised me, because *I love the Blessed Virgin* so much that it ought to be easy for me to pray in her honor prayers that are pleasing to her. Now I'm less sorry, because I think that since the Queen of Heaven is *my Mother*, she must see my good will and is happy with it.

Sometimes when my mind is in such dryness that it's impossible for me to pull a thought out of it to unite myself to God, I *very slowly* recite an "Our Father" [the Lord's Prayer, Mt. 6:9–13] and a "Hail Mary" [cf. Lk. 1:28]. Then those prayers delight me; they nourish my soul more than if I had recited them hurriedly a hundred times. . . .

The Blessed Virgin shows me that she's not angry with me; she never fails to protect me as soon as I invoke her. If some sort of worry, some difficulty, overtakes me, quickly I turn toward her and always, like the most tender of mothers, she shoulders my interests. . . . How many times, as I've been speaking to the Novices, has it happened to me to invoke her and to feel the blessings of her motherly protection! . . .

Often Novices tell me, "But you have an answer for everything. I thought this time I would stump you. . . . Where do you get what you say?" Some are even candid enough to think I read their soul because it's happened that I've caught them off guard by telling them what they were thinking. One night one of my Sisters had resolved to hide from me a painful thing that was making her suffer a lot. I met her in the morning, and she spoke to me with her face smiling, and I, without responding to what she was saying, told her with a convinced tone of voice, "Something is troubling you." If I had made the moon fall at her feet she wouldn't have looked at me with more astonishment. Her stupefaction was so great that it took me over, and for an instant I was seized with a supernatural fright. I was quite sure that I didn't have the gift of reading souls, and it surprised me that much more at having hit the mark so squarely. I knew that God was very near, and that, without my being aware of it, I had said, like a child, words that were not coming from me but from Him.

Beloved Mother, you understand that for Novices everything is allowed. They have to be able to say what they're thinking without any restriction, the good as well as the bad. That's so much easier for them with me since they don't owe me the respect that they would give to a teacher.

I can't say that Jesus makes me walk *externally* by the way of humiliations. He contents Himself to humble me *in the depths* of my soul. To the eyes of creatures everything is successful for me. I follow the path of honors, as much as that is possible in a religious order. I understand that it's not for me, but for others, that I have to walk along this path that seems so perilous. In fact, if in the eyes of the community I were to pass for a nun who is full of defects, incapable, without intelligence or good judgment, it would be impossible for you, Mother, to be helped by me. That's why God has thrown a veil over all my interior and exterior defects. That veil at times brings me a few compliments from Novices. I feel that they don't do this out of flattery but that it's the expression of their naïve feelings. Truly there would be no way for that to inspire vanity in me, because I have unceasingly present in my thoughts the memory of who I am.

However, sometimes the strong desire comes to me to hear something other than praise. You know, beloved Mother, that I prefer vinegar to sugar. My soul also gets tired of food that is overly sugary, and Jesus then allows it to be served a good little salad, topped with lots of vinegar and spices, with nothing lacking except *oil*, which gives it one more flavor. . . . That good little salad is served to me by the Novices at the moment when I expect it the least. God lifts the veil that hides my imperfections, and then my dear Sisters, seeing me as I am, no longer find me quite to their taste. With a simplicity that delights me, they tell me all the struggles that I give them, what they don't like about me. In short, they don't worry any more than they would if they were talking about somebody else, knowing that they give me great pleasure in behaving this way. Oh! Truly, it's more than a pleasure, it's a delicious banquet that floods my soul with joy. I can't explain how a thing that is so displeasing to nature can cause such great happiness. If I hadn't experienced it, I wouldn't be able to believe it. . . .

One day when I had particularly desired to be humiliated, it happened that a Novice took it on herself so well to satisfy my desire that I immediately thought about Shimei's cursing David [cf. 2 Sam. 16:5-13], and I told myself, "Yes, it's truly the Lord who has told her to say these things to me. . . ." And my soul savored deliciously the bitter food that was served it with such abundance.

This is how God deigns to take care of me. He can't always give me the fortifying bread of outward humiliation, but from time to time, He allows me to feed on the crumbs that fall from the *children's* table [cf. Mt. 15:27]. Ah! How great is His mercy; I will be able to sing of it only in heaven.

Beloved mother, since with you I'm starting to sing of this infinite mercy on earth, I must go on to tell you a great blessing that I got from the mission that you entrusted to me. It used to be when I saw a Sister who was doing something that I didn't like and that seemed irregular to me, I would tell myself, "Oh! If only I could tell her what I think, show her that she's wrong, that would do me good!" Since I've practiced the trade a bit, I assure you, mother, that I've completely changed my mind. When I happen to see a Sister doing an action that seems imperfect to me, I heave a sigh of relief and I tell myself, "What happiness! She isn't a Novice, so I'm not required to correct her." And then very quickly I try to excuse the Sister and to see in her the good intentions that she no doubt has.

Oh! Mother, since I've been sick, the care that you've lavished on me has taught me so much more about charity. No remedy seems too costly to you, and if it doesn't work, then, without becoming weary, you try something else. When I used to go to the recreation periods, what attention you gave to seeing that I was well sheltered from the wind. In short, if I were to say everything, I would never finish.

Thinking about all these things, I've told myself that I ought to be as compassionate toward the spiritual infirmities of my Sisters as you are, dear Mother, in caring for me with so much love.

I've noticed (and it's quite natural) that the holiest Sisters are the most loved. People seek out their conversation, and they render services to them without their asking for them. In short, these souls who are capable of enduring the lack of consideration and tact find themselves surrounded with the affection of everyone. One can apply to them this word from our father St. John of the Cross: "All good things were given to me when I no longer sought them out through self-love."

Imperfect souls, on the other hand, are not sought out. No doubt people remain on their behalf within the boundaries of religious politeness, but perhaps out of fear of saying some not-so-nice words to them, people avoid their company.

By saying "imperfect souls," I don't mean to speak only about spiritual imperfections, since the holiest of persons will be perfect only in heaven. I mean to speak about the lack of judgment, of manners, of susceptibility in certain characters—all the things that don't make life very pleasant. I know well that these moral infirmities are chronic. There's no hope of cure. But I also know full well that my Mother would not stop caring for me or trying to comfort me even if I were to remain ill for my whole life.

Here's the conclusion that I make from this: I must seek out during recreation periods, during free time, the company of the Sisters who are the least pleasant to me, and fulfill among those blessed souls the role of the good Samaritan. One word, one pleasant smile, are often enough to cause a sad soul to brighten up. But it's not absolutely to attain that goal that I want to practice charity, because I know that soon I would be discouraged: A word that I might have said with the best of intentions might perhaps be interpreted all wrong.

Therefore, so as not to waste my time, I want to be pleasant with everyone (and particularly with the least pleasant Sisters) in order to give joy to Jesus, and to respond to the counsel that He gave in the Gospel more or less in these terms: "When you give a feast, don't invite your family members and your friends out of fear that they won't invite you in turn, and thus you will have received your reward. But invite the poor, the lame, the crippled, and you will be happy that they won't be able to pay you back, because your Father who sees in secret will reward you" [cf. Lk. 14:12–14, Mt. 6:3-4].

What feast could a nun offer to her Sisters if it isn't a spiritual feast comprised of pleasant and joyful charity? For me, I don't know of any other, and I want to be like St. Paul, who rejoiced with those who rejoice [Rom. 12:15]: It's true that he also mourned with those who mourned, and tears must sometimes appear in the feast that I want to serve, but always I will endeavor that at the end those tears will change into joy [Jn. 16:20], since the Lord loves those who give cheerfully [2 Cor. 9:7].

I remember an act of charity that God inspired me to do when I was still a Novice. It was a small thing, but our Father who sees in secret, who looks at the intent rather than at the greatness of the action, has already rewarded me for it without waiting until the next life. It was at the time that Sister St. Peter was still going to the choir and the refectory. At evening prayers she was placed in front of me. Ten minutes before six o'clock, a Sister had to take the trouble to guide her to the refectory [the dining room], because at that time the nurses had too many other patients to come get her.

It cost me a lot to offer myself to render that little service, because I knew that it wasn't easy to make poor Sister St. Peter happy, she who was suffering so much that she didn't like to change guides. However, I didn't want to miss such a beautiful opportunity to practice charity, remembering that Jesus said, ". . . whatever you did for one of the least of these brothers and sisters of mine, you did for me" [Mt. 25:40]. So I offered myself quite humbly to guide her—and not without some difficulty, I managed to get my services accepted! Finally I set my hand to the work, and I did it with such good will that I succeeded perfectly.

Each evening when I would see Sister St. Peter shake her hourglass, I knew that that meant, "Let's go." It's unbelievable how much it cost me to take this trouble, especially in the beginning. Nonetheless I did it immediately, and then a whole ceremony would begin. I had to move and carry the bench in a certain way, and above all, never hurry. Then the walk would take place. It was a matter of following the poor invalid, supporting her by the waist. I did this with the greatest gentleness that was possible for me. But if, through some misfortune, she took a false step, instantly it seemed to her that I was supporting her poorly and that she was going to fall.

"Oh! Good Lord! You're going too fast. I'm going to break something." If I tried to go still more slowly, "Well, follow me, now, I can't feel your hand, you've let go of me, I'm going to fall. Oh! I was right that you're too young to guide me."

Finally we would arrive without accident in the refectory. There, other difficulties would crop up. It was a matter of taking Sister St. Peter to her seat and of acting nimbly so as not to hurt her. Then I had to roll back her sleeves (again in a certain way), and then I was free to go. With her poor crippled hands, she would arrange her bread in her bowl as best she could. I soon noticed this, and each evening, I left only after having rendered this one more little service to her. Since she hadn't asked me to do this, she was very touched by my attention, and it was through this means, which I hadn't sought out on purpose, that I gained her good graces completely, and especially (I found this out later) because after cutting her bread, before leaving her I would give her my most beautiful smile.

Beloved Mother, perhaps you were surprised that I'm writing you about this little act of charity that happened such a long time ago. Oh! If I did so, it's because I feel that because of it I have to sing of the mercies of the Lord: He deigned to leave me with this memory, like a perfume that leads me to practice charity.

I sometimes remember certain details that for my soul are like a spring breeze. Here's one that presents itself to my memory: One winter evening I was as usual fulfilling my little task [of guiding Sister St. Peter to the refectory]. It was cold, it was night. . . .

Suddenly [in a vision] I heard in the distance the harmonious sound of a musical instrument. Then I was able to make out a well-lit room, quite brilliant with gilding, with elegantly dressed girls giving each other compliments and worldly politeness. Then my glance fell on the poor invalid that I was holding up. Instead of a melody I heard from time to time her plaintive moaning; instead of gilding, I saw the bricks of our austere cloister, dimly lit by a weak glimmer.

I can't express what happened in my soul, but what I do know is that the Lord illuminated it with the rays of truth that so far surpassed the dark glitter of worldly feasts, that I couldn't believe my happiness. . . . Oh! In order to enjoy worldly feasts for a thousand years, I wouldn't have given up the ten minutes spent in fulfilling my humble office of charity. . . . If already when suffering, in the midst of battle, one can enjoy for an instant a happiness that surpasses all the happiness of earth, at the thought that God has taken us out of the world, what will it be in heaven when we will see, in the midst of gladness and eternal rest, the incomparable grace that the Lord has given us by choosing us to live in His house, the veritable gate of heaven? [Gen. 28:17, Ps. 27:4] . . .

It's not always with these transports of gladness that I've practiced charity. At the beginning of my religious life, Jesus wanted me to feel how sweet it is to see Him in the souls of His brides. Therefore when I was guiding Sister St. Peter, I would do it with so much love that it would have been impossible for me to do better if I'd had to guide Jesus Himself.

The practice of charity hasn't always seemed so sweet to me, as I was telling you just now, dear Mother. To prove this to you, I'm going to tell you about certain little battles that will certainly make you smile. For a long time, at evening prayers, I was placed in front of a Sister who had a funny idiosyncrasy, and I think . . . a lot of inner illumination, because she rarely used a book. Here's how I noticed it: As soon as this Sister had arrived, she would begin making a strange little noise that sounded like one that would be made if you rubbed two shells against each other. I was the only one who noticed it, because I have extremely keen hearing (a little too keen sometimes).

To tell you, Mother, how much that little noise tired me out would be impossible. I really wanted to turn my head and look at the guilty one, who, of course, didn't notice her tic. That was the only way to let her know what was going on. But in the depths of my heart I felt that it was better to suffer that for the love of God and not to give the Sister any trouble.

So I kept quiet and tried to unite myself with God and to forget the little noise. . . . It was all of no use: I felt sweat pouring out of me, and I was obliged to simply pray a prayer of suffering. But as I was suffering, I was seeking the way to undergo it, not with agitation, but with joy and peace, at least in the innermost part of my soul. So I made every effort to love that little noise that was so unpleasant. Instead of trying not to hear it (which would be impossible) I placed all my attention on hearing it well, as if it had been a delightful concert, and my whole prayer (which was not the prayer of quietude) was spent in offering that concert to Jesus.

Another time I was doing laundry with a Sister who kept throwing dirty water in my face each time she picked up the handkerchiefs on her bench. My first movement was to draw back and dry my face, in order to show the Sister who was sprinkling me that she would do me a service if she would move gently, but immediately I thought that I was quite silly to refuse treasures that had been given to me so generously, and I took great care not to let my struggle show. I made every effort to desire to receive a lot of dirty water, so that in the end I had really taken a liking to this new form of sprinkling with holy water, and I promised myself to come back another time to that happy place where one received so many treasures.

Beloved Mother, you see that I am a *very little soul* who can offer to God only *very little things*. It still happens often that I miss out on doing these little sacrifices that give so much peace to the soul. That doesn't discourage me—I endure having a little less peace, and I try to be more vigilant another time.

Oh! The Lord is so good to me that it's impossible for me to be afraid of Him. He's always given me what I've desired, or rather, He's made me desire what He wanted to give me. So a short time before my trial against faith was to begin, I told myself, "I really don't have any great outward trials, and in order to have inward ones, the good Lord would have to change my way. I don't think He'll do that, but I can't always live this way, at rest. . . . So what means will Jesus find to test me?" The answer wasn't long in coming, and it showed me that the One I loved isn't short on means. Without changing

my way, God sent me the trial that was to mix a health-
ful bitterness with all my joys. It's not only when He
wants to test me that Jesus makes me sense His presence
and desire Him.

For a long time I had a desire that seemed quite unob-
tainable, namely to have a *priest brother*. I often
thought that if my little brothers hadn't flown up to
heaven I would have had the happiness of seeing them
step up to the altar. But since God chose them to make
little angels out of them, I could no longer hope to see
my dream come true. And yet, not only did Jesus give
me the grace that I desired, but He also united me
through ties of the soul to *two* of His apostles, who
became my brothers. . . . Beloved Mother, I want to tell
you in detail how Jesus granted my desire and even surpassed it, since I wanted only one priest brother who
would think about me each day at the holy altar.

It was our Mother St. Teresa who sent me my first
little brother as a birthday bouquet in 1895. I was in
the laundry, quite immersed in my work, when Mother
Agnes of Jesus [who was then prioress] took me aside
and read me a letter that she had just received. It came
from a young seminarian [Maurice Bellière], inspired,
he said, by St. Teresa, to ask for a Sister who would
devote herself especially to the salvation of his soul and
help him through her prayers and sacrifices when he
became a missionary, to the end that he might be able
to save many souls. He promised to always keep in
remembrance this one who would become his Sister,
when he would in the future be able to offer the Holy
Sacrifice. Mother Agnes of Jesus told me that she wanted

me to be the one who would become the Sister of this future missionary.

Mother, it would be impossible for me to tell you how happy I was. My desire, fulfilled in an unhoped-for way, gave birth in my heart to a joy that I would call childish, because I would have to go back to the days of my childhood to find the memory of those joys that were so lively that the soul is too little to contain them. For years I've never felt that type of happiness. I felt that because of it my soul was new. It was as if for the first time musical chords were played that had until then fallen into unconsciousness.

I understood the obligations that I was taking on, so I set to work trying to redouble my fervor. I have to admit that at first I had no consolations to stimulate my enthusiasm. After writing a charming letter full of heartfelt, noble sentiments to thank Mother Agnes of Jesus, my little brother showed no sign of life until the following July, except when he sent his letter in November to say that he was starting his required military service.

It was to you, Beloved Mother, that God had reserved the task of completing the work that had begun. No doubt it's through prayer and sacrifice that missionaries can be helped, but sometimes when it pleases Jesus to unite two souls for His glory, He permits that from time to time they may be able to communicate their thoughts to each other and excite one another to love God more. But that requires the *express desire* of authority, for it seems to me that otherwise that correspondence would do more harm than good, if not to the missionary, at least to the nun who is continually led through her lifestyle to withdraw within herself. Therefore, instead of uniting her to God, that correspondence (even at a distance) that she might have solicited would occupy her mind, making her imagine she's moving mountains and doing marvelous things. She would do nothing at all except to bring on herself, under the guise of zeal, a useless distraction.

For me it's the same with that as for everything else: I feel that for my letters to do good they have to be written out of obedience, and I feel repugnance rather than pleasure in writing them. So when I'm talking with a Novice, I try to mortify myself as I do so. I avoid asking her questions that would satisfy my curiosity. If she begins an interesting topic and then passes on to another that annoys me without finishing the first one, I take care not to remind her about the subject she has left aside, because it seems to me that you can't do any good when you're seeking yourself.

Beloved Mother, I notice that I'll never change and do better. Here I am, having wandered quite far from my subject, with all my dissertations. Forgive me, please, and let me start again at the first opportunity, since I can't do otherwise! . . . You behave as does God, who never gets tired of listening to me, when I tell Him quite simply my pains and my joys as if He weren't acquainted with them. . . . You also, Mother, have known for a long time what I think and all the little memorable events of my life. So I wouldn't know how to tell you anything new.

I can't help laughing when I think that I'm writing you scrupulously so many things that you know as well as I do. Well, dear Mother, I'm obeying you, and if now you don't find any interest in reading these pages, perhaps they will entertain you in your old age and will then serve as fuel for your fire, so I won't have wasted my time. . . . But I'm having fun talking like a child. Don't think, Mother, that I'm looking for what usefulness my little work can have. Since I'm doing it out of obedience, that's enough for me, and I wouldn't feel any distress if you were to burn it in front of me after reading it.

It's time for me to go back to the story of my priest brothers, who now hold such a big place in my life. Last year at the end of May, I remember that one day you sent for me before a mealtime. My heart was pounding when I entered your office, dear Mother. I was wondering what you could have to say to me, because this was the first time you had sent for me like that. After you told me to be seated, here's the proposal that you made: "Would you please take on the spiritual interests of a missionary who is to be ordained a priest and depart very soon?" And then, Mother, you read me the letter from that young priest [Fr. Adolphe Roulland] so that I might know just what he was asking for.

My first response was a feeling of joy that soon gave way to fear. I explained to you, beloved Mother, that since I had already offered my poor merits for a future apostle, I believed I wouldn't be able to do it again for the intentions of another one, and that, besides, there

were many Sisters better than I who would be able to
respond to his desire. All my objections were of no use;
you replied that one could have several brothers. Then I
asked you if obedience couldn't double my merits. You
answered yes, and told me several things that made me
see that I had to accept, without scruple, a new brother.

In my heart, Mother, I thought like you, and even,
since "the zeal of a Carmelite nun should set the world
on fire," I hope with the grace of God to be useful to
more than *two* missionaries. And I would never be able
to forget to pray for all of them, without setting aside
simple priests whose mission is sometimes as difficult to
fulfill as that of apostles preaching to the unconverted. In
short, I want to be a daughter of the Church as was our
Mother St. Teresa, and pray for the intentions of the
Holy Father the Pope, knowing that his intentions
embrace the whole world. There is the general goal of
my life, but that wouldn't have prevented me from praying and uniting myself especially to the works of my dear
little angels if they [my deceased brothers] had been
priests.

Well! Here's how I've united myself spiritually to the
apostles that Jesus gave me as brothers: Everything that
belongs to me, belongs to each of them [Lk. 15:31]. I
feel clearly how the *good* Lord is too *good* to divide His
inheritance. He's so rich that He gives without measure
everything that I ask of Him. . . . But don't think,
Mother, that I'm going to get lost in long enumerations.

Since I have two brothers and my little Sisters the
Novices, if I wanted to ask for what each soul needs
and set it out in detail, the days would be too short, and

I would be very much afraid of forgetting something important. To simple souls, complicated means aren't required. As I'm among that number, one morning during my time of thanksgiving prayers, Jesus gave me a *simple* means of accomplishing my mission. He made me understand this word from the Song of Songs: "Draw me: we will run after thee to the odour of thy ointments" [Song 1:3 D-R]. Jesus, therefore it's not even necessary to say, "By drawing me, draw the souls that I love." This simple word, "Draw me," is enough. Lord, I understand it. When a soul has let itself be captivated by the intoxicating fragrance of Your perfumes, it wouldn't know how to run all by itself. All the souls that it loves are brought along in its train. That's done without constraint, without effort. It's a natural consequence of its attraction toward You.

Just as a flooded stream, spilling impetuously into the ocean, carries along after it everything that it has encountered on its passage, in the same way, Jesus, the soul that plunges into the shoreless ocean of Your love draws with it all the treasures that it possesses. . . . Lord, You know that I have no other treasures than the souls that it has pleased You to unite with mine. Those treasures You've entrusted to me, so I dare to borrow the words that you addressed to the Heavenly Father on the last night that saw You still on our earth as a traveler and a mortal. Jesus, my Beloved, I don't know when my exile will end. . . . More than one night will see me still in exile singing of Your mercies [Ps. 89:1], but finally, for me as well, the last night will come. Then I would like to be able to say to You, my God:

I have brought you glory on earth by finishing the work you gave me to do. . . . I have revealed you to those whom you gave me. . . . They were yours; you gave them to me. . . . Now they know that everything you have given me comes from you. For I gave them the words you gave me and they accepted them . . . and they believed that you sent me. I pray for . . . those you have given me, for they are yours. . . . I will remain in the world no longer, but they are still in the world, and I am coming to you. Holy Father, protect by the power of your name those whom you have given me. . . . I am coming to you now, but I say these things while I am still in the world, so that they may have the full measure of my joy within them. . . . My prayer is not that you take them out of the world but that you protect them from the evil one. They are not of the world, even as I am not of it. . . . My prayer is not for them alone. I pray also for those who will believe in me through their message. . . . Father, I want those you have given me to be with me . . . Then the world will know that you . . . have loved them even as you have loved me. [cf. Jn. 17:4-26]

Yes, Lord, this is what I would like to repeat after You before flying away into Your arms. Is this perhaps impudence? No! For a long time You've allowed me to be audacious with You. Like the father of the prodigal son talking to his elder son, You've said to me, "Everything I have is yours" [Lk. 15:31]. So Your words, Jesus, are mine, and I can use them to draw the favors of the Heavenly Father upon the souls who are united with me. But, Lord, when I say that where I will be, I want those You have given me to be as well, I'm not claiming that they can't arrive at a higher glory than the one that it will please You to give me. I simply want to ask that one day we may all be reunited in Your beautiful heaven.

You know, God, I've never desired anything else than to love You. My ambition is for no other glory. Your love informed me beginning in my childhood. It grew with me, and now it's a chasm the depth of which I cannot fathom. Love attracts love, so, my Jesus, mine shoots up toward You. It would like to fill up the chasm that draws it, but alas! It's not even a drop of dew lost in the ocean! . . .

To love You as You love me, I have to borrow Your own love; only then do I find rest. Oh my Jesus, it's perhaps an illusion, but it seems to me that You can't fill a soul with more love than You've filled mine. It's because of that, that I dare to ask You to love those whom You have given me as You have loved me [Jn. 17:23]. One day, in heaven, if I discover that You love them more than me, I'll rejoice at that, since I recognize even now that those souls merit Your love much more than I do. But here below I cannot conceive of a greater immensity of love than the one that it has pleased You to pour out so lavishly on me, without any merit on my part [Rom. 3:23-24].

Dear Mother, I'm finally coming back to you. I'm quite surprised at what I've just written, because I had no intention to do so. Since it's written, it will have to remain, but before coming back to the story of my brothers, I want to tell you, Mother, that I don't apply to them, but rather to my little Sisters, the first words borrowed from the Gospel, "For I gave them the words you gave me" [Jn. 17:8], etc., because I don't think I'm capable of teaching missionaries. Fortunately I'm not yet proud enough for that! Nor would I have been capable of giving some counsel to my Sisters, if you, Mother, who represent God for me, hadn't given me leave to do so.

On the contrary, it's your dear spiritual sons who are my brothers that I was thinking about when I wrote those words of Jesus and the ones that followed, "My prayer is not that you take them out of the world. . . . I pray also for those who will believe in me through their message" [Jn. 17:15, 20]. How in fact could I not pray for the souls that they will save in their distant missions by means of suffering and preaching?

Mother, I think that it's necessary for me to give you a few more explanations about the passage from the Song of Songs, "Draw me, we will run" [Song 1:3 D-R], because what I tried to say about it doesn't seem to me to be very understandable. "No one," said Jesus, "can come to me unless the Father who sent me draws them" [Jn. 6:44]. Then, through inspiring parables, and often without even using that method that was so familiar to the common people, He taught us that it's enough to knock and the door will be opened, to seek and we will find, and to humbly hold out our hand and we will receive what we ask for [Lk. 11:9–13]. . . . He also said that everything that we ask of *His Father* in His name, He will grant it [Jn. 16:23]. It's for that purpose, no doubt, that the Holy Spirit, before the birth of Jesus, dictated that prophetic prayer, "Draw me, we will run."

What then does it mean to ask to be *drawn,* if not to unite ourselves in a personal way to the object that captivates our heart? If fire and iron had the faculty of reason, and the latter said to the former, "Draw me," wouldn't it prove that it desires to be identified with the fire in such a way that it penetrates and takes in its burning substance and seems to become only one with it?

Beloved Mother, this is my prayer: I ask Jesus to draw me into the flames of His love, to unite me so closely to Himself, that He may live and act in me [Gal. 2:20]. I feel that the more the fire of love will inflame my heart, the more I will say, "Draw me," the more also, souls will come close to me (poor little useless dross of iron, if I were to move away from the divine clear glowing fire), and the more those souls will run quickly toward the fragrance of the perfumes of their Beloved.

For, a soul aflame with love can't remain inactive. Doubtless, like Mary Magdalene, it clings to Jesus' feet, it listens to His sweet and blazing word. Seeming to give nothing, it gives much more than Martha, who was upset about many things and would have liked for her sister to be like her. It's not Martha's works that Jesus blamed. Those works are the ones His divine Mother humbly accepted to do her whole life, since she had to prepare the meals for the Holy Family. It's only the anxiousness of His eager hostess that He wanted to amend [Lk. 10:39–42].

All the saints understood this, and more particularly perhaps those who filled the world with enlightenment of the Gospel doctrines. Isn't it through prayer that Sts. Paul, Augustine, John of the Cross, Thomas Aquinas, Francis, Dominic, and so many other well-known Friends of God plumbed that Divine knowledge that delights the greatest minds? One scientist said, "Give me a lever, a point to support it, and I will lift the world." What Archimedes was unable to obtain because his request wasn't made to God and was made only from a material point of view, the Saints obtained in all its fullness. The Almighty gave them, as a point of support, *Himself,* and Himself *alone.* As a lever: prayer, which sets ablaze a fire of love, and that's how they lifted the world. That's how all the Saints who are still fighting the battle lift it, and that's how until the end of the world the Saints to come will lift it as well.

Dear Mother, now I would like to tell you what I mean by the fragrance of the Beloved's perfumes [Song 1:3]. Since Jesus went back up into heaven, I can follow Him only by the prints that He left behind [Acts 1:9]. But those prints are so resplendent that they're perfumed! I have only to cast my eyes on the Holy Gospel, and immediately I breathe the perfumes of Jesus' life, and I know in which direction to run. . . . It's not to the first place, but to the last one, that I cast myself [Mk. 10:31]. Instead of pressing forward with the Pharisee, I repeat, full of confidence, the humble prayer of the tax collector [Lk. 18:10–14].

But above all I imitate Mary Magdalene's behavior, her surprising—or rather her loving—audaciousness that charmed Jesus' Heart and captivates mine [Lk. 7:36–38].

Yes, I feel it. Even when I might have on my conscience all the sins that can be committed, I would go with a heart broken with repentance to throw myself into Jesus' arms, because I know how much He cherishes the prodigal who comes back to Him [Lk. 15:20–24]. It's not because God, in His kind mercy, has preserved my soul from mortal sin that I rise and go to Him in confidence and love.

Important Dates for St. Thérèse of Lisieux

1873 January 2: Birth of Marie-Françoise-Thérèse Martin

1873 January 4: Baptism

1877 August 28: Death of Zélie Martin, Thérèse's mother, of breast cancer

1882 October 2: Thérèse's "second mother," her sister Pauline, enters the Carmelite convent at Lisieux.

1883 March 25: Thérèse becomes seriously ill.

1883 May 13: The Blessed Virgin's smile; Thérèse recovers from illness.

1884 May 8: First Communion

1884 June 14: Confirmation

1886 October 15: Marie, Thérèse's eldest sister and godmother, enters Carmel.

1886 December 25: Conversion on the Feast of the Nativity

1887 November 20: Audience with Leo XIII

1888 April 9: Thérèse enters Carmel.

1889 January 10: Thérèse takes the Carmelite habit.

1890 September: Thérèse receives a Blessing from Pope Leo XIII.

1890 September 8: Thérèse makes her Profession (takes her vows as a nun).

1890 September 24: Thérèse takes the veil.

1890 December: Influenza breaks out at Carmel.

1893 February 20: Sr. Agnes of Jesus (Thérèse's sister Pauline) is elected prioress; the outgoing Prioress, Mother Marie de Gonzague, takes over responsibility for the Novitiate; Thérèse is assigned as her assistant in the spiritual formation of the Novices.

1894 July 29: Death of Louis Martin, Thérèse's father

September 14: Thérèse's sister Céline enters Carmel.

Winter: Out of obedience, Thérèse begins writing the memoirs of her childhood (manuscript A, chapters 1–8 of this edition).

1895 June 9: Thérèse offers herself to Love.

1896 March 21: Mother Marie de Gonzague is re-elected Prioress; she retains oversight of the Novitiate and asks Thérèse to devote herself totally to the Novices.

April 2-3: Thérèse has her first episode of hemoptysis (coughing up blood, a symptom of tuberculosis).

September: Various writings (Manuscript B, chapter 9 of this edition) for Sr. Marie of the Sacred Heart

1897 June: Out of obedience, Thérèse writes Manuscript C (chapters 10-11 of this edition).

September 30: Death of Sr. Thérèse of the Child Jesus of the Holy Face

1898 September 30: Publication of 2,000 copies of *The Story of a Soul*

1914 June 9: Cause of Beatification introduced in Rome

1923 April 29: Beatification (Thérèse is now called "Blessed")

1925 May 17: Canonization (Thérèse is declared a Saint)

1927 December 14: Pope Pius XI proclaims Thérèse joint Patron of the Missions with St. Francis Xavier.

1956 A facsimile edition of Thérèse's manuscripts (including the original, unedited version of *The Story of a Soul*) is published.

1988 The Centenary Edition is published (a critical edition of Thérèse's complete works).

1992 The New Centenary Edition is published (presented to Pope John Paul II on February 18, 1993).

1997 October 19: Pope John Paul II declares St. Thérèse of Lisieux a Doctor of the Church.

About Paraclete Press

Who We Are

Paraclete Press is an ecumenical publisher of books and recordings on Christian spirituality. Our publishing represents a full expression of Christian belief and practice—from Catholic to Evangelical, from Protestant to Orthodox.

Paraclete Press is the publishing arm of the Community of Jesus, an ecumenical monastic community in the Benedictine tradition. As such, we are uniquely positioned in the marketplace without connection to a large corporation and with informal relationships to many branches and denominations of faith.

We like it best when people buy our books from booksellers, our partners in successfully reaching as wide an audience as possible.

What We Are Doing

Books

Paraclete Press publishes books that show the richness and depth of what it means to be Christian. Although Benedictine spirituality is at the heart of all that we do, we publish books that reflect the Christian experience across many cultures, time periods, and houses of worship.

We publish books that nourish the vibrant life of the church and its people—books about spiritual practice, formation, history, ideas, and customs.

We have several different series of books within Paraclete Press, including the bestselling *Living Library* series of modernized classic texts; *A Voice from the Monastery*—giving voice to men and women monastics about what it means to live a spiritual life today; award winning literary faith fiction; and books that explore Judaism and Islam and discover how these faiths inform Christian thought and practice.

Recordings

From Gregorian chant to contemporary American choral works, our music recordings celebrate the richness of sacred choral music through the centuries. Paraclete is proud to distribute the recordings of the internationally acclaimed choir Gloriæ Dei Cantores, who have been praised for their "rapt and fathomless spiritual intensity" by *American Record Guide,* and the Gloriæ Dei Cantores Schola, which specializes in the study and performance of Gregorian chant. Paraclete is also the exclusive North American distributor of the Monastic Choir of St. Peter's Abbey in Solesmes, France, long considered to be a leading authority on Gregorian chant performance.

Learn more about us at our Web site:
www.paracletepress.com, or call us toll-free at
1-800-451-5006.

Other Classics from Paraclete Press

The Way of Perfection

Teresa of Avila
Edited and Mildly Modernized
by Henry L. Carrigan, Jr.

$14.95
Trade Paper, 198 pages
1-55725-248-3

In this classic work, Teresa of Avila, one of the world's most beloved mystics, offers guidance for the religious life and shares her own deeply felt reflection on the Lord's Prayer. Teresa's luminous mystical classic is enlivened by her passion for an active life of prayer and her down-to-earth suggestions about ways to achieve it.

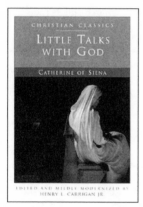

Little Talks with God

Catherine of Siena
Edited and Mildly Modernized
by Henry L. Carrigan, Jr.

$14.95
Trade Paper, 210 pages
1-55725-272-6

In this intense and searching work, the holy saint of Siena offers up petitions to God, filling her conversation with instruction on discernment, true and false spiritual emotion, obedience, and truth, and revealing her famous image of Christ as the Bridge. Catherine's brilliant insights into the nature of the spiritual life and the character of the Church will motivate contemporary Christians who seek to unite a life of prayer with a life of action.

Available from most bookstores or through Paraclete Press:
www.paracletepress.com; 1-800-451-5006
Try your local bookstore first.